Daniel H Klinger

Books by Joseph C. Goulden

Jerry Wurf: Labor's Last Angry Man   1982

Korea: The Untold Story of the War   1982

The Million Dollar Lawyers   1978

The Best Years   1976

The Benchwarmers   1974

Meany: The Unchallenged Strong Man of American Labor   1972

The Superlawyers   1972

The Money Givers   1971

Truth is the First Casualty   1969

Monopoly   1968

The Curtis Caper   1965

Mencken's Last Campaign (editor)   1976

JERRY WURF

LABOR'S LAST ANGRY MAN

JOSEPH C. GOULDEN

JERRY WURF

LABOR'S
LAST ANGRY MAN

NEW YORK   *Atheneum*   1982

Library of Congress Cataloging in Publication Data

Goulden, Joseph C.
 Jerry Wurf, labor's last angry man.

 Includes bibliographical references.
  1. Wurf, Jerry, 1919–   . 2. Trade-unions—
United States—Officials and employees—Biography.
3. AFSCME. I. Title
 HD6509.W87G68   1982   331.88'1135'0000924 [B]   81-70110
 ISBN 0-689-11291-2   AACR2

For

Mildred,

Nicholas, Abigail,

Susan,

and Al

Foreword

Jerry Wurf and AFSCME. The words were synonymous. During his seventeen years as AFSCME's president, Jerry Wurf built the union member by member. But numbers alone can't measure the influence that Jerry had on public employees during his career in the labor movement.

Dignity, respect, and fairness. These are the things that AFSCME has stood for since 1964 when Jerry was elected head of the union. Dignity on the job. Respect at the bargaining table. Fairness in public employment, whether the worker is white, black, or Hispanic, male or female, blue collar or white collar.

Jerry never saw the union as just a labor institution. AFSCME has also become a social mechanism. The union doesn't just represent workers at the bargaining table. AFSCME, under Jerry Wurf, has led the fight for civil rights, human rights, and women's rights. It's no accident that Jerry was one of the first labor leaders to oppose the Vietnam War or to support women's rights. He believed that labor unions represented workers more than eight hours a day. Jerry believed AFSCME should work for its union members as they struggled for change in their communities and in the political arena.

Jerry had a passion and he lived it. He never lost that fire in his heart. He never had to search for indignation against injustice. It walked with him as an old companion. In this pursuit he could be, and often was, impatient and abrasive. That's because he wouldn't compromise when it came to AFSCME and public employees.

Jerry believed in the dignity of work. He believed with equal intensity that working men and women were entitled not only to personal dignity but to fair treatment.

The political, social, and labor institution called AFSCME continues the struggle. AFSCME has helped forge a partnership between public employees and the public that has delivered care to the sick and elderly, kept our streets and roads maintained, provided clean water for our cities, and helped raise and educate our youth. The union will continue to be a conscience of the labor movement. Union democracy, civil rights, and pay equity are not just slogans for AFSCME. They are hard-won principles, forcefully enunciated by Jerry Wurf, that guide the behavior of the union.

It is difficult to say whether AFSCME is a reflection of Jerry Wurf or vice versa. Both have been demanding, aggressive, driven, and thoroughly egalitarian in outlook. Tennyson once wrote, "I am a part of all that I have met." The same might be said of both AFSCME and Jerry Wurf!

GERALD W. McENTEE, *president,*
American Federation of State,
County and Municipal Employees

Contents

Illustrations

(FOLLOW PAGE 138)

Prologue

They came to the Washington Monument grounds by the hundreds of thousands and stood on the grass under a brilliantly blue sky. Semptember 19, 1981—Solidarity Day for the American labor movement, unionists assembled to protest the budget cuts and economic policies of the first nine months of the Reagan administration. Never before had the American Federation of Labor–Congress of Industrial Organizations put its imprimatur on a demonstration intended to affect public policy. Its longtime president, George Meany, had preferred to do his lobbying quietly, in the Congress, rather than loudly, on the streets. But Meany was gone now, dead since January, and the AFL-CIO was showing faint signs of change. And now what had been planned as a rally of perhaps a hundred thousand people had swelled to a crowd of half a million persons, the largest demonstration in America since the Vietnam War.

People in the crowd carried banners and placards and wore T-shirts identifying their unions. Auto workers. Steel workers. Electrical workers. Teachers. Here and there was a cluster of men with PATCO placards—the professional air controllers who had been dismissed from their jobs the previous month by President Reagan for striking. But none of these groups was more conspicuous than a contingent clad in bright green T-shirts imprinted "AFSCME In The Public Service." They rallied beneath a massive helium-filled balloon, also emblazoned with AFSCME's name—public workers from many cities and many states, including people from Iowa and Illinois who had endured an all-night bus ride to reach Washington.

Around noon the demonstrators moved onto Constitution Avenue, and soon the broad thoroughfare was crammed from curb to curb as the march moved toward the Capitol, some eighteen blocks distant.

Meanwhile, a black sedan pulled up beneath the speakers' platform erected on the plaza just west of the Capitol grounds. A man in the rear seat with wiry gray hair sat with notes in his lap, his lips twisting intently as he scribbled changes. Now he was out of the car, carefully, and with a supporting arm from his driver, a muscular former White House guard named Bernard Harvey.

Jerry Wurf studied the approaching marchers with the gaze of an experienced crowd-counter and said *sotto voce,* "Hey, we're really getting them out today. This is gonna be great."

Harvey looked at the ladder leading to the top of the platform. It was metal, with hand rails, and it went straight up for some fifteen feet. Then Harvey looked at Wurf, who had left his hospital bed the day before to prepare for the march. He saw a sick man, one gasping from emphysema, limping from the polio that had left his left foot a dead but nonetheless aching mass of flesh and bone, suffering from an ulcer that denied his frail body the nourishment he needed to survive. But Harvey knew Jerry Wurf. "He was going up that ladder, and I just had to figure out a way of getting him there."

What Wurf did was this: He grasped the side rails with both hands and pulled himself up a step at a time, Harvey's bulk below him to catch him if he fell. Wurf stopped after every step and gasped for breath. Then he resumed his painful climb. By the time he reached the top, his pain had etched deep lines in his face and sweat dampened the green AFSCME T-shirt he wore beneath a windbreaker. He sat for a few minutes to revive himself, then grinned at Harvey. "I have to be here for my troops," he said.

Jerry Wurf limped to the side of the platform. Many in the union knew he had been hospitalized; some staff members as late as the previous day doubted that he would be able to attend the rally.

When the massed AFSCME marchers came by, Wurf waved his cap at them, and called out the names of people he knew.

They saw him and pointed up to him, waved back. They began a chant,—"JER–REE WURF, JER–REE WURF, JER–REE WURF!"

Wurf grabbed the arm of Lane Kirkland, the AFL-CIO president. "Look at them, look at them! These are my people, these are my troops!" he said excitedly.

Later, with other speakers, Wurf berated "Reaganomics" at caustic length. His voice rising shrilly as the public address system boomed his words out over the crowd, Wurf decried "the Reagan administration's fight against workers, its fight against the poor and the disadvantaged, and the attempt by corporate power to take over every rule and role in this society." Wurf wanted Solidarity Day to be the "beginning of a united attempt" to change things.

Later, Bernard Harvey helped Wurf down the ladder, preceding him as a sort of human safety net in case he slipped. Jerry Wurf had made the last major speech of his life.

That Jerry Wurf would ignore his own agony to talk on behalf of workers was not an unusual event; he did so most days of his professional life, over a forty-year period. The results are rather visible. When he first began organizing public workers in New York City in the 1940s, they had no legal right to strike, they had no mechanism for collective bargaining with employers. As Wurf would say, "We had no collective bargaining—all we had was collective begging." Wurf thought this outrageously unfair, and he transmitted his fury to his membership. At a meeting early in his career, when some Water Department employees were taking a strike vote, a man arose and asked, "What happens if my foreman tells me I can't take off that day and I gotta come to work?"

"Well," Wurf replied, "tell him to go fuck himself." If only two hundred members walked out, he continued, "those two hundred guys will be destroyed. But if five thousand of you hit the bricks, we'll destroy them."

Using such damn-the-torpedoes tactics, Wurf built the American Federation of State, County and Municipal Employees into a million-member union, largest in the AFL-CIO. By daring to strike—even when strikes were illegal—Wurf forced governments to face the reality that antistrike laws did not work. His confrontational tactics forced many—but by no means all—governments to adopt formalized procedures for dealing with public employee unions.

Which did not make him a loved man among mayors and governors. A business magazine once captioned a profile of Wurf, "This man can shut down your city." The labor columnist Victor Riesel wrote that "Wurf has invented more ways to besiege a community than anyone since Spartacus." The *Portland Oregonian* said Wurf "comes on like a war admiral, the Beatles, and the front four of the Los Angeles Rams all at the same time."

When Wurf began organizing for AFSCME, his first "troops" were the economic serfs who do the scut work of any city—laborers, drivers, hospital aides, oftentimes black or Hispanic, people passed over by society. Wurf got them something more than a union. As he frequently told AFSCME training seminars, "Most organizers think they're peddling better wages and working conditions, but essentially they're peddling dignity." A teacher once asked elementary pupils in a Washington school their parents' occupations. Wurf's son Nicholas replied, "My father fights for justice." He did.

Wurf's "troops" certainly understood this point, which was the wellspring of his support in AFSCME. In many jurisdictions, AFSCME membership is voluntary and not a condition of employment. Hence the union delivers, or the members drop out and quit paying dues. That AFSCME grew while most other labor organizations were losing membership is a tribute to the union's ability to deliver "dignity."

As I discovered in my research, there were several Jerry Wurfs, which together put him in a class by himself. In an era when many union presidents became union *bureaucrats*, Jerry Wurf never lost his ability to raise hell. Wurf for years denied that he was hot-tempered; when a *Wall Street Journal* story once so described him, he complained loudly for a couple of hours to his wife, Mildred. He then grinned sheepishly. "Maybe so," he said. To outsiders he would concede that he had a "Donald Duck streak," which would cause him to yell and storm at subordinates (and governors). Wurf was capable of directing this rage at anyone who offended him, whether mayor, staff member, waiter, or cab driver.

For years AFSCME staff members favored a restaurant near the union headquarters building in downtown Washington. Wurf came in once with another person after the lunch hour rush had subsided, and asked for a table for four persons, saying the extra space would give him more room for his lame leg. The maître d' insisted on seating them at a table for two persons. Wurf looked around the dining room. Perhaps half the customers there worked for AFSCME. "All my people," Wurf yelled, "get out of this crummy place right now!" The restaurant emptied. Wurf then stood outside the door for awhile, telling people who tried to enter that the place was a "lousy joint."

The owner, alarmed, sent Wurf a peace offering, a bottle of Scotch. Wurf sent it back. Until he died, some staff members still avoided the restaurant.

Wurf had a gentler side seldom seen by persons outside his immediate circle. His home in Cleveland Park, a neighborhood favored by Washington liberals, was crammed with stereo equipment, and Wurf could sit and listen to classical music for hours. He followed the theater, he skimmed more books in a week than most citizens do in a year. Table talk in the Wurf household tended to be on a high plane, intellectually and politically, for Wurf was a self-confessed "brain picker."

Wurf particularly liked talks with old Socialist friends from New York, for as he would say, "All the new ideas in this country come from the radicals." Although Wurf spoke warmly of his days as a young Socialist, he abandoned Socialism when he entered the labor movement, for he recognized that he was now working within the capitalistic system. He would not be a "guy who is a raving socialist on Monday, and who on Tuesday happily trots off to some Democratic Party meeting. Work one side of the street or the other."

When a listener once questioned whether he abandoned Socialism for political reasons, Wurf replied, "The average stiff in AFSCME wouldn't have cared if I was a nudist, so long as I delivered."

AFSCME was Jerry Wurf's life. When he involved himself in political and social issues, he did so on the assumption that anything that affected the course of American life affected AFSCME members. To Wurf, summer "vacation" meant going to his cottage in Wellfleet, Massachusetts, on Cape Cod, a pleasant place set on a sandy hill amidst pine trees. But with him went a secretary, a battery of telephones, and a photocopying machine; and there would be a constant flow of staff members from Washington and elsewhere. Wurf was also a rarity as a public figure, in that he insisted on listing his home telephone number in the Washington directory. "Nuts did bother him occasionally, but he felt he should be accessible to the members," Mildred Wurf said.

In a talk several years ago with the writer Nat Hentoff, Wurf decried that the American labor movement did so little for the people it represented. A rational society would not accept the poverty that existed in America, yet labor had not stepped forward to assume the lead in any fight for change. As Wurf told Hentoff:

> We at the top of the House of Labor don't do nearly enough! You know why I am angry? I am angry because there is no anger among most of my brothers. And I am angry because they piss away the power they could have. The power, by *really* organizing and using political clout, to actually change priorities in this country. The power to inform their own members, and everybody else, about what's actually going on in this country. About, for example, what a terrible class weapon for the rich the tax structure is.

This book is intended to explain where Jerry Wurf got his anger, and how and why he used it. A secondary purpose is to sketch the history of AFSCME, and how it grew to its present status. After some months I feel I understand a good deal about Jerry Wurf, but some parts of his complex persona continue to perplex me. I am not alone. I mentioned this point to Victor Gotbaum, who for years was Wurf's closest friend in the union. He laughed and related a conversation he once had with Eric Polisar, an academic labor specialist and also a Wurf friend. "We spend three hours roaming all over the field, talking about Jerry. Suddenly Eric backs up and bursts out laughing. He said, 'You can hate him, you can love him, but you can't ignore him.'"

Washington, D.C.
March 2, 1982

JERRY WURF
LABOR'S LAST ANGRY MAN

CHAPTER ONE

"Mal'ach Hamaves"

People in Brighton Beach came to know the boy in the wheelchair as a familiar and sympathetic figure. On warm afternoons his mother would push his chair to the boardwalk along the Atlantic Ocean, find a bench, and sit and chat with other women as they sunned themselves. The boy was thin for his age, and he sat in the chair with his shoulders slightly pitched forward, as if seeking to lean away from the pain of his withered left foot. His darting eyes and prominent nose made him look like an angry falcon.

Sometimes, when the chatter of the women bored him, he would grasp the wheels of the chair and propel himself down the boards until he found a quiet place of his own. Then he would rummage in the side pocket of the chair for a book—usually something thick and heavy, on economics, politics or history—and prop it in his lap and read. As he flipped through the pages at the pace of a speed-reader his brow would tighten, and he would tap the page with a forefinger, as if to emphasize a point for himself. His right index finger would unconsciously go to his forehead, pause there for a moment, then slip backward into his tight black curls and twist them.

Other kids his age would rush by during the afternoon, whooping with the exuberance of youth, bound for a baseball game or a splash in the ocean. Occasionally one would spot the boy in the wheelchair and call, "Hey, Jere, how's it going?" The boy would sometimes look up, sometimes not. His world had tightly-defined bounds: what he could do from his wheelchair, which was not much, and what he could do with the mind he was methodically, determinedly schooling. Jerry Wurf had learned, cruelly, in his early boyhood, that whatever mark he might make upon the world—indeed, whether he even *survived* in the world—would be due to factors other than his crippled body. His only viable resource was his intellect, and he intended to make the most of it.

The Brighton Beach section is where Brooklyn meets the Atlantic Ocean, and it is where Jerry Wurf spent his early years. In the 1920s and the 1930s, Brighton Beach was a neighborhood where second-generation Jews began to shed ghetto memories and build better lives for their families. (The 1930 census showed a population that was 77 percent Jewish.) Densely populated, a jumble of small bungalows and crammed apartment buildings, Brighton Beach had a personality of its own. To the immediate west was the glittering yet tawdry holiday resort of Coney Island. On quiet days the crash of roller coaster cars and the shriek of the boardwalk calliope could be heard above the soft surf sounds. To the immediate east was Manhattan Beach, a more affluent community, also mostly Jewish, where incomes seemed to have more chance of meeting aspirations.

In the words of social critic Milton Klonsky, "Brighton itself was the middle-class axis of this seesaw, sometimes tipping its families up and sometimes down." Median family incomes there ($3,780 in 1930) lagged behind such second-generation neighborhoods as Flatbush ($4,320) and Washington Heights ($4,030). Nonetheless, it was an important social and economic step upward from the East Side ($1,360) or the East Bronx ($2,770). To one commentator, Brighton Beach was "considered a miniature East Side," albeit one with a distinctive character. Street peddlers sold bagels, knishes, hot peas, and, on Fridays, candles for the Sabbath. Families liked Brighton Beach because year-round residences gave it a stability lacking in transient Coney Island, which shut down after Labor Day.

Although Jerome Wurf was not born in Brighton Beach, he seldom spoke of any other area when remembering his childhood. His father, Sigmund Wurf, was an Austrian. The youngest of four brothers, Sigmund Wurf came to the United States at the turn of the century, went into the textile business, saved sufficient money to pay the passage of his brothers to America, and seemed bound for middle-class comforts. His eye fell upon a younger woman in his shop, Lena Tannenbaum, a Hungarian immigrant. They married and set up housekeeping in an apartment on Jerome Avenue in the Bronx. Illiterate in English, Lena Wurf was a strong-spoken, prideful woman, one who knew how to change a button on a frock to make it *just* right, and who, when she left her house, "looked like a little doll."

Jerome Wurf—no one ever called him other than Jerry—was born May 19, 1919, in the Bronx. His brother Albert (Al) followed eighteen months later. Exact information on family circumstances in those years is murky, for reasons to be stated later. Sigmund Wurf comes through Al's memory as a man with a goatee and a gray moustache, autocratic and aloof in his household, the owner of perhaps a LaSalle automobile (the smell of the leather seats is remembered more than the father), an interest in a textile plant in Paterson, New Jersey, and an export-import business.

To Jerry Wurf, the first and most vivid memory was polio. He was four years old, and in the course of an agonizing summer his left foot, in sequence, "hurt like hell," went limp, and then "sort of dropped off the end of my leg, although it was still attached." Muscular control disappeared, the flesh atrophied. Jerry Wurf was left with a foot that would not support his weight and that hurt him more or less constantly the rest of his life.

Medically, three courses were available: physical therapy, and the almost impossible hope that life could be coaxed back into the dead muscles; a brace, with its metal and stiff leather; and surgery, wherein the functionable remnants of flesh and bone could perhaps be fashioned into something resembling the original limb.

"My mother was reluctant to have a brace," Al Wurf remembered, so over the course of several years she entrusted Jerry's lame foot to a surgeon who operated two, three, perhaps four times. There was family dissension as to whether this was the proper course. Al Wurf said, "The brace, I think would have kept his foot as long as his other foot. Anyway, mother was against the brace and he had the operations."

For a child of less than ten years of age, this succession of surgeries assuredly was a devastating experience, both emotionally and physically. As an adult, Jerry Wurf would speak a few words about what he felt at the time, and then suddenly—and firmly—shove the subject aside. "Every so often," Al Wurf observed, "it would pass my mind that he's not going to have any fun in life, or wasn't having any fun as a kid. He was the 'sick one,' he was in a wheelchair a lot. He became an adult, I suppose, because he never had a childhood."

So Jerry Wurf read. When confined to the wheelchair he would give his mother a list of desired books, and persuade her to get them at the library. Books were piled on the table before him, books piled in his lap, books strewn wherever in the room his wheelchair could negotiate. Wurf as a pre-teen contracted that most pleasant and incurable of childhood compulsions, *bibliomania*. Whatever was printed, he would read. Books are a unique refuge for kids who are not quite as swift or as strong as their contemporaries; books enable the introvert to construct mythical conflicts in his mind and through deduction learn how to solve them. To learn to skim a book is to learn to skim a subject, to strip away the parts that are really essential, and to store them in one's head for future use. A fast reader becomes a fast thinker, a person who can comprehend and communicate in a verbal shorthand that often leaves him minutes ahead of the person with whom he is speaking.

In his wheelchair, Wurf had only a damaged body, an active mind, and his books. Al Wurf used to feel sorry for him, in a brotherly sense. "I was always out playing ball or something. And here he was, in that damned wheelchair."

The operations continued through Jerry Wurf's childhood. Each time he would be told of "hope," and he would endure the postoperative pains and permit his hopes to build. Each time, afterward, he would hear, "I'm sorry, Jerry, it didn't work." So eventually the doctors had him fitted with a thick built-up shoe for his left foot, one sturdy enough to support an appendage now horribly maimed by the surgeons' knives. And with the finality of the shoe came another family tragedy. Al Wurf:

> My father went broke and tried to commit suicide. I remember that part of it. It was in a bathroom, and then it stops. He 'died from pneumonia' but I'm not sure that he did die from pneumonia. My mother took the pictures, threw [them] away, never talked about him again, that's the end.

Sigmund Wurf did leave insurance money, and Lena Tannenbaum Wurf remarried, to Samuel Baron, a textile jobber like her late husband. Several years later they had a daughter, Dianna— "Deenie" to the family.

Jerry Wurf had had minimal contact with his own father; although he and Al called Baron "Pop," no true intimacy existed between the surrogate father and the stepsons. By the time his family moved to Brighton Beach just before his teens, Wurf was a child who had reason to resent both physical and personal indignities. Such experiences often transform a person into a misanthrope satisfied only when other humans are unhappy. The psychological motivations of Jerry Wurf are a subject to which we shall occasionally return. But at a most early age Wurf made an important decision: His own condition was a *fait accompli*; however damnable and unfair, it was not reversible. He would hurt the rest of his life; he would walk with a hop. He tried sports, yet not too happily. (Al, by contrast, had local renown as a baseball player; he was so skilled at handball that he picked up spending money by hustling unsuspecting opponents.) Years later Jerry Wurf looked at himself as "a guy who is brought up that he never plays baseball when there are eighteen other guys around to play; it's only when there are seventeen that he's chosen last to play because he can't run as fast as the other guys." But when he did get onto the field, Jerry was a ferocious competitor. "Knock him down, he'd be right back up, with fire in his eye," Al said.

Several happenings propelled Wurf into political activism. One was the family's recurrent financial crises. During the mid-1930s, Samuel Baron was periodically out of a job. The family took refuge in a summer bungalow on the beach, where they lived rent-free and stole furniture from other vacant houses to burn in the stove. Al Wurf got a job delivering groceries. "We were sort of desperate, and I started stealing fruit. You have a series of deliveries, you leave five apples rather than six, or four oranges instead of five, you have a pile of fruit at the end of the day." During one particularly desperate period, when sister Deenie was ill, "I sold the [delivery] bike to a kid in the street, then called up the food store and said that someone had stolen the bike from me." The grocery owner's wife did not believe the story—"These women from the other side could look at your soul."—and her husband "beat the stuffing out of me, but I got that five bucks." Sometimes the family meal—for two days—was a loaf of pumpernickel or raisin bread and a quarter pound of sweet butter. The strains of poverty inevitably affected the family life. "My mother was a very angry woman and was constantly beating the hell out of me because she couldn't beat Jerry," Al said. "What the hell? He was sick all the time. But if she was angry at him, she'd beat up on me."

Jerry Wurf, meantime, read books and newspapers that told why the American economic system had collapsed. His rage against the flaws of capitalism grew more heated the more he read and learned. Whatever capitalism's virtue, this economic system had left his neighbors—and his family—scratching for survival. The Nye-Wheeler Senate hearings on World War I munitions dealers—the so-called "merchants of death" who sold indiscriminately to all adversaries—particularly disgusted him. Jerry Wurf was definitely leaning to leftist politics. But which of the competing causes should he choose?

Leftist politics were a veritable subculture for New Yorkers of the middle and late 1930s, with two groups offering especial appeal to the youth. The noisiest, and the largest, organization, was the Young Communist League (YCL), an adjunct of the Soviet Union's Communist International (COMINTERN), and Mos-

cow-dominated. Jerry Wurf came into contact with the YCL early because in Brighton Beach "there were probably more Communists in a square mile than any other place in the whole damned world, including Moscow." To a sickly, lame teenager such as Wurf, the Communists offered appeals other than ideology. "Girls," he said. "You'd go to one of these Commie functions, and girls would be all over you, smart college girls. They really went for kids like me who had nothing really going for them. It was pretty cold-blooded, you realized after a while; they were in effect whoring for the Commies. But the first few times, it was kind of . . . well, kind of impressive."

But as Wurf was to reminisce to the Socialist historian and editor Harry Fleischman, "I turned my back on them [the Communists] because they wanted me to hate so many things. [Although] I am still a rather abrasive personality, I am not somebody who hates comfortably, or easily, or persistently. There [were] *so goddamned many* things and institutions that they hated."

Thus Wurf gravitated toward the Young People's Socialist League (YPSL), founded in the 1920s by leftists repelled by the excesses of the Russian Revolution and the subjugation of the American Communist Party to the USSR. The democratic socialism espoused by the "Yipsels"—as the YPSL members called themselves—sprang from leftist Jewish intellectual thought, a philosophy that argued vociferously for man's betterment under the auspices of a benevolent but nondomineering state. The democratic socialists felt that society could be changed without the destruction of existing institutions; that given the proper leverage the "masses" could bring about changes in the way the nation worked.

Wurf did not see the Yipsels as the ultimate solution; when he opted for Socialism over Communism, "The Socialist Party was going down the drain." But he could not accept the "terrible pervasive influence" the Communists exercised over "those small New York circles that I moved in." The Hitler-Stalin Pact of 1939, the agreement that ensured Hitler protection to his east while he invaded France and Belgium, was proof enough to Wurf of the perfidy of Communism. Regardless of its lofty words about justice and mankind, "The Communist Party was nothing but totalitarianism operating under another brand name." So Wurf adopted the Socialist leader (and many-time presidential candidate) Norman Thomas as an intellectual mentor. To Wurf, Thomas's greatest contribution to American radicalism was "a concern for the democratic process; he emphasized the critical importance of nonviolence and made the left legitimate for millions of Americans." Thomas's philosophy was to guide Wurf for decades. "I still believe that the resort to violence leads to the temptation to adopt totalitarian means, and is fundamentally dangerous as a social philosophy." Wurf heard Thomas speak at a public rally in Brighton Beach while a high school student, and "my mind was made up."

Wurf's first direct political activism came during his years at James Madison High School. He and perhaps half a dozen other "rather scrawny, introverted boys" formed a peace club and announced their intention to hold a "Peace Day" on April 22, the anniversary of the day the United States entered World War I. The football team wished no such event to sully the school's reputation, and announced that any protesters would be beaten up. The police also became involved—although given Wurf's description of the group, they seemed no true menace to the peace and dignity of Brighton Beach. In any event, a uniformed officer appeared in French class and asked the teacher to produce one Jerome Wurf.

> He wanted to take me out of the class and prevent me from demonstrating. The teacher looked me straight in the eye and said, "He isn't here today."
>
> There was a gasp in the class, but the cop went away. Then I had to go to the principal's office. Up until then I had been ambivalent, but now I was forced to demonstrate. I went out through the principal's window just before he got there and joined two other guys walking around the school with picket lines. That was my first step as a militant activist.

One person most unimpressed by the demonstration was Wurf's mother. Afterward, she was summoned to Madison High School, where she heatedly denied that her son was a "radical" or a "Bolshevik." The immigrant Lena Wurf now considered herself part of the *bourgeoisie;* that her son would involve himself in radical activities threatened her own sense of identity. "I don't think she ever recovered from it," Wurf told Harry Fleischman, "even though by the time she died, I was a fairly well-known and somewhat respectable labor figure."

But for an agitator, Wurf lacked a basic and essential skill. As an early English teacher told him, Wurf had trouble communicating verbally. She gave him a provisional failing grade, and a suggestion: practice speaking publicly.

It is most unlikely that English teacher had political soap box oratory in mind, but that was the self-help route Wurf chose. Wurf and fellow Yipsels sought out rightists for debate. "With great manliness we would go down to Columbus Circle, where in those days the Fascists in New York used to stand on soap boxes and denounce Jews." Wurf would mount a box of his own and shout back at the Fascists, while the police prevented any serious mayhem.

After graduating from Madison High School, Wurf wished to attend Tufts College (now University) in Medford, Massachusetts, with the aim of becoming a lawyer. Lena Wurf, mindful of his physical frailty, said no; she insisted that he not leave New York. "So I wound up at New York University instead. Think of that: If it hadn't been for my mother, I'd probably have become a Wall Street lawyer." So Wurf rode the subway daily to the NYU campus at Washington Square in Greenwich Village, a vibrant area teeming with political activity. By his own admission Wurf was not a very attentive student because "I spent more time being a radical than a student. So I never graduated. I kind of crapped out."

For a youth in search of causes, Greenwich Village was a veritable supermarket of challenges. Wurf and other students raised funds for refugees from the Spanish Civil War; they continued to debate Fascists who praised the Hitler and Mussolini regimes; they took up any cause on behalf of social justice that came into view. One fleeting—and disillusioning—experience even involved a labor union.

The painters' union was picketing one of NYU's Washington Square buildings because the university was using spray guns or rollers instead of brushes. A few of us who were activists wanted to join the picket line. The painters chased us away like we were bringing malaria. They didn't want radicals involved in their job action.

Yipsel activities dominated Wurf's life during his college years. As an unpaid volunteer he worked at Socialist Party headquarters in Brooklyn—first in a "little cellar on Ocean Parkway, and then a little storefront on Coney Island Avenue." No money was involved, only the "pleasure of driving your adversaries crazy." These years were important to Wurf because the organizational and publicity techniques he learned as a Yipsel were directly transferable to unionism. As he told Harry Fleischman, he learned how to use a mimeograph machine—the oldfashioned kind on which one painted the ink with a brush—and how to grind out five thousand leaflets advertising a rally. He said of his Yipsel experience:

> You learn how to deal in group situations, you learn how to give leadership, you learn how to mount a demonstration. You learn how to write a press release, you learn how to use a mimeograph machine. . . .
>
> There were no resources other than our own resources—the thinkers and the writers were also the mimeograph machine operators and the . . . leaflet distributors. Then, when you got to the meeting, you made the speech, too.

Looking back on these experiences later, Wurf credited much of his New York organizing success to "some of the pedestrian things you have to do in a party like the Socialist Party or the Young People's Socialist League."

But were not park speeches and leaflets essentially worthless? If you wished to have an impact, you had to find a mechanism; otherwise, your entire life could be spent in windy discussions in coffee shops. As he told Harry Fleischman, ". . . One tragedy . . . was that we spent too much time and effort diddling around with the Communists, whose power was incredible. . . . [While] we were busy pointing out their shortcomings, they relegated us to the ashcans of history, to put it in Marxian terms. And they were right. We had no power, but we did do important things."

In those years Wurf, by his own self-description, was a "*very* serious kid, a greasy grind type." But he learned something about himself during a Yipsel convention in Washington in 1940, "held in the kind of slimy, cheap hotel that the Socialist movement managed to find in every city." Some of the side events excited Wurf. When delegates learned the National Press Club would not serve blacks, even as guests of members, he joined a picket line with Norman Thomas. The frivolity of other Yipsels upset the grim Wurf. As he told Nat Hentoff:

> Just before the first session, I'm standing watching my comrades jitterbugging. I am very disapproving of this very unserious thing they are doing while there are so many dreadful problems in the world. Besides, I couldn't dance.
>
> A wonderful woman was there, Angelica Balabanoff*, a self-exiled Russian revolutionary who made great contributions to democratic socialism. I went up to her and I asked how people like these jitterbugs throwing their bodies around could possibly make a revolution.
>
> Angelica Balabanoff turned toward me, and with great concern and great anger, she said in a voice that stopped all the dancers: "The only way you will be able to accomplish anything in our society is to be *of* our society—to be with the people of our society. You will never accomplish anything if you stay inside some strange sectarian group that is not part of the totality of the working class. That is why these people dancing are much more likely to make a revolution than *you*."

* Balabanoff was the first secretary of the COMINTERN in the 1920s; she broke with the Communist Party and aligned with the Socialists.

Wurf took Balabanoff's admonition to heart. In his soap box speeches on Fourteenth Street, near the NYU campus, he frequently drew off-duty workers from the neighborhood cafeterias. Wurf could tell by a glance that these people were unhappy with their status in life: They wore greasy uniforms, they had the hangdog looks of men who knew that the next pay check would not make much difference in their lives. So Wurf talked to these men about organizing. The Yipsels had an "industrial committee," with a nebulous mandate to organize workers into unions patterned after the United Auto Workers. (The UAW in the late 1930s became a major industrial union in the United States—a union that included all workers in the industry, regardless of their trades. The American Federation of Labor, in contrast, was composed of unions organized by crafts.)

Jerry Wurf's first organizing techniques were rather rough. To attract the boss's attention, he, Al Wurf, and other Yipsels would stage lightning raids on cafeterias during rush hours, grab trays of silverware, and dash out onto the street. During the turmoil Jerry Wurf would lecture the workers on the benefits of unionism. Understandably, he had no significant impact other than to attract attention to himself.

But Wurf's gutsiness—and unorthodoxy—did attract the attention of a fellow Socialist named Max Siegel, who worked for the Hotel and Restaurant Workers Union. Siegel "fixed me up with a job in the evening as a cafeteria cashier and occasionally as a busboy and other things," Wurf remembered. Siegel sensed in Wurf the dynamism that could persuade the cafeteria workers to unionize. As Wurf has stated,

> Cafeterias were a big industry in those days, because you could get food cheap and you could hang around and talk indefinitely. In the depression and the postdepression era, this was a very useful place in our society.

And also a tough and dirty place to work. His built-up shoe biting into his leg, the diminutive Wurf would stagger through the cafeteria, heavy trays of dirty dishes balanced on his shoulder, trickles of grease going down his arms and fouling his body. On the better days, when he worked at the cashier's booth, he would keep a hundred different prices in his head, and punch them into the cash register; any error meant money out of his own pocket, so he was careful, even at the shank end of a twelve-hour day. Nothing glamorous can be said about cafeteria work: It is a scut job, a greasy ordeal. The comfortable early family background and the years at NYU notwithstanding, during his cafeteria worker days, Jerry Wurf was about as low as one could get on America's economic ladder, both in terms of pay and job dignity. Years later a big-city mayor, during a negotiation, would say to Wurf, "What in the hell do you know about real work? All you do is sit on your ass in Washington and run a labor union." Wurf bit back his temper, because he was near a settlement. "I've worked a day or two," he finally said.

The cashier jobs were a pretext to get Wurf inside the cafeterias. What Siegel wanted was organizing. Very quietly, Wurf and Siegel distributed representational cards to cafeteria workers. Almost overnight they were able to found what became Local 448, Food and Cashiers Local of the Hotel and Restaurant Employees International Union. They rented an office on Court Street in Brooklyn, and went after workers in cafeterias in Manhattan, Brooklyn, and the Bronx. They also took in a man who had had vague roles in the past as an "organizer" of salesmen who dealt with cafeterias and restaurants. Wurf was suspicious of him (let us call him John Smith) because of his past associations, but he remained silent.

For organizing strategy, Wurf decided to target the Garden Cafeteria, located in the same block as the *Jewish Forward*, the most respected Jewish daily on the Lower East Side. The selection was pragmatic. Because of their social orientation, Jewish residents in the area "wouldn't go through a picket line," whether they were Trotskyite, left wing, right wing, or Socialist. Wurf knew he could win the strike, and once the Garden was organized, he could go after other cafeterias in the area.

However, "John Smith" protested against any action against the Garden Cafeteria. "I thought he was full of it and went on. I persuaded Max to get a couple of pieces of cardboard and start picketing. Whereupon the Commie leader [of a hotel and restaurant workers local] came along and said, 'What the hell is going on? Why are you picketing this place?' "

Wurf explained that he had jurisdiction over the cashiers. "Like hell you do," the other unionist retorted. He insisted that "John Smith" had signed a contract with the restaurant owner. Wurf immediately recognized that he had fallen victim to a "sweetheart contract," a pact signed without reference to the workers covered or the full union. Wurf's rage had a sincerity that impressed the other union man. As Wurf told writers Richard Billings and John Greenya:

> This guy smelled the plot, and he said, "I tell you want I'm going to do, Jerry. I don't know what the hell you are doing, and I don't know what this is all about, and I'll probably regret doing it. I'm going to shut this joint down. I'm going to pull all the workers out."
>
> So they shut down the joint. They pulled the workers out, the boss comes out screaming, and I in my own inhibited way said, "Fuck you, you probably paid off somebody, you and your fuck cafeteria." He screamed that he had a deal with "Smith."
>
> So, I said, "If you got a deal with 'Smith,' why don't you go tell Tom Dewey about it?" [Dewey was then the New York district attorney, a racket-buster who eventually was to become governor.]

Wurf eventually managed to squeeze out "Smith," who had decided on his own that running a cafeteria union was unprofitable. Max Siegel also drifted away, under pressure from his wife, who wished him to make more money. "So Wurf has his union," Wurf recollected in the third person, "and he goes about organizing." It was a decidedly one-man operation run on a frayed shoestring. "I had no bookkeeper, nobody to answer phones. The way I kept the union going was by kiting checks. I was probably the most efficient check-kiter in New York. You cash a check at one cafeteria, you had to go cash a check somewhere else the next day to cover it. I kept this circle going in hopes that I can get some of these SOBs to hand me some dues money to keep the union going—which was really rent and my miserable twenty-five to thirty dollars a week."

Despite his combativeness and his awesome energy, no one took Wurf seriously his first months with the cafeteria workers. "The bosses thought I was a big joke." Many of the people working for them were their own relatives, mostly either overage or underage, and they were working for twelve hours a day." So the bosses would appeal to familial loyalty to try to persuade the workers to scorn unionism. But Wurf knew how to argue. Sure, he would say, our union is weak, and it does not have many members, but it gives you a chance to speak together. Wurf played rough. He learned to call walkouts at the height of the lunch hour rush—the owner risked losing an entire day's profits if he would not bargain. Or he would "suggest" that a willing busboy drop a tray laden with dirty dishes at the end of a serving line.

So militant was Wurf that Yiddish-speaking cafeteria owners called him *mal'ach hamaves*, the "angel of death." The shock-headed Wurf would limp into a restaurant or cafeteria, ignoring the pain in his left leg, and speak of unionism. Why should you work fifty, sixty, seventy hours a week, he demanded. You are *men*, you deserve consideration, you deserve a chance at a decent life. The people to whom he spoke were often the debris of society—winos searching for the dollar that would keep them unconscious through a night or a weekend, Orientals who did not speak enough English to enable them to seek work elsewhere (or even to understand the terms of the job they had accepted), Greeks, Puerto Ricans, Jews, a few blacks (although even the scruffiest of New York cafeterias in those years would not employ Negroes). Wurf would look for the leader, a worker who could command the attention of other workers. He would take him across the street, down the block, talk with him over coffee, demand of him, "Who will go with us? When we start passing out the cards, who will sign them, who will fink and run to the boss?" Wurf would gather one, two, half a dozen people at the informal coffee talks (always finding the dollar or so to pay the tab) and talk of such things as a forty-eight-hour week, rather than the accepted fifty-six, and breaks and meal money.

These activities eventually made Wurf a marked man in his own union. On orders from the international office, his cashiers local was folded into a larger group, with the awesome name, Local 325, Cooks, Countermen, Subdispensers, Cashiers and Assistants of the Hotel and Restaurant Employees International Union. As bait, Wurf was told he "was to be a political force," with the specific job of helping administer a welfare fund that the international had just formed. Once inside the larger local, Wurf did not like what he saw. "Being a dumb bastard, I raised questions about the administration of the union, about democratic process. I go to membership meetings. I ask for financial statements. Pretty soon they sent me running. They fired me, on grounds that are still not clear to me. They held on to jurisdiction over the several hundred cashiers I had brought to them. I was on the street."

Sudden unemployment was an especial disaster for Wurf because now he had a wife and child to support. In the summer of 1940 he and some friends had been enjoying the ocean at Brighton Beach when his eye had fallen upon a lithe young brunette in a daringly cut black bathing suit. Sylvia Spinrad remembered, "I weighed all of ninety pounds in those days, but I did have a good figure. Jerry had been out at an all-night party, and he hadn't shaved, and with his black beard he looked rather disreputable. But I looked at him, and I loved him."

Sylvia Spinrad was one of five children of a boisterously political family whose members touched about every point of the leftist spectrum. One brother, a member of the Young Communist league, detested Jerry because he was a Yipsel, and said so. Sylvia herself attended YCL meetings, but she found the talk about dialectical materialism weighty to the point of incomprehensibility. She also found it outrageous when YCL officers ordered her not to speak to her own brother because he was a Trotskyite. So she never joined the party.

"After that day on the beach we were together constantly," Sylvia said. "We would take long walks up and down the boardwalk, and Jerry would talk ideas, and how he wanted to become a labor leader. Or we would sit in a cafeteria and nurse a cup of coffee for hours, maybe splitting an English muffin, and talk." Sylvia's father, Max, a scholarly if not often-employed man, took an instant liking to the young man. "They would sit and talk politics and the like for hours. Jerry found the sort of home environment he never had elsewhere, even at his own home." After a year of courtship, Jerry and Sylvia married on July 23, 1941, in a rabbi's study in Brooklyn. Their daughter, Linda Susan, was born three years later, on February 24, 1944.

Given the catch-as-catch-can nature of Wurf's income, those were tough years for the family. Whatever money Wurf took home depended on the dues he could collect from his members. No checkoff system existed whereby the employer automatically collected dues for the union. Wurf had to seek out each member personally and collect a handful of change. (Because of this experience, Wurf was to make dues-checkoff a key demand when he began bargaining for public employees in late years.) Some weeks the family had to survive on twenty or thirty dollars or whatever Wurf could find.

Susan Wurf, who was to become an AFSCME organizer (over her father's objections) remembered both the deprivations and the pleasures of those years. To Susan, Jerry Wurf was a father who always managed to sneak over to her bed for a hug and a pat, regardless of how late union business had kept him away from home. The Wurfs lived in a succession of apartments in Brooklyn—some good, others not, such as a dank basement so near a hospital that ether fumes drifted across from the operating room. There were months when her embarrassed parents gave young Susan the rent money to deliver to the landlord; later, she came to understand they were paying late, and used her as messenger to avoid a personal confrontation. But although Susan might have lacked the occasional dime her playmates spent for ice cream, she enjoyed the company of a father who took her for long rides in the country on Sundays in a battered old Nash and who introduced her early to music, the theater, and good books. The succession of apartments lacked rugs and substantial furniture, but Susan remembered them as being "as neat as a pin, spick-and-span." When new clothes were bought, they came to Susan; Sylvia made do with the same dress for years.

But circumstances forced Wurf to play an additional parental role. Early in the marriage, Sylvia began losing her eyesight. Susan would wonder why Daddy cut her toenails, rather than her mother, and why Daddy changed her dressings when she had an appendectomy at age six. Sylvia could make her way around the house and do simple chores; but she could not see well enough to read a book or drive a car. The internal dynamics of the marriage were a subject Jerry Wurf did not discuss. Regardless of the "insights" offered by outside observers, only two persons really know the circumstances involved in any marital situation.

"I had been an extrovert all my life," Sylvia said. "When there were school plays, I always had the lead. But as Jerry's wife, I had to take the side seat, or the backseat. I must admit this caused me some unhappiness, for I was no longer my own person." Wurf would not permit her to work, insisting that "your job is to take care of Susan." Also, Sylvia argued back when Jerry lost his temper. "Later, I wondered if things would have gone differently had I just remained silent and let his anger run its course."

Decades later, Sylvia remembered her years with Wurf as "sometimes terrible, because of his hours and the lack of money, but often very exciting as well." He was home before midnight only a couple of nights a week; he would be out addressing night meetings of workers, trying to organize. Then he would telephone that he was en route with Chinese food, and a sleepy-eyed Susan would hear her parents chatting, and come into the kitchen and sit in her Daddy's lap.

Even as a small child, Susan realized her father was in constant pain. When he came home in the evenings he would take off the built-up shoe, and massage his foot, and prop it on a table or a stool. She remembers him shouting at night, "I'm going to cut the fucking thing off!" A shoemaker made molds of Wurf's foot, and

tried to fashion shoes that would permit him to walk with a semblance of comfort, but during cold snaps, the foot would contract
and hurt; Susan would watch her Daddy try to walk, and shudder
along with him when he felt pain.

In 1946, for a number of reasons, Jerry Wurf was ready to abandon unionism as a career. Al was out of the army and the brothers
decided to open a delicatessen restaurant in Freeport, Long Island,
just outside the city. When Al Wurf talks about this venture today,
his face takes on a pained expression, and his hand involuntarily
covers his eyes. The most that can be said of the Wurf brothers' restaurant—Al refuses to even *try* to remember its name—was that it
was an unmitigated disaster.

Jerry operated the machine that sliced corned beef and pastrami,
at constant risk to his fingers. Although business seemed booming,
profits did not match volume. "It turned out that Jerry was stuffing
the sandwiches with three or four times as much meat as required
and, on top of that, he refused to take money from many friends he
knew couldn't afford it," Al said. Relatives discovered the deli and
there were days when every second person seemed to be a cousin or
an uncle, hungrily dining at the brothers' expense. "We were feed-
ing everybody in New York free," Al Wurf said. "We were losing
money like crazy." A climax of sorts came when Jerry Wurf came
in one day from picking up supplies of pastrami and corned beef.

"The side window in the car is broken in," he said to Al.

"What do you mean, the side window. . . ?"

"I hit a horse, and the horse ended up in the car," Jerry said.

Al collapsed on the floor with a mixture of laughter and exaspera-
tion. The restaurant closed shortly thereafter, and the brothers
went their separate ways.

The next months were tough ones for Jerry Wurf. The problems
of the delicatessen aggravated a severe case of colitis, and as Sylvia
remembered, "For several weeks he was rather seriously ill. He lost
weight, and he looked like an old man." When Wurf was well
enough to look for work, he had another disappointment. Men he
had known for years in the New York labor movement would not

even let him into the office, much less give him a job interview. "Jerry would come home in frustration and tell me that when he got to be a boss, he would *never* refuse to talk to someone who needed a job, even if he couldn't help. This was probably the bitterest I ever saw him."

So Jerry Wurf did the only thing he knew how to do: He returned to the cafeterias, this time as a cashier, not as a union officer. "The union was afraid of him," Al Wurf said. "He was so much smarter than the guys running things that they didn't want him around." As Jerry realized, "I had no alternative. I had no skills, I had no abilities. I was a professional agitator without a cause." What Wurf intended to do was to bull his way back into the union, from the grass roots. The union tried to stop him. He went daily to the union's central hiring hall and insisted that he be given a ticket for a day's work at a specified cafeteria. He would work the first hour, then be send home as "incompetent." This happened day after day.

> After a while, even a dumb bastard like me begins to feel that there might be a conspiracy. The boss might have gotten a phone call to shove me out.
>
> So I did something which I thought was very intelligent. I can't remember the name of the cafeteria, but as the boss was paying me off—car fare and maybe a dollar or whatever for a half-hour's work, I said, "I want to tell you something, boss. I think you got a call to do this to me because you know I'm a decent union man and I want to do right in that union, and I'm being starved out of the union. I started out in the street, and you're not going to leave me in the street. I'm not going to leave the union; and, you son of a bitch, the day will come when I'm a union official, and I want you to know, man, you're going to have the best fucking paying contract in the union."

By now Wurf was desperate for money. "It was really clear to me that those guys were out to get me, and it was also quite clear to me that I might starve and die in the process." But Wurf kept trying, and finally a friendly steward permitted him to begin working at the Concord Cafeteria in Brooklyn even though he did not have the required card from the union. After several days, two officials of Local 325, Harry Dallas and Abe Silverstein, "walked into the shop and very dramatically walked over to me and asked me who the hell gave me permission to work at this job and where was my ticket." Wurf stood his ground. He needed the work, he had been systematically blackballed, he intended to stay on the job.

"Get him from out behind the counter," Dallas told the cafeteria owner. Wurf pulled out his cash register drawer and began counting the money; he had no choice.

The shop steward argued with Dallas, saying, "Unions are supposed to help people, not screw people." Other workers crowded around, all siding with Wurf. The steward waved his arm. "OK, everyone off the station." Wurf was astounded. " 'We're going out on strike against the union'—this whole really wild crowd of excited Greeks, Jews, Orientals. The boss panicked. He put me back to work. Dallas and Silverstein left. This was one of the great moments of my life."

But the victory was pyrrhic. Harry Dallas made plain to Wurf he wanted him out of the union. By this time Wurf did not care what happened to the restaurant workers. "You bang your head against a particular wall for so long a time," he said, "and you look at your head in the mirror, and the scars might be trying to tell you something." With Dallas's earnest blessing, Wurf looked for another union. By happenstance, a Socialist friend, William Becker, told him of an organization called the American Federation of State, County and Municipal Employees, whose New York operations were something of a mess. Would Wurf be interested in talking with the AFSCME president, Arnold Zander, who would be in town a few days later for a dinner of the Workers Defense League? Wurf would.

Uncharacteristically, Wurf and his friend stopped for drinks before the dinner, and he put down three martinis, a voluminous amount of alcohol by his standards. He was "half-stupefied" when he finally spoke with Zander, who, although a teetotaler, paid no notice to Wurf's breath.

Zander offered Wurf a temporary job for six weeks, at sixty dollars per week, plus expense money, which was far more than he had been making from his haphazard cafeteria work. That was in 1947. Jerry Wurf had found a home.

CHAPTER TWO

An Agitator Finds a Home

Jerry Wurf approached his new job with misgivings. All that he knew of AFSCME in 1947 was that "It didn't have much impact, and it was treated with a kind of contempt by the rest of the labor movement at the local level." But he needed a job, and "I really didn't want to work as a cashier." After getting a bit deeper into AFSCME, and recognizing its potential for membership, Wurf came "to believe that perhaps this was the kind of movement that could be changed. It was clear to me that it was susceptible to ideas and agitation."

Public employee unions had had to push their way through extraordinarily rocky soil, opposed by both employers—that is, government—and the rest of the labor movement. The idea took hold early in America that a person who worked for the government—any government—was a public servant who should be thankful for the privilege of holding the job. The state was the sovereign, whether a small county in Texas or the U.S. Post Office, and serfs did not argue with kings. The early history of public employee unions can be boiled down to a few words: They tried, and they did not get very far. The formal labor historians make much of strikes by highway repairmen and garbage collectors in such places as Cincinnati, Johnstown, Pennsylvania, and Ithaca, New York, during the late 1800s. In fact, however, history digested those local mutinies without even a burp.

For one thing, the American Federation of Labor, dedicated to the welfare of such building tradesmen as plumbers, carpenters, and bricklayers, felt no fraternal empathy for city workers. When some Cincinnati policemen organized a union, and asked the AFL for a charter in 1897, they were turned away on the grounds that the police were "too often controlled by forces inimical to the labor movement." The firemen had somewhat better luck. They lived together for hours on end; when not putting out fires they talked, and they griped, and they discovered that they spoke loudest when they spoke together. A firemen's "association" founded in 1902 grew to fifty-six chapters by 1918 and obtained an AFL charter as the International Association of Firefighters (IAFF). Despite an IAFF constitutional provision that it "shall be deemed inadvisable to strike or take active part in strikes," the firemen left their jobs some thirty times during 1918. These actions so alarmed the Congress that it passed a law making it a misdemeanor for policemen or firemen in the District of Columbia to join any labor organization. Many cities passed similar ordinances.

But the event that was to plague public employee unions for decades occurred in Boston in 1919. Here reality and public perception clashed, to the detriment of the unions. For thirteen years Boston policemen had maintained a "social club" through which they tried to better their pay and working conditions. Unsuccessful, the policemen then decided to affiliate with the AFL, which through a policy change had now become amenable to police members. The police commissioner ordered the men not to join the AFL; when they persisted, he fired their leader, and the officers struck in protest. The Massachusetts governor, Calvin Coolidge, said, in the most oft-quoted anti-union statement of the century, "There is no right to strike against the public safety by anybody, anywhere, at any time." President Woodrow Wilson called the strike "an intolerable crime against civilization." Coolidge sent state troopers to Boston, and broke both the strike and the union. The defeat destroyed the policemen's trade union movement and set back unionism among firefighters, whose own strikes had attracted unfavorable public attention. The surviving IAFF locals abandoned trade union tactics and turned to political activity and lobbying.

The Boston police strike did have a prominent winner. Coolidge, an obscure New England governor, became an overnight national figure. The Republicans put him on their ticket as Warren G. Harding's vice-presidential candidate in 1920; one fatal bellyache later, he was president.

What was generally overlooked in the public praise for Coolidge's firm stand was that (a) the policemen had a legitimate grievance, as recognized by the Boston mayor; and (b) the replacements received exactly the same pay that had been demanded by the strikers. As Wurf pointed out repeatedly in speeches a half-century later, the Boston action pointed up the need for collective bargaining procedures; for it was the police commissioner's "obdurate denial of all compromise and mediation proposals which precipitated the strike."

But to elected officials across the nation, the truncated version of the Boston strike was preferable. Coolidge's meteoric rise to the presidency afforded them a lesson: Public employees are convenient stepping-stones for someone striving for higher office; and if you kick them and wipe your feet on them along the way, so much the better.*

Labor militancy and strikes certainly did not intrude upon a quiet meeting in the spring of 1932 between Henry Ohl, Jr., president of the Wisconsin State Federation of Labor, and Colonel A. E. Garvey, the state director of personnel. The old friends could speak frankly with one another, and they believed in common goals. Under the leadership of Republican Governor Philip La Follette (who later served [1935–39] as governor under the aegis of the Progressive Party) Wisconsin had established a civil service system

---

* President Reagan and his supporters cited the Boston police strike as a precedent for firing striking air traffic controllers in 1981. Jerry Wurf walked his last of hundreds of picket lines that summer, at O'Hare Airport in Chicago, in support of the fired controllers.

that, despite some technical weaknesses, had put state employment on a merit basis. But Ohl sensed troubles in the coming elections. The Democratic Party, out of power for years, seemed certain to win control of the Wisconsin state government, and Ohl heard that a first intention after victory was to replace civil service employees with patronage appointees. Ohl's protective solution, which Colonel Garvey readily endorsed, was formation of a state employees' union to speak for all workers in arguing for the preservation of civil service.

In 1932 the working day for state employees ended at four in the afternoon, and on May 10, 1932, at ten minutes past the hour, several score administrators and fiscal, clerical, and technical workers gathered in a hearing room of the state capitol building. Within the hour they formed the Wisconsin State Administrative Employees Association, which through evolution was to become AFSCME. E. E. Gunn, Jr., who worked for the State Board of Vocational Education, was elected president. A gangling Swedish-American named Arnold Zander, a senior personnel examiner working under Colonel Garvey, was elected financial secretary. Zander soon became the dominant figure, despite his lesser rank, and he got the union busy organizing. Of the ten thousand workers for the state, the union estimated that 1,768 were eligible for membership; by the end of the first fiscal year, some 710 had joined. The idea of unionism clearly appealed to many state employees. The American Federation of Labor chartered the group as a "federal local" for public employees in Wisconsin. (Under the AFL structure, a "federal local" is chartered directly by the executive council and has no affiliation with a national union. The AFL used this procedure in unique organizing situations where no existing union had claimed jurisdiction.)

The advantages of unionism became starkly clear to state workers soon after the 1932 elections, when the Democratic Party gained control of the governorship and both legislative houses. The Democrats came into office with the unveiled intention of purging the state payroll of Republicans. As the *Milwaukee Sentinel* reported on December 23, 1934:

> Repeal of the state civil service law and abolition of the
> state bureau of personnel will be sought by Democratic lead-
> ers as soon as the legislature meets in January.... It is neces-
> sary to wipe out the entire civil service organization ... in
> order to give the state a completely Democratic administra-
> tion for the next two years.

What the Democrats intended had long been considered traditional, and acceptable, in state government. In political warfare, the
spoils went to the victor, even if this meant displacing nonpartisan
employees. Civil service had attempted to supplant patronage by
establishing a nonpolitical cadre of state workers whose future
would not depend upon the ballot box. The civil service argument
was that the bulk of state workers did not affect policy. They were
technicians who followed mandated laws, and they were scrupu-
lously impartial in what they did. Immunity from political displace-
ment supposedly made these workers more secure and proficient
and enabled them to make judgments on objective facts, not politics.

Preservation of civil service was enough of an issue to keep the
seedling that was to become AFSCME alive. In December 1932,
Arnold Zander persuaded the state to let him work half-time at his
regular job and half-time for the union—at $150 a month—to
build a campaign against the Democratic effort to end civil service.
The Democrats indeed sought Draconian changes. A bill introduced by State Senator W. D. Carroll would have eliminated the
entire civil service system. As the Madison *Capital Times* summarized in a headline:

> Hungry Dem Hordes Await Spoils Chase;
> Haunt Assembly Galleries For
> Carroll Bill Passage.

With lobbying help from the American Federation of Labor, the
Wisconsin State Employees Association managed to beat off the
Democratic changes. What Zander had accomplished, against
overwhelming political odds, was noticed not only in Wisconsin

but elsewhere in the country. And Zander saw the Wisconsin experience as one that could be repeated elsewhere in the country. He joined the AFL staff, on a three-month trial basis, and traveled the country, talking to other public employees who had formed their own little local unions, and preaching the merits of merging into a national union.

Then, however, the AFL suddenly turned uncooperative. In October 1934, the AFL executive council decided to affiliate the Wisconsin State Employees Association with the American Federation of Government Employees (AFGE). Originally a union for federal workers, AFGE had recently amended its constitution to extend its jurisdiction to state, county, and municipal employees. The disturbed Zander appealed to AFL President William Green, with no success. All he could wheedle was a promise by AFGE leaders that Zander's group—which by now had taken the name of American Federation of State, County and Municipal Employees—would be an autonomous department. Nonetheless, since the dues money would go to AFGE, AFSCME would not have the separate identity that Zander felt was essential to organizing. Further, AFSCME would be the eternal stepchild of the older, recognized AFGE.

Against William Green's urging, Zander called an AFSCME constitution convention in Chicago in December 1935. If the AFL did not want AFSCME, Zander warned Green, perhaps he would be better off affiliating with John L. Lewis's Committee on Industrial Organization, the block of industrial unions that were on the verge of breaking away from the AFL. (They did so two years later, as the Congress of Industrial Organizations, and remained apart from the AFL until the 1954 merger that created the AFL-CIO.) But the threat proved unnecessary. E. Claude Babcock, the AFGE president, arrived in Chicago as an invited guest, but never made it to the convention. As Zander told Richard Billings and John Green years later:

> Babcock arrived the night before the convention and was
> having a drink with some friends in a bar. After a few drinks
> an argument began, which Babcock ended by getting up and

throwing a bottle through the mirror behind the bar. It seems that such conduct was frowned upon, and he found himself in jail.

The episode effectively ended Babcock's power within his own union. Zander, meanwhile, ran AFSCME's first convention, and was elected president. Another Wisconsin resident, Roy E. Kubista, was elected secretary-treasurer. Formally, AFSCME still remained a department of AFGE. But Zander and others intensified pressures on William Green and the AFL for autonomy. With Babcock discredited—and eventually suspended from the AFGE presidency—the executive council yielded, and on October 8, 1936, AFSCME was granted a national charter, with jurisdiction over state, county, and municipal employees.

But in reality, what did the charter mean? Two cornerstones of New Deal legislation were the LaGuardia Act and the Wagner Act, measures that established collective bargaining procedures for workers and so touched off massive organizing drives. No such statute covered public employees. To the contrary, what statutory law existed in the public employee field forbade strikes. Further, AFSCME was predominantly white collar, the kind of professional employees who held themselves aloof from labor union militancy.

Much of this attitude stemmed from Arnold Zander. A second-generation Socialist, Zander held a doctorate in public administration from the University of Wisconsin. To Zander, the civil service system was holy, a means of ensuring that public employees hired under it were well-qualified and assuredly more intelligent than the run-of-the-mill worker. An austere man, not given to small talk, Zander was conservative both professionally and personally. He flinched at profanity or an off-color story. He neither smoked nor drank, and he frowned disapprovingly at conventions when delegates spent their evenings in long barroom talks. "Arnold never learned to slap backs," summarized Joseph L. Ames, an AFSCME organizer who was to become secretary-treasurer.

The thought of public employees striking was abhorrent to

Zander. Nor did local unions need any external guidance from a
national union office. Given the superior intelligence of members,
they could bargain with government officials as gentlemen and as
equals. Thus Zander was content to charter innumerable small
locals, each of which would function on its own. An example: If a
large city had three municipal hospitals, Zander chartered a local in
each, rather than relying on the strength-in-numbers that would
have been provided by city-wide bargaining by a single local.

One AFSCME strength, however, was its essentially voluntary
nature. During its first years AFSCME had no checkoff agreements
with employers; AFSCME stewards had to track down each member monthly and collect dues. Nor was AFSCME membership a
requirement for holding a job, in contrast, for example, with the
auto industry and the United Auto Workers. If a worker became
angry with AFSCME, or decided he did not need the union, he
quit, and continued on the job. Thus an employer knew that if a
worker belonged to AFSCME, he did so by choice, and hence was
apt to be very devoted to the idea of unionism.

In the early years Zander ran the union from Madison, Wisconsin, and with little money. In the 1930s and early 1940s the union's
monthly per capita tax (or dues) was two dollars, of which thirty-
five cents went to Madison. With such a niggardly income, the
union constantly fought to stay alive. The situation was classic
chicken-and-egg: With no money, the AFSCME national office
could provide minimal services; with minimal services, the membership did not wish to give the national office extra money.

But the mere existence of AFSCME encouraged public employees to join the union, albeit in minute numbers. AFSCME had a
membership of 9,737, at the end of 1936, the year it was chartered.
Eleven years later, when Jerry Wurf joined the staff in New York
City, the membership had grown to slightly more than seventy-
three thousand. As Wurf sensed, AFSCME's greatest asset was its
unfulfilled potential.

AFSCME held a tenuous foothold in New York City, largely
because of a moment of indignation by Mayor Fiorello LaGuardia.

According to Wurf, LaGuardia "got sick of independent associations in the sanitation department, one for each of the five New York boroughs." So LaGuardia summoned Arnold Zander and the heads of each of the five associations to a meeting. "LaGuardia said, 'You bastards are going into the AFL,' and Zander said, 'Fine.' The five bosses said, 'How much does it cost?' and Zander told them thirty-five cents a member. LaGuardia chiseled them down to twenty cents and there we had five unions."

That was in the early 1940s. Growth was slow thereafter for several reasons, the lack of any meaningful local leadership chief among them. One so-called "leader" held the city job of "motor vehicle operator." But through some arrangement Wurf never pretended to understand, the man spent most of his time doing political chores for the Manhattan borough president, from the comfort of a chauffeured car that picked him up at home each morning and drove him around the city all day. These activities boosted his nominal city salary of $1,200 a year to upward of $15,000; whatever work he did for AFSCME District Council 37 was more or less an afterthought.

Another AFSCME "strong point" was a melange of small locals banded together as the Joint Board of Hospitals. As Wurf saw it, "They had about twenty or fifty members in every hospital in New York and they were the 'joint board,' except they never met, they never negotiated, they never did anything, they didn't even have a checkbook." In the Welfare Department, AFSCME had chartered a local union for each of the scores of separate welfare centers around the city. Some of these locals existed only on paper; nonetheless, they had voting strength at AFSCME national conventions; and had they chosen to do so, their mythical strength would have enabled them to elect national officers. In reality, however, they were creatures of Zander and the international staff, and their votes went where directed.

Despite its AFL charter, AFSCME by no means had unquestioned jurisdiction over New York City employees. Within the ranks of the AFL, it competed with the Teamsters, the Service Employees, and any number of craft unions, the last insisting on the principle that a worker's job skill, not his employer, determined the union he should join. By this definition, a carpenter was a carpenter, and belonged in the carpenters' union, regardless of whether he worked for a private building or a city. Non-AFL organizations abounded. The Civil Service Forum, as its name implied, was dedicated to the perpetuation of the civil service system. Rather than strive for great numbers of members, the CSF seemed "to prefer . . . a manageable nucleus of leaders and members in an agency or an occupational group who could assert representation of the whole," according to political scientists William S. Sayre and Herbert Kaufman. The United Public Workers of America (UPWA) consisted of militants who had split from AFSCME in 1937 and received a charter from the Congress of Industrial Organizations (CIO). Another nuisance was the catchall District 50 of the United Mine Workers of America, to which John L. Lewis had given buccaneer rights to raid any AFL target in sight.

But this competition did not disturb the New York AFSCME leaders, who simply ignored it—as they did the prospect of organizing any members. The director of District Council 37, one Walter Pavenek, had the dual misfortune of being both diabetic and hopelessly alcoholic. Through a private arrangement with a distiller, according to Wurf, "he used to buy whiskey by the barrel, he'd keep a barrel in the office. It was a pretty gay place." AFSCME's "offices" on lower Broadway consisted of two small rooms and an entrance lobby, for which the union paid $100 a month rent. Recollections of persons who visited this place are uniform in calling it dismal; one former AFSCME organizer remembered it as a "beat-up, disheveled place."

There was little communication between the District Council and its constituent locals. Although the sanitation workers' local was headquartered in the same ramshackle building, they were separated by what one Wurf associate called a "wisely-locked door." Its boss, Harry Feinstein, "didn't want any more members," according to a longtime Wurf associate.

He had enough to 'do a little of this and a little of that,' as he put it, to make a comfortable living. He wanted no one out organizing and upsetting his own little apple cart. The idea was that if the District Council began organizing, it would just stir up activity by other unions and make everyone's life more difficult—that is to say, they'd have to go out and work.

The other unions gladly went along. The sanitation workers, for example, in those days consisted of people who ran raffles with unnumbered tickets. Where did the money go? Well, if the tickets were not numbered, who can win? But buying a ticket helped you keep a job.

Wurf's first assignment from Zander was audacious. A group of dissident city transit workers had just broken away from the powerful Transport Workers Union, run by the redoubtable Michael J. Quill. An Irishman of wild temperament, his speech so full of brogue as often to be incomprehensible, Quill inspired either utter devotion or utter contempt from the people who dealt with him. His strength in New York rested upon his ability to shut down the subway system vital to the daily transportation of hundreds of thousands.

Quill was an off-and-on member of the Communist Party, a fact that made him a pariah to the American Federation of Labor. Indeed the evidence suggests that the AFL encouraged the insurgents to break away from Quill in the hope their group could become the nucleus of a new transit union.

Wurf soon saw the absurdity of the assignment. The dissidents numbered perhaps a thousand men, led by a man named Barney Brophy, out of the forty thousand in the TWU. Wurf, although staunchly anti-Communist, felt that Brophy and his followers went a bit far. He could understand why they opened their meetings with the *Star-Spangled Banner* and the Pledge of Allegiance to the flag. But then the anti-Communist oratory would begin. "It was the kind of super-nationalism that you heard in Columbus Circle, put out by the Fascist groups that used to meet up there. This mandate to put Mike Quill out of business was like trying to melt an iceberg with a matchstick."

Wurf also sensed ulterior motives by Zander: The raid against the TWU, he decided, was an attempt by the AFSCME president to court favor with AFL President William Green, the anticipated reward being a seat on the AFL executive council. "I spent a few weeks with the foolish thing and I came to a hard conclusion that it's antiworker to go on with the situation [to fight the TWU]: that whatever Quill is, he is trying to get bread for his people." Further, Quill was sincere in trying to obtain collective bargaining for public employees, which Wurf felt was essential.

A particularly distressing moment came at a meeting of the New York Central Labor Council, where affiliates were asked to provide "volunteers" to run the subways in the event Quill called a transit strike. "That did it for me," said Wurf, "using the central body to recruit finks." The council leadership—chiefly Martin T. Lacy of the Teamsters—were doing nothing other than trying to please the then mayor; Wurf wanted none of it. He angrily told Walter Pavenick, "I don't like Commies, I don't like Quill, I don't like the mayor, I don't like the central body, and I don't like being a scab-hunter." He made the first of several attempts to quit AFSCME; Arnold Zander, however, persuaded him to try the job a bit longer.

But hypocrisies continued to confront Wurf at every turn. The small clique of barons controlling labor could turn on an unpopular Mike Quill and try to break his union. But no union could count on their support during a strike if the labor establishment decided it offended the city's politicians and other power brokers. Wurf learned this lesson in 1948 when a struggling local of the office workers union tried to organize clerical workers in the Wall Street brokerage houses. "Their international union, which was kind of finky—it still is—treated them with contempt," Wurf said. "The strike was lost not because the workers didn't want a union, but because the whole labor movement, the mayor, the police department, the whole establishment, put the knives into the backs of these workers." Angered, Wurf called around and found the strikers' only support was coming from Paul Hall, president of the Seafarers Union—one of the toughest and most honest men of the labor movement of the past century.

Wurf and Hall came from wildly divergent backgrounds, yet they shared a common rage when they saw workers being abused. The son of a poor white family in rural Alabama, Hall was "getting into knife fights at age eleven" (according to stories he later told his friend Wurf) and boxing professionally by his mid-teens. He went to sea at age sixteen, lived in whorehouses in New Orleans and Baltimore, earned a reputation as a tough fighter, and to undiscerning outsiders seemed an archetypal Southern cracker who had somehow wound up as a seaman. But as Wurf discovered, "Hall played this dumb role deliberately." Through a combination of brawn and intellect, Hall eventually became a port agent for the Seafarers Union on the New York docks, and then the international president.

The two unionists—the Brooklyn Yipsel, the Alabama cracker—found common ideological and strategical ground in the Wall Street strike; they were to share it time and again in other causes the next three decades. Wurf decided, on his own, to set up kitchens to give hot meals to workers walking the picket lines. "I called some of the food wholesalers, people I had known from my cafeteria days, and told them I was asking them for a favor, and got food for these workers." To Wurf's surprise, he learned that Paul Hall had already sent sailors to the picket lines to add some beef to the clerks. Hall's reaction, as he later told Wurf ("Maybe fifty times he told me, it must have really impressed him.") was that Wurf was a unionist who would "stick his neck out on behalf of somebody else in trouble." Wurf even went to Wall Street to join the officer workers' picket line. To his astonishment the District Council 37 president, Pavenick, ordered him to stop, and to disassociate AFSCME from the strike. "He didn't want to offend the central labor body [the New York labor council] because it would have scared the whole labor movement. This would have been supporting a small local union and in effect giving the finger to their international union.

"Paul sort of passed the word, 'Tell this fucking Pavenick if he ever comes down here, he gets dumped on his ass, but I would sure like to get this Jerry Wurf guy, who apparently told his boss to go fuck himself.' Paul figured that if a guy says this to his boss, if you support a strike your boss is not supporting, your days might be numbered. Because that is the way things are in those days. But Pavenick wasn't sober long enough to can me, although he did threaten to."

Wurf and Hall came out of the Wall Street strike firm allies, outsiders who felt the union hierarchy in New York City cared more about self-preservation and deals than the betterment of workers. They spent long evening hours together, drinking in bars in lower Manhattan and Brooklyn; they ate dinner together two and three nights weekly. The talk generally centered on how they could bring some sense to organized labor, and whether any levers of power existed that could make unions decide to organize, rather than spend their time in mutual back-scratching.

Wurf's deep dissatisfaction with the labor movement in general, and with AFSCME in particular, was coming to a head. "I had been jousting in a utopian fashion with the world, and I had come to the intellectual conclusion that it was about time to have some impact." But was AFSCME the place to spend his life? The union, he said, was a "shit house. It wasn't corrupt, but it bordered on it." The president of one AFSCME local kept his top desk drawer open, and visitors could see stacks of ten and twenty dollar bills in it. "If you had a grievance, you dropped some money in the drawer, and the grievance was taken care of."

I wanted out, yet I had no place to go. I sure didn't want to go back to being a cashier in the restaurant workers' union, and I needed a job. I had a wife and kid. It was important to me. I didn't know if I could get another job. Jobs were hard to come by in those years, unless you were ready to peddle your ass, and I wasn't ready to peddle my ass. There were a lot of guys hopping on all kinds of wheelie-dealie things, but I was still going through my scrupulous period.

But Wurf saw a long-range potential in public-employee unionism, the glaring flaws of AFSCME notwithstanding. "By this time it was dawning on me that this wasn't a silly thing, that these workers, who had no rights, represented a new kind of frontier. I realized that I had this golden opportunity to be involved in the pioneering of a new thing."

In an angry confrontation with Pavenick, Wurf announced he was quitting, that he could no longer work with AFSCME. When Arnold Zander heard of Wurf's intention, however, he persuaded him to come to Wisconsin to talk. Zander told the younger man, in effect, that he recognized he would always be a rebel. Zander offered Wurf the position as executive director of District Council 37, which would give him *de facto* control of all AFSCME locals in the New York City metropolitan area. Wurf would have freedom; all Zander expected of him was personal loyalty. Would he have the authority to rid AFSCME of some of the encrustations of corruption it had acquired over the years? It's your operation, Zander replied, do as you wish. Wurf accepted. The year was 1948. Jerry Wurf had taken the first step up in the hierarchy of AFSCME.

As an international union representative for New York and environs, Jerry Wurf held a bifurcated role. He had free-lance credentials to organize any workers who fell within AFSCME's loosely-defined jurisdiction, and to help nourish new local unions to maturity. Yet his salary and direction came from Arnold Zander, not the workers he was organizing. Wurf, in his own words, was "Zander's fair-haired boy. I looked up to him, I admired him. It was by no means a father-son relationship, but I could do business with Arnold. In those years, at any rate."

Wurf early on decided on some guiding principles. He would not make deals with politicians in exchange for vague promises for future contracts. He would organize what workers he could, and wherever he could find them, and with little regard for the artificial "jurisdictions" staked out by the AFL. To be sure, AFSCME was weak and minuscule for the moment, but Wurf felt that he could build it into a viable union that in the long run would benefit city employees.

The words "unorthodox" and "confrontational" do not begin to describe Wurf the organizer. Wurf would carry his battles to the enemy's home ground. He built a network of allies upon whom he could call for the small favors that could tilt an organizing situation in his direction. Paul Hall was the first such ally. Another was Eric J. Schmertz, who had graduated from Union College in upstate New York and gone on to Washington to study at the School of Advanced International Studies in the hope of entering the foreign service. But Schmertz's father died, and he did not have money to continue. A friend suggested he obtain union experience and enter the diplomatic corps as a labor attaché. Schmertz wrote letters to every union in the Yellow Pages; replies came from only two persons, Wurf and Gus Tyler of the International Ladies Garment Workers Union. He interviewed both, but went to work for the ILGWU. Wurf nonetheless called him a few months later with an unusual request.

"The Service Employees Union, which is raiding my ass off, is holding a meeting in your union hall [Roosevelt Hall] tonight, and I need to get in. If they see me, they'll throw me the hell out. Now what I want from you is this. How can I slip in and hide until the meeting starts, so that I can make a speech?"

Just what did Wurf have in mind? the suspicious Schmertz asked.

"I want to stand up and disrupt the meeting," Wurf said.

Wurf's intrigue appealed to Schmertz, and he showed him a door leading to the balcony. Once Wurf was hidden away, Schmertz went home.

"The next day one of my superiors in the ILGWU called me over and said, 'The damnedest thing happened here last night. The building service people had just started their meeting when this firebrand named Jerry Wurf stands up in the balcony and starts hollering. Fistfights broke out all over the place." Schmertz acted properly surpised. "Jerry was forever grateful," Schmertz remembers. Shortly thereafter he left the ILGWU to go to work for AFSCME as an organizer.

A few months later even a more important person came into Jerry Wurf's life, professionally and personally. Marriage is a peculiar chemistry in which opposite characteristics often mix better than similar personalities. From his early manhood Jerry Wurf had been impetuous, quick of emotion, a man who often did things without even pausing to think about them. Although shrewd of strategy, Wurf could let the fire of the moment seize control of his actions. A long-time friend has described Wurf as a "slightly off-center flywheel—the faster he goes around in a circle, the more erratic he becomes. What he needed was someone to say, 'Whoa, boy, sit back and think a minute, and slow things down.' "

That someone proved to be Mildred Kiefer, a young graduate student at Columbia University in the spring of 1951. A woman of poise, control, and quiet common sense—and an iron-willed intellect on a par with that of Wurf—Mildred Kiefer could listen to Jerry Wurf, and believe in him, yet not be swept away by him. A native of San Francisco, Mildred had come to New York via the University of California at Berkeley, where she had been a student activist; and the National Student Association, first in Madison, Wisconsin, and then in NSA's international office in Boston. NSA in the late 1940s and early 1950s was a magnet for bright collegians who saw a need for an extracampus youth network that would give them an input into national policy. Internationally, NSA served as a counterfoil to the Moscow-dominated World Youth Federation, which was covertly financed by the Soviet Union. (In self-defense, the United States, by presidential decision, gave NSA money through the Central Intelligence Agency, thus ensuring that the Soviets did not go unanswered in their appeals to world youth.)

In the spring of 1951 Mildred Kiefer was at Columbia, holding down a succession of part-time jobs. One day a friend of a friend remarked, "I know the perfect job for you." A union named AFSCME, run by a "real fireball" named Jerry Wurf, needed a researcher. "Many of my friends at Columbia, although thoroughly altruistic, had no sense of the realities of the outside world. I had held down four separate part-time jobs to finance my way through Columbia. I decided to apply to AFSCME just to show one of these friends how people get jobs."

The day of the interview turned out to be April 20, 1951, which coincided with the ticker-tape parade for General Douglas Mac-Arthur, who had been fired by President Truman for not faithfully executing United States policy in the Korean War. The General had not been in the United States since the late 1930s, and the welcome promised to be rambunctious, with the public eager to honor his World War II career and to express displeasure at Truman for the firing. "I felt no need, no urge, to go all the way downtown through all that nonsense," she remembered. She phoned Wurf to break the appointment, but he was insistent. Reluctantly, she went.

Mildred Kiefer found the interview interesting, even if in unimpressive surroundings, a railroad-flat layout of rooms with Wurf's office at the rear. AFSCME, Wurf explained, had been given a half-hour weekly program over a labor radio station, and he needed material to fill the time. Shouts from Broadway interrupted their talk; MacArthur's caravan was outside. "Let's get up on the roof and watch this SOB," Wurf said.

MacArthur sat in the rear of a convertible and waved regally at the thousands of New Yorkers cheering his return. That he had bungled his Korean command, and almost lost his army to a Chinese intervention he refused to recognize until well past the eleventh hour, was of no concern to the shouting hordes. America wanted a hero, and MacArthur looked the part. To everyone, that is, save Jerry Wurf. As Mildred Kiefer listened in astonishment, Wurf unleashed a savage flow of billingsgate at the general. "Would you look at that ———?" he roared. Mildred stepped back in shock. "I had never heard people speak that way," she thought. "He was rather odd." She made her exit and went back to work at Columbia.

Two hours later she listened to other graduate students discussing MacArthur. "Two of them spoke of him as the latest manifes-

tation of the 'Promethean legend,' and another as the replacement
for the lost god-figure, and on and on in that vein. I sat and stared
at them. I remembered what Jerry had said that morning. Mac-
Arthur was no 'Promethean legend.' He was a ———— who had not
followed his orders in the war. I got a dime and I phoned Jerry and
I said, 'OK, I'll do it, I'll take the job.' I realized I had been in graduate school long enough, even too long."

The labor radio program she had been hired to produce proved
an ill-conceived idea, and it soon died; thirty years later, Mildred
could not remember the subject of a single broadcast. However, attracted by Wurf's vibrance, if still somewhat wary of his language,
she stayed with AFSCME as a general research functionary. "This
was a most disorganized operation," she related. "Our main concern at times seemed to be avoiding any confrontation with the
Teamsters. I once had to put out a mailing, and I asked Jerry for a
list of our locals. 'Oh,' he replied, 'we couldn't possibly keep anything like that. If we did, the Teamsters would steal it and go raiding.' "

The elevation of the militant Wurf to the head of AFSCME operations in New York alarmed traditionalists, who sensed a threat
to their power. Johnny DeLury, the head of the sanitationmen's
local, sent word to Arnold Zander, "There's no room for Jerry and
me both in this union." When Zander did nothing to curb Wurf,
DeLury hurried over to Martin Lacy and offered to defect to the
Teamsters. Lacy accepted, for DeLury controlled hundreds of
members. But could such a raid be condoned under AFL rules
about one union snatching away members from another? Legal
strictures deterred neither Lacy nor DeLury. As Wurf related,
"Lacy had had enough. He came to a central body meeting, and he
made the announcement that the 'jurisdiction had been changed,'
and the Teamsters were assuming jurisdiction over public employees. I got up and told him he was full of shit, and they would have
to fight every inch of the way. He had about as much right to
change that jurisdiction as I have to impound the funds of the
Treasury of the United States."

Lacy handled Wurf's protests by ignoring them, and AFSCME

did not have sufficient power in the AFL to challenge the raid. Emboldened by success, Lacy next persuaded Harry Feinstein to take even more locals out of AFSCME and affiliate with the Teamsters. Thus within a few weeks Wurf found himself heading an empty shell of a District Council, with only six hundred or so members left.

In retrospect, the departure of Feinstein and DeLury was a blessing for Wurf. Although the defections left him with only a few members, he nonetheless had a clean slate. All the deals that had been made over the years with politicians and other unions were now void. He could begin organizing without having to recognize the "arrangements" that had tainted AFSCME in the past. So Wurf began the tough job of organizing—the every-night appearances wherever he could gather a few workers, the talking, the promises. Some health inspectors heard of the new man at AFSCME, came in and told Wurf they wanted a union. He issued them a charter. Harry Feinstein, the newly-minted Teamster, made a counteroffer, but Wurf argued him down, and the health inspectors stayed with AFSCME. The addition to Wurf's "power base" was minute—but it was his first victory over the Teamsters in a head-to-head situation.

In building an organizing staff, Wurf of necessity had to look to other unions for manpower. The first professional he hired was William Evans, who had worked for the retail clerks union and then the American Federation of Television and Radio Artists.

> I talked with Jerry, and we impressed one another. He told me he wanted to start a campaign to sign up blue-collar workers. AFSCME had practically nothing at that time in New York, so he had to start somewhere.
>
> Now these were men who earned about $1,750 a year, which comes to a few cents over thirty-three dollars a week. Nonetheless, a New York law said that laborers and mechanics working on public roads and structures were entitled to the "prevailing wage" in the private sector, which of course was considerably more than thirty-three dollars a week. But

the city kept insisting that the laborers did not come under the law.

Over the years, various lawyers had signed up these men and filed a class action suit aimed at getting the pay increased, and also back pay. As a fee, they would take 20 percent or so of the recovery. Because of the number of men involved, maybe five thousand or so, and the time, they stood to collect an enormous amount of money in fees.

So Wurf and Bill Evans offered the laborers a counterproposal: AFSCME would take up their cause, and the expense of obtaining a settlement would be paid from dues, not the contingency fees. To the workers, this meant a considerably larger cash return. "We told them we would have the muscle of the whole American Federation of Labor behind us," Evans said.

Evans persuaded hundreds of the laborers to sign statements abrogating their agreement with the contingency lawyers. "The lawyers at first ignored us. When we started to make headway, the lawyers suddenly saw fit to start talking with us," Evans said. He and Wurf called on the lawyers and told them, "We are going to win this case; play ball with us or we leave you in the lurch."

Wurf formed the laborers into Local 924, AFSCME granted them a charter, and they were ready to do business. He called a meeting at Werderman's Hall on lower Third Avenue, and the crowd flowed over onto the sidewalks outside. The preponderance of the men clearly wanted AFSCME as their representative, rather than the lawyers. "Jerry laid it out. No longer would they have to hire lawyers to get what was due to them. AFSCME would get it for them. Jerry, now, is an incredibly effective speaker, and he had them eating out of his hand."

AFSCME eventually settled the back pay claims for about four million dollars and signed the vast majority of the five thousand-odd city laborers as members. The earlier lawyers did press a successful claim for about half a million dollars as fees, based on work they did before AFSCME intervened. But thereafter such contingency deals did not exist.

"This was the breakthrough, the visible success that established AFSCME in New York," Evans stated. "This led directly to Jerry's success elsewhere in New York City—and eventually, in the United States."

Organizing New York public workers had visible advantages and disadvantages. On the negative side, New York law did not recognize public employee unions, nor did it provide for collective bargaining. A particularly Draconian section of this law, the Condlin-Wadlin Act, passed during the anti-union fervor of the post-1945 period, mandated a jail term and automatic firing for any public employee who dared to strike. The "go-along-to-get-along" system prevailing in New York City in the late 1940s called for unions to support the proper politicians, and then to accept whatever largess they cared to distribute.

Several positive factors did work on Wurf's behalf. New York was and is a town with a strong union base in certain areas. The idea of workers "forming a union" is not foreign to a city whose building tradesmen had enjoyed the benefits of collective bargaining for almost a century. Then there was Wurf himself. He could identify with the menials in New York's work force, for he was a limping man who had hustled cafeteria trays and done the dirty work. Because of his background, Jerry Wurf carried credibility. And because of this credibility, the people in his unions responded when he spoke. A case in point:

During the early 1950s, Wurf negotiated with the city Board of Estimate for an appropriation that would give city laborers a pay increase. The city controller, Lazarus Joseph, was not impressed. Wurf was a relatively new labor leader; how could he come before a city board and claim to speak for men who had worked for the city for years? Joseph strongly implied that Wurf was on a personal power trip, that he was making demands that even his own membership did not support. Why should the Board of Estimate take the wage request seriously?

Wurf decided that the only way to knock Lazarus Joseph off dead center was through a show of force. He was uneasy. He could talk to the laborers at their union hall, they seemed responsive—

but how far would they actually follow him? Not knowing what would happen, Wurf asked the laborers to demonstrate at City Hall the day the Board of Estimate was to decide their wage request. Mildred Wurf, who was there, described what happened:

> Unfortunately, this turned out to be a day of pouring-down rain, one where you couldn't walk five feet without being drenched. As we rode toward City Hall, we wondered whether any of our people would come.
>
> City Hall Plaza was empty—a few taxi cabs, the policeman on the door, people running across the street holding umbrellas. But when Jerry got out of the car, the laborers came out of doorways and basement foyers where they had been waiting. There were hundreds of them, many soaking wet, but determined to make their appearance.

Wurf paused to talk with some of the leaders. A policeman sidled over to Mildred, a seeming outsider in such a gathering. "Why are you here with all *these people?*" he asked, his inflection showing his scorn for the crowd. Mildred cut him down with a glance.

Inside the City Hall chamber, Wurf's followers took off their yellow rain slickers and rubber boots and sat in orderly if aromatic array before the Board of Estimate—one of the first times that city officials who made decisions about workers' well-being had been confronted with the workers themselves en masse. The demonstration of direct democracy shook Lazarus Joseph. He shrieked to Wurf, in Yiddish: "What do you want? What do you want?"

Wurf arose and strode toward the hearing table. A lot of things, he said. These men, some of them, they work forty-four, even forty-eight, hours a week. For starters, that should come down to a decent forty-hour week. We'll be back to you. We just want to let you know that we are united.

A few days later Wurf gathered the laborers in a meeting hall. He outlined a series of complicated options to the men, in effect asking them the same question that Lazarus had posed, "What do *you* want?"

There were some mutterings, and a pause, and finally one of the laborers arose. "You understand all this," he said to Wurf. "You make the decision. The one decision we could make was to choose you to represent us. You tell us what the best deal is. You are qualified." To Mildred Wurf, the episode was a striking demonstration of leadership. "This was the real world at work," she said. The laborers received a satisfactory settlement.

Wurf's reputation as a hard-nosed bargainer began to spread. Eric J. Schmertz, who by now had joined AFSCME, was given the assignment of servicing union members who worked at three state mental hospitals, in addition to the responsibility of organizing area garbage workers on the side. This odd juxtaposition of duties was no fluke: Wurf had few people, and he dispatched them where he could. So it happened that Schmertz was handed a letter from a group of garbage workers in three small townships in Nassau County. They had heard of AFSCME, and they had formed a union. Now what should they do? Schmertz set out to investigate.

They were so afraid of the county officials that I couldn't even come around the work places or the shops in the beginning. We'd have to meet at night in the backrooms of bars. These people had formed their union without anyone's knowledge. They worked under intolerable conditions even by early 1950s standards—six or six and a half days a week, with no vacations, no sick pay, no holidays. What they wanted was recognition.

Schmertz talked with county officials, who essentially told him to get lost. "They looked at me and saw a twenty-two-year-old kid, and they threw me out." As an excuse, the Nassau County officials pointed to the Condlin-Wadlin Act.

Cognizant of this law, Wurf and Schmertz plotted, and waited. "Each summer," Schmertz said, "the sanitation department would hire temporary workers. It just so happened that one of these temporaries, a college kid, was fired. He showed up the next day carrying a picket sign, colored with crayons, protesting his dismissal as 'unfair.'

"The other workers refused to cross this one-man picket line. They closed down the sanitation department. Now they were not striking *themselves*, they were simply honoring another fellow's picket line."

How did the college student know that a one-man picket line could stop sanitation workers from going to their jobs in three Nassau County townships? Schmertz laughed. "Jerry told him what to do. Jerry even made the picket sign for him."

The strike worked, and garbage went uncollected for three hot and smelly weeks. When Nassau County officials complained to Wurf about his "violation" of the Condlin-Wadlin Act, he snapped back, "Condlin-Wadlin sounds like a vaudeville team. We're not striking. We're supporting a poor kid who was fired."

Schmertz was standing on the picket line one morning when a limousine glided to the curb. From the depths of the car came an angry voice. "Kid, come the hell here. Who the hell are you?"

Schmertz peered into the car and saw William DeKonig, the head of the Nassau County labor council, a man with a reputation for using muscle against anyone who offended him. "DeKonig berated me at great and profane length. I was a 'dumb college kid' who had no business running a strike in his county. Who the hell did I work for? Who the hell told me I had a right to put up a picket line?" DeKonig ordered Schmertz into the limousine, and they rode to the Nassau Labor Lyceum. DeKonig's tirade continued.

Fearful of his physical safety, Schmertz telephoned Wurf, who hurried to the office by train. Once he arrived, DeKonig told him, "Get this snot-nosed college kid out of here; he don't know nothing about running a labor union."

Wurf did not flinch. "You're damned right he's a college kid," he told DeKonig, "but he went to *Union* College, and that should mean something to a labor leader such as you. Furthermore," Wurf said, roaring past this piece of irrelevancy, "you are looking at a war hero. You call this fine young man a snot-nosed college kid? Have you heard of the goddamned Medal of Honor? Do you know how brave you've got to be to win that medal? This man is a naval hero of the Pacific, and Douglas MacArthur himself pinned the Medal of Honor on him."

"DeKonig started apologizing," Schmertz said. " 'Gee, I'm sorry,' he told me, 'I didn't know anything about your war record.' As a matter of fact, neither did I, because Jerry made it up on the spot. I had been in the navy, but I had nothing approaching the Medal of Honor. But Jerry saw a chance to appeal to DeKonig's patriotism, and it worked. From that day on, I could do no wrong where DeKonig was concerned. I even visited him in his house when he was sick. Whether he found out the truth about my 'war record,' I do not know."

DeKonig's support also ended the garbage strike. DeKonig arranged meetings with the political powers in Nassau County. Mildred Wurf attended one of these sessions, held in a box at Roosevelt Raceway while the races were in progress. "Somebody slipped us a program with a horse marked in each race," she said. " 'Bet these,' he said, 'these are going to be the winners.' Labor affairs were run rather peculiarly in those days."

Wurf asked for formal recognition of the union, which the county would not give, since the Republican leadership of New York state did not want to set a precedent for other towns. But the sanitationmen did receive an effective doubling of their pay, and a fair contract. "Those were probably the highest-paid garbagemen in the whole world," Schmertz said, "and Jerry Wurf was the reason."

Schmertz was not to work for Wurf long; he enrolled in New York University law school while with AFSCME, and attended classes at night, while working for the union during the day. But in the months he was at Wurf's side he came to understand the man's style. "Jerry had a great facility for indignation," Schmertz said. "He would yell a bit, he would murmur a confidential aside, he would appeal to the other party's emotions. When all else failed, out came the bombast. But there was a reason. Jerry had no substantive strength, no staff, no money, no legislation in his favor. You had to stretch things to call AFSCME a union. But Jerry could size up a situation and think of a way to handle it."

Schmertz cited a time when he and Wurf met with a public official just after lunch. Wurf glanced at an errant strand of spaghetti stuck to the man's coat. He whispered to Schmertz, "We can handle this guy. Any guy dumb enough to come away from the lunch table with spaghetti splattered all over him, we can take." They did, too.

Wurf realized, however, that all this energy was being wasted: What was needed were basic changes in the way New York City dealt with public employee unions. He began talking about ideas that sounded truly radical at the time. He wanted a statutory right for city workers to bargain with government. He wanted a dues checkoff, as provided in most contracts in the private sector. He wanted his people to be considered public *employees*, not public *servants*. But achieving these goals meant overcoming the fierce opposition not only of New York politicians but of other unions as well.

AFSCME's major handicap was the lack of any effective forum for collective bargaining. During the first years he ran District Council 37, pay raises were granted either by mayoral fiat or by a Salary Appeals Board consisting of three city representatives and two persons from labor. Understandably, labor seldom received what it requested. And, as Wurf charged, the imbalance was greater than the three-to-two statutory ratio would suggest, because the labor representatives were often "civil service politicians subservient to their employers."

But Wurf recognized realities. Unless public employee unions won the *right* to collective bargaining, they would be perpetual supplicants in dealing with government agencies. Occasional stunts won isolated victories. For instance, in the early 1950s, the multi-hatted Robert Moses, whose New York fiefdoms also included city zoos, would not countenance the thought of "his workers" being organized. Wurf put several Parks Department employees in cages and brought them to City Hall to demonstrate the hardships they claimed to suffer under Moses. Moses was angry for several weeks, but he eventually made the desired concessions. However, as Wurf said, "You weren't about to organize New York City properly with a succession of tricks. You needed some law on your side."

Wurf shrewdly saw the importance of *procedure:* that the very existence of a systematic approach to resolving problems could ensure fairness to both parties. Lacking formal procedural rules, every dispute had to be resolved on an *ad hoc* basis, without regard to either precedent or fairness. Would he have to dream up tiger-cage stunts each time a contract expired? By the early 1950s Wurf knew what he wanted:

> Public workers are not going to be satisfied by having public officials unilaterally and patronizingly determine their social and economic destiny. They demand collective bargaining. Public employees want the kinds of organizations and representation which their fellow workers in private industry have as a matter of right. There must be reasonable, workable systems for implementing those rights.
>
> All workers should have the right to form, join, and assist in the management of organizations of their own choosing. They should be able to do this without interference, coercion, or reprisal: [They should be able] to bargain collectively with their employers in the determination of their wages, hours, and conditions of work; to be protected by written, signed agreements; to be able to participate in elections to determine whether they want such representation; to be able to handle grievances in a reasonable fashion; to obtain that kind of dignity which has not characterized the public employee.

Wurf recognized the impossibility of pushing any collective bargaining law through the New York legislature, so conservative in the 1950s that it refused even to consider repeal of the Condlin-Wadlin Act. So Wurf decided to work on Robert F. Wagner, Jr., Manhattan borough president, and a slightly-favored candidate for mayor in 1954. Wagner's father, as a United States senator, had authored the National Labor Relations Act, which vastly broadened the right of unions to represent workers and negotiate collective bargaining agreements. The Wagner Act, "labor's Magna Carta," permitted the mass industrial union organization of the 1930s. Why not, Wurf reasoned, ask young Bob Wagner to declare a "little Wagner Act" covering New York City employees.

Wurf contacted Wagner and asked if he would address a meeting of AFSCME "shop stewards and local union officials." Wagner agreed. What Wagner did not know was that Wurf called on his troops to "turn out every living body you can find." Thus Wagner appeared at a midtown Manhattan hotel to find thousands of AFSCME members milling about in the streets, a mass demonstration that pointed up the union's growing strength.

Wurf had two main questions for candidate Wagner: Would he grant a dues checkoff for city employees? And would he issue an executive order extending collective bargaining rights to city workers?

Wagner's political eye carefully counted the crowd, and his mind computed the number of votes represented by the men crowding the meeting room and standing outside in the streets. Yes, he said, "if elected" he would give AFSCME what it wished on both points.

"We went out and knocked up the city for Bob Wagner," Evans said. "We got the votes for him. He kept his promise."

But only after some pressure. Once elected, Wagner seemed to lose interest in Wurf. Phone calls to City Hall went unanswered. Wurf sought out Ida Klaus, counsel to the City Labor Department. Wurf struck Klaus as a "poor boy, with very bad teeth and bad clothes," but his fervor impressed her. "He was probably the most idealistic trade union leader I've ever seen. He was a fighter with fire in his eyes. He was particularly good with blue-collar workers, which is funny because he was an intellectual. He was really concerned with their problems, which was not true of other labor leaders who represented those workers."

At Ms. Klaus's urging, Wagner agreed to proceed with the promised order. "He was a pretty weak mayor," Wurf said, "so I supposed he was looking for something to leave behind in history."

Executive Order 49, drafted by Ms. Klaus and signed by Mayor Wagner in 1958, gave unions representing municipal workers the right to organize, bargain collectively, and serve as exclusive bargaining agent for an employee group. As Wurf said, "This was probably my most significant achievement in New York. This gave AFSCME the opportunity to go head to head with other unions, on a winner-take-all basis. Hell, I wasn't afraid of elections, I *wanted* elections. We had the reputation of being a service union, not a rip-off outfit."

But even the issuance of the formal order by Mayor Wagner did not convince die-hard anti-unionists that they must bargain with Wurf. One of Wurf's chief antagonists, Robert Moses, refused even to give him an audience, must less bargain with his local. Moses considered himself an extra-governmental power in both the city and the state; he answered to neither mayor nor governor, nor to an obscure leader of a relatively unknown union. Wurf took to the megaphone. He rallied Parks Department workers, and told them they had to show muscle, otherwise he could do nothing for them. He wanted them to march on City Hall. In earlier demonstrations Wurf had often worried about the staying power of his members. This time he was confident.

> We threw three thousand men onto a picket line around Parks headquarters in Central Park, and then we marched down to City Hall. It was a cold day, and Abe [A. H.] Raskin, who was covering us for the *Times,* bet me we'd lose two-thirds of our membership on the way downtown. He lost. Almost all of our people turned up, all protesting because Moses wouldn't follow Wagner's order.
>
> We marched around City Hall chanting, 'Which Bob is boss?' That did it. The next day, when we went back to Central Park, Moses was waiting to see me.

By one account, Moses greeted Wurf, "You do that to me again, you little ———, and I'll cut your ——— balls off." But he cooled, and said, "OK, what kind of contract do you want?" "I want a representational election," Wurf replied. About 94 percent of the Parks Department employees voted, and of these, 98 percent chose AFSCME as their union.

Wurf still expected a battle royal over the contract, Mildred Wurf remembered. Moses surprised him. "This was the first election held in the city, and we're going to write the best contract ever," Moses said.

Wurf next moved against another Moses domain, the Triborough Bridge and Tunnel Authority. Anticipating further troubles with Moses—the parks victory could have been a one-time win—Wurf cast around for leverage. Someone on the AFSCME staff found an obscure provision of the New York humane laws. If a bird or animal was found in a tunnel used for highways, the tunnel had to be closed until it was caught and removed. According to William Evans, Reese Hammond of their staff came up with a most devious idea. He found a flatbed truck, and arranged to have it loaded with crates of live chickens, rigged so that the driver had only to pull a single lever, and the Brooklyn-Battery Tunnel would be filled with chickens, from portal to portal. "This, we felt, would give Brother Moses no end of problems." The idea delighted Wurf. "Get the chickens," he said. Moses settled the dispute before AFSCME had to use them.

In ensuing years, Wurf became very friendly with both Moses and the Bridge Authority general manager, George E. Spargo, even going so far as to give them rare praise in the District Council 37 newspaper. Spargo, in turn, called on Wurf for advice on occasional problems. Once he complained that the uniformed bridge and tunnel employees insisted on carrying guns, which he felt was unnecessary. Wurf agreed. "The next time you buy them uniforms, get gray ones, rather than the dark blue stuff they wear now," Wurf suggested. "That way they won't look like cops and feel they need pistols." Spargo did as advised; no more talk was heard of weapons.

In the early 1960s Moses called in Wurf and made him a lucrative offer. He had undertaken general supervision of the 1964 New York World's Fair, and he would pay Wurf twenty-five thousand dollars to thirty thousand dollars a year to oversee labor relations during the project; once the fair ended, a place could be found for Wurf elsewhere in one of the agencies he controlled. Wurf at the time earned thirteen thousand dollars from AFSCME; Mildred perhaps another eleven thousand dollars through her work. When he told Mildred of the offer, she replied, "That's crazy, you can't work on that side of the street." Wurf nodded. "I thought so, too, but I was obligated to tell you. There are two of us, you know." He declined the offer.

An issue in which Wurf took an early, and keen, interest was civil rights, although he was disturbed by his organization's lack of activism. "This union [although] . . . it passed all the civil rights resolutions and was very proud of the fact that it was on the right side of all the good issues . . . really didn't do a goddamn thing about the basic problems of race and indecency." But in his own District Council 37, Wurf actively pushed civil rights. Economic and social acceptance of blacks moved at a glacial pace in the United States at that time. Wurf saw then, and later, the necessity for combining the causes of labor and civil rights. Workers and blacks were foremost among the disadvantaged in America, and he felt they should work together for mutual benefits. Among his activities, he helped form the New York branch of the Congress of Racial Equality (CORE), which in the 1940s was an integrated organization. More than that,

> The body supply for the early Freedom Rides came from District Council 37. When white thugs moved in to beat up blacks who used a chain of hamburger joints in New York, we took our heaviest and fattest laborers and legally and properly saw to it that black people had access to this chain. When they needed bodies to picket airlines because they wouldn't hire black staff, our union in New York led this.

Wurf's original New York constituency came from predominantly Caucasian ethnic groups, especially Italians and Irish, and he recognized that many of his members carried the inbred racist attitudes of other big-city white Americans. Nonetheless, "We were able to show our people that the black workers were not their enemies but their essential allies." So the ethnic whites supported Wurf's efforts to organize blacks and other minorities. The reasons might have been pragmatic, but they were successful. Lacking the right to bargain collectively, "the only thing we had was *force majeure*, strength of numbers. We were . . . dealing with an employer—government—who was interested not in production or profit, but in its public image and its ability to progress politically.

"If we had sufficient numbers, we could make an impact on the city government and obtain the working conditions we wanted. So we sold strength, and in the course of building that strength, we sold racial brotherhood. Everybody was predicting our doom, but it worked."

As the 1950s neared a close, Jerry Wurf could look with pride upon what he had done with District Council 37. Membership had swelled from the original four hundred-odd to well beyond twenty-five thousand. Mayor Wagner's executive order had opened potentials for vast future organizing; Wurf knew that in a matter of years he could have one hundred thousand members, perhaps even more. He had won the forty-hour week for most persons under his jurisdiction. Because of his explosive temper, administrators now tended to give in on minor demands without a fight. (A minor instance: Workers at Bellevue Hospital had complained for years of a leaky pipe that left an inch of water on a corridor floor. Someone finally mentioned the problem to Wurf. One growl, and it was repaired overnight.) Wurf was the most talked-about labor leader in New York City, if not the most powerful.

Nonetheless, Wurf was increasingly unhappy about AFSCME. The reason was Arnold Zander, the international president and his mentor.

The breaking of any relationship, especially one of long standing, is a matter to be approached cautiously. Friendship implies mutual trust, the willingness to overlook a stray flaw of personality, a respect for the other person's innate honesty. Arnold Zander, by the account of everyone who knew the man, was a labor leader of undenied probity—a nonsmoker, nondrinker, and prude who once visibly recoiled when a friend congratulated him, "Good going, chief, you really kicked that guy's balls off."

Hence an irony: Jerry Wurf's first stirrings of distrust of Arnold Zander's judgment came not on strictly union matters, but because of Zander's naïve willingness to believe he could deal with unsavory characters, use their influence and contacts to help AFSCME—and not be corrupted by them. As a New Yorker, street wise in the ways of the Mob because of years of personal observation, Wurf knew that any alliance with organized crime, however tenuous, would eventually prove disastrous. "I think this had to do with my background, my views, my training, my outlook. I felt the same way I felt about the government: In no way can you have any kind of relationship with these people, no matter how limited, without compromising your mission, your usefulness, without corrupting what you're trying to achieve."

Zander, however, frequently listened earnestly to people who proposed that AFSCME join in shady operations. Wurf remembered vividly a year Zander invited him to Florida coincident with an AFL-CIO executive council meeting. ("Arnold wasn't a member, but he liked to go down and pal around with the big boys.")

> A guy sat down with Zander in my presence and told him that we really weren't doing the right things in New York and New Jersey, and that we were not taking advantage of making the "right contacts." This guy said that I was "a nice guy and useful guy," but I frankly was "creating obstacles towards getting my job done."
>
> Arnold pressed him as to what could be done. He pointed out that the important thing was that I didn't have the right relationship with the right people, and that there were a couple of friends of his there [at the convention] who had the

"right relationships" and he insisted that I sit down with
"these friends."

Wurf asked the identity of these insiders, and the man mentioned the name of two brothers prominent in a union. "I of course
knew that the brothers, if not Mob guys, were very friendly with
the Mob. Their reputation was very unsavory—the kind of people I wouldn't be found dead with." Wurf refused to speak with
the brothers. "Zander insisted that I was prejudiced and that his
great problem with me was that I was so stubborn and unreasonable."

Zander's naïveté—even in anger, Wurf would call it nothing
else—continually caused him to give serious attention to ap-
proaches from outrageous personages. One of these instances resulted in Wurf receiving a quasi-serious death threat. Wurf was
directed to Jersey City, New Jersey, to organize workers at a medical center founded by the late Mayor Frank Haig. Part of the leverage was "strike insurance" that was to be sold to the center by a
shadowy background figure. "I began organizing and was somewhat surprised when a very substantial city official served notice on
me that I'd be killed. I don't think they meant it figuratively."
Wurf hurried to Zander and reported what had happened. Zander,
in due course, told Wurf that the person who could straighten
out the situation was Abner "Longie" Zwillman. What Zander
apparently did not know was that Longie Zwillman was a Mob
figure of more than three decades' standing, a trusted lieutenant
of the notorious Charles "Lucky" Luciano. But as Wurf put it,
"Arnold was quite intrigued with the idea of taking North Jersey
and putting it in his back pocket . . . through these forces that
he thought were substantive." Once again, Wurf confronted
Zander.

I took the position that the day he sat down with Longie
Zwillman was the day that the kind of union I thought I was
working for was over. Even if Longie would help, the price
involved in that kind of relationship was incredible. "Arnold,

this is a mistake, I want no part of it. If I'm to be involved in it, I'm taking off."

Zander backed away, the idea died.

These episodes are significant only because they raised questions in Wurf's mind about the soundness of Zander's judgment and his ability to lead AFSCME. In the years to come, Wurf would be called upon either to side with Zander or lead a drive to depose him. He would cast his lot with the rebels.

CHAPTER THREE

A Successful Insurgency

"Beating the incumbent president of an international union isn't all that big a deal," Jerry Wurf once said. "It's not any tougher than overthrowing the pope, say, or the king of England." Wurf's remark was facetious, but not all that inaccurate. Union presidents, once in power, tend to stay there, and for many sound political reasons. The paid field staff ostensibly spends its time organizing workers; anyone who had been around labor more than a few months knows that an important secondary job is keeping the rank and file in line behind the president. There is patronage. Staff jobs carry no tenure; everyone serves at the pleasure of the president, a fact that ensures loyalty. The president usually has broad discretion on how he spends union money. If in his wisdom he decides on an "inspection tour" that also brings him into areas where his political fortunes are in need of shoring up—well, who can quibble with a man following the time-honored examples of many presidents of the United States? The president controls the union newspaper, where he is a frequently-pictured man of quotable wisdom. The president's domination of union disciplinary machinery is a constant threat to any rival: Any charge, however slight, must be answered, and a man spending his days before hearing panels tends to be distracted from union politics.

Arnold Zander enjoyed all the advantages of incumbency as AFSCME entered the 1960s. Perhaps that is why he didn't take the union insurgency seriously enough. One of Wurf's chief allies, Joseph L. Ames, is quick to point out, "We didn't win the election, Arnold Zander blew it. Zander and his sidekick Leo Kramer." Wurf felt the same way. "We didn't set out to take the union away from Arnold. We asked him to make some changes. He dug in his goddamned stubborn heels and wouldn't move, and he left us no choice. So what did we do? We kicked his ass for him."

The campaign—run by Wurf, Joe Ames, Robert Hastings, Victor Gotbaum, Al Bilik, Norm Schut and others—is a classic case study in the realities of intra-union politics. Unions and the people in them played hard-ball politics long before Nixon aides invented a name for it. And, as Wurf said, what began as a quiet drive for technical changes in the way AFSCME conducted its internal affairs ballooned into four years of savage guerrilla warfare. When they ended, Jerry Wurf ran AFSCME.

Jerry Wurf tried one afternoon to remember when he first decided that something must be done about Arnold Zander. He had noted, and chosen to overlook, many flaws in his mentor. "For many years," he said, "I was Arnold's guy, I was Arnold's mechanic, I was Arnold's hatchet man." At one convention, for instance, Zander knew he did not have the votes to win a needed increase in the per capita tax; so he told Wurf, in effect, "Get a roll call vote going, and keep people coming to the microphone as long as you can. Give me enough time, and I can swing the votes." For two days Wurf marshaled a flow of speakers to the floor microphones, dragging on the proceedings while Zander wore down and won over opponents. "My willingness to really destroy my credibility on the floor of the convention, in his behalf . . . made me very unpopular with most of the people in the union. But I felt that my loyalty was to Arnold and that Arnold would return that kind of loyalty."

On reflection, Wurf felt he followed Zander because he "at least had a superficial allegiance to the things that I believed in: consumer cooperation, housing, a sound position on the war, a feeling for Gene Debs, an admission that Norman Thomas was probably the clearest voice of our time. I was so forgiving. I was looking for a hero. I was looking for somebody to follow. A guy who can't swim as well as the other kids, or play punchball with the other kids, is the kind of guy who looks for heroes and, although he is not insensitive to their flaws, is willing to rationalize."

But after more than a decade of watching Zander at firsthand, Wurf decided he was a "decent, well-meaning, but befuddled man."

Ironically, when the revolt began, Jerry Wurf was still very much Arnold Zander's man, and indeed worked with him to try to put down the dissidents. The first murmurs of opposition came just before the 1958 AFSCME convention in Long Beach, California, when a small group of rank-and-filers wrote to AFL-CIO President George Meany protesting Zander's policy of permitting paid international representatives to come to conventions and vote as delegates of locals or councils. Meany wanted no part of the dispute, writing in crisp response, "I do not gather from your letter that this practice is in violation of the international's constitution." (Meany was correct.) Zander, in remarks opening the convention, was sternly critical of the protesters. He said he would rather devote the talk to how "we have gloried together in being known throughout the land as a highly respected and the most rapidly growing union in the movement."

> I must, however, speak to evil. I address myself to it, briefly, I hope. I address myself to evil, not to evildoers, to those who have not been able to get satisfaction from the record which has been established, but who seem instead to be irked by success; who would, it seems, be much more satisfied if we had fallen on our faces and come to you with a report of failure. . . . [It] seems one reaches down inside himself and comes up with venom and bile to spew out against this organization . . .

Many delegates felt Zander's use of the word "evil" offensive: unduly harsh language to use against fellow unionists. One of the proponents of the "evil" of which he spoke was a highly respected Minnesotan, the Rev. Albert Blatz, a Catholic priest who was a chaplain at a state mental hospital, and president of the Minnesota AFSCME Council. Father Blatz, a strapping, soft-spoken man in his late thirties, was the antithesis of "evil" in the minds of most of the delegates. But he, too, had his differences with Zander.

Father Blatz's major fight with Zander in 1958 was over the president's decision to abolish the position of administrative vice president. This was complex. The AFL and CIO had merged in 1954, and part of the compact called for AFSCME to absorb the CIO's Government and Civic Employees Organizing Committee (GCEOC), which had about thirty thousand members. In return for these members, AFSCME agreed to create the post of administrative vice president for GCEOC's former president, Milton Murray. Zander, however, decided he could run the union "more efficiently" if he were AFSCME's sole elected official. Previously Zander had tried—and failed—to have the convention eliminate the position of secretary-treasurer; he had effectively made this officer little more than a bookkeeper. Father Blatz, arguing for the retention of Murray, would not accept Zander's assertion that it was "too cumbersome" to have three elective officers. "I would like to see enough people at the top," he said, "so that I know one man isn't going to take the reins in his mouth and take off any way he wants to go." Father Blatz lost; Murray's position was eliminated.

Another issue attacked by the dissidents—and one that turned out to have long-range significance—was the so-called "special arrangements" provision under which Zander was systematically shifting control of AFSCME from the local level to Washington. The 1950 AFSCME convention authorized "special arrangements" through a constitutional amendment. The stated purpose was to "furnish organizational assistance, to assist in servicing, and to render other assistance of a research, technical, or legal nature that may be required in the course of collective bargaining or otherwise." These services were made available to any council or local that paid a higher per capita tax to the international union than required. But the price was high.

In practical terms, acceptance of a "special arrangement" meant that a local or council had to give Zander the right to take over its treasury and hire and fire staff. Although even skeptics agreed that "special arrangements" could be of short-term value during an organizing drive for which a council or local did not have money, their quarrel was with Zander's gross abuse of the system. "What Zander did, in effect, was to use these damned 'special arrangements' to stomp anybody who raised a voice against him," Wurf said.

Once Zander got his hooks into a local or a council, Christ Almighty couldn't make him turn loose. A council in, say, Michigan, would go under special arrangement and expect help. What the hell does Zander do? He fires the full-time organizer and sends in some part-time jerk who doesn't know diddle about Michigan labor, the local situation. He closes the damned office and installs one of those telephone answering machines—you ever try to carry on a conversation with one of those things? He shuts down the newspaper, so that members don't know what is happening. He gets all the money he can out of the council to pay for his guys who are running around three states distant, lining up votes for the great Arnold Zander.

Now the local officers, the guys who had been elected by the membership, get tired of this chickenshit stuff, and they appeal to Zander to lift the special arrangement. They are ready to work on their own. What does he say? "Oh, no, we couldn't possibly do that until your council repays the monies advanced to you by the international." Which, of course, is goddamned impossible because nothing is happening in the council.

Arnold pulled this kind of stunt all over the country. One hint of any dissent, and he'd have his men in there on the next plane, and the locals would be out the door.

By May 1964 when Wurf was elected president forty of the sixty-eight councils in the union were either under "special arrangements" or trusteeships. "Literally hundreds of local unions were being administered from international headquarters," Wurf said. "We had to put an end to that."

But when attacks were made on the special arrangements at the 1958 convention, Wurf stood with Zander, and he helped knock down the dissidents. In the end, Zander let the dissidents have one seemingly minor resolution with which he disagreed, that the name of "Public Servants Week" be changed to "Public Employees Week." Father Blatz submitted the resolution, and as he explained, "The word 'servant' implies that the government is the worker's 'master,' a concept I certainly do not accept. It precludes any chance of the worker being treated with dignity. Although on the surface, this was a cosmetic change, it did denote a sharp shift in the way AFSCME members conceived of themselves. It was, I suppose, an important step on the road to dignity."

Zander did not think much of the change, "because I insist I stand here as your humble servant, and think well of the virtue of humility." But he let it pass.

For years Wurf had managed to rationalize Zander's shortcomings. But after the 1958 convention, Wurf seriously questioned Zander's judgment. He knew the union was a political tinderbox, and that although Zander had contained the opposition, it was real and growing. Wurf was unhappy that Zander had taken on a new protégé, Leo Kramer, his executive assistant, and given him much authority over AFSCME. Further, Zander seemed to be spending a lot of time on matters having nothing to do with trade unions. He had taken State Department and Agency for International Development (AID) contracts to help develop unions in "emerging nations," and he was constantly busy on a program under which AFSCME with government assistance was to build low-cost housing for workers.

Soon after the convention, "My tolerance is going rather low. I'm in Washington for some reason or another, and Zander tells me that he's going off to Africa for several months. He asked me if I wanted to join him, which was idiotic, because the New York situation was in a serious state of flux." Wurf declined, but he did suggest that Zander take along James Farmer, an articulate black intellectual serving on the District Council 37 staff. As Farmer quipped later, "While Arnold and I toured Africa, talking to the natives, Jerry Wurf toured America, talking to AFSCME members. Arnold was too dumb to know what was going on."

During Zander's absence, Gordon W. Chapman, the secretary-treasurer, ran the union, along with an appointive business manager. "Between the two of them, these ———— wouldn't pay the electric bills in New York and the power company turned off the electricity because I didn't send out the appropriate notice. Then one day they turn off the telephones for the same reason. Now we're a fair-sized union, and we're willing to let our bills be paid out of international. But the thing is that while Zander is gone, the whole national union is a mess."

Wurf roared into Washington and confronted Chapman, who "is so distressed with my complaints . . . that he treats it as a personal offense." Chapman missed the point: Leo Kramer had assumed so much authority in AFSCME that Chapman, a constitutional officer, was working as a "bookkeeper" (Wurf's word). Wurf ran AFSCME's largest-growing council, he was gaining members faster than any other part of the union, yet he could not rely on the international office for even elementary logistical support.

When Zander returned from his African trip, Wurf told him he was through. "I want to resign. I just can't live this way." Zander tried to dissuade him, and the confrontation was "painful," in Wurf's word. "There were no voices raised, there was no anger. But for me it was a turning point, a milestone in a deteriorating situation." Wurf stated flatly that he would no longer answer to people whom he did not respect. He went off the international payroll and immediately became executive director of District Council 37. "I reached the conclusion that here was going to be a fair-sized council, and I was going to be an independent operator."

Cutting Zander's apron strings gave Wurf freedom in another

sense as well: He could now consort with the forces in the union that wished to force Zander to make basic reforms in AFSCME— or else force him from office.

Just as Jerry Wurf predicted, the quixotic backbench fights against Zander in the 1958 convention soon coalesced into a more potent force. In describing the group later, Wurf uncharacteristically used the cliché "young Turks." Two of them shared Wurf's New York Socialist background: Al Bilik, an intense political scientist lured into AFSCME by Wurf and assigned to Cincinnati, where he ran the AFSCME local and served as president of the Central Labor Council; and Victor Gotbaum, a shaggy intellectual who had worked briefly for the State Department, then gone to Chicago on the perhaps impossible assignment of persuading Mayor Richard Daley's patronage workers to join a union. ("Gotbaum almost wore his hair off, running his head up against Daley," Wurf said.) There was also Joseph L. Ames, a hulking Missourian who had been badly wounded in World War II—he had lost part of a leg, and his face bore deep scars—and returned to St. Louis to work for the International Ladies Garment Workers Union, the Teamsters, and lastly AFSCME. A complex man, intellectually and emotionally, Ames had helped found the Congress on Racial Equality (CORE), and from this was friendly with Jim Farmer, who worked with Wurf at District Council 37. Another mover was Robert H. Hastings, a lawyer by training, then with AFSCME's council in Columbus, Ohio. The final member was Norm Schut of Washington state.

Each man had his own complaint against Zander. To Ames, who came from an industrial union background, Zander was profligate in chartering local unions. "Arnold had this philosophy that you issue as many charters as you can and the organizing will take care of itself," Ames said. "They had issued, I think, in excess of twenty local union charters in the St. Louis city service and for some pretty weird jurisdictions. One was for the imposing name of 'Operators of Hospital Emergency Vehicles.' This consisted of maybe ten ambulance drivers at one hospital, and that was the local union all by itself." But each of these minute locals meant extra convention votes for Zander, so he resisted attempts to merge them into larger, more manageable groupings.

To Gotbaum, Wurf's strong point was a willingness to "go down in glorious defeat" in a hopeless cause—if the cause was worthwhile. Gotbaum had managed to organize a few small locals in Chicago.

> One of the locals I had put together was the Chicago University Hospital Group, and in order to keep union conditions going, I knew I had to organize some of the other voluntary hospitals. I organized them, but they wouldn't give me recognition.
>
> Both Jerry and Zander didn't want me to strike. I felt that I had to, even though I agreed with both of them that it was going to be very tough.
>
> The big difference was that Zander disappeared. Jerry gave me help. He had people go through [Chicago] walk on a picket line with me; [he] sent me a few bucks, even though I think he believed it was hopeless. I respected him for that. This led, however, to my disenchantment with Zander.

The initial meeting was held in Columbus. The group kicked around exactly what they wanted from Zander. "I don't think at that point it ever occurred to anybody that Zander could be taken," Wurf said. Gradually a consensus emerged. The group wished decentralization, with more power given to officers elected directly by the membership. Under the existing constitution, vice presidents (who in turn made up the international executive board) were elected at large. The board was self-perpetuating. The incumbent board would meet, and put forth names that became the "administration slate." Those annointed would be notified in dramatic middle-of-the-night fashion, with a knock on the hotel room door and an invitation to "join the ticket." Another complaint was the allocation of convention votes, which was so tilted in favor of smaller locals that a numerical minority could control AFSCME. Wurf and Ames, especially, felt that larger locals needed a larger voice.

But what leverage could be brought against Zander to make him yield to these reforms?

At a meeting in Chicago in 1960 the group, still nameless, hit upon a strategem. At the previous convention Zander had pleaded for an increase in the per capita tax—the amount paid the international each month by each member—from sixty-five cents to one dollar. Increasing one's own taxes, even by a few cents a month, is seldom done with enthusiasm, so Zander had been unable to win the issue. However, the group decided to make an offer to Zander: If he would approve regional election of board members, they would help him win the per capita increase.

This meeting, held in the grimy old Sherman Hotel (now defunct) in downtown Chicago brought to the surface the divergent temperaments and strong personalities that in later years were to bring on painful splits. At one point, according to Ames, Wurf became so enraged he "picked up a glass ashtray that must have weighed two pounds and threw it at me." Wurf missed, but the ashtray left a "big dent" in the wall. Another person remembers Ames starting to throw a punch at Wurf. And Wurf and Gotbaum standing on opposite sides of a bed shouting obscenities at one another—ignoring a man who was lying there trying to work a crossword puzzle beneath the din.

Wurf's role at these meetings was somewhat ambiguous. He saw himself as the "voice of reason," commissioned by Zander "to see if I can handle these young red-hots, many of whom are critical of me." According to Wurf, the understanding was that he would relay the thrust of the meeting to Zander to see if an agreement could be struck. Ames denied that others attending knew any such thing. "Unbeknownst to the rest of us," he said, "Wurf was going from these meetings directly to Zander and reporting to him about it." Had the group known of these reports, Ames said, Wurf "very likely" would have been excluded.

In any event, Wurf tried to meet with Zander in Philadelphia as delegates gathered for the 1960 convention. "He's too busy to see me, and he's too busy to see the guys. I said, "Oh, ——— him, if he can handle these ———, he can handle them; if he can't, he can't." Wurf knew, however, that Zander was due for a rough convention; for his opponents "knew how to make a speech, knew a point of order, knew how to read the constitution." Although Zander commanded a majority vote, because of the large number of international representatives doubling as delegates, he would not be able to win the per capita increase, which required two-thirds approval.

The Sunday before the convention opened, Wurf sat in the hotel coffee shop with Norman Schut of Washington State. Mrs. Zander, at an adjoining table, said, "Why don't you two boys go down and talk with Arnold?" Wurf replied, "Well, I used to think I could communicate with Arnold, but it isn't that easy anymore." Mrs. Zander insisted, and so Wurf and Schut spent several hours with Zander.

This meeting proved fatal to Zander's presidency, for it marked the beginning of the final break with Wurf. According to Wurf, Zander agreed to support regional election of vice presidents in return for dissidents' support of the per capita tax increase. Relieved, Wurf saw the settlement as an end to the internal dispute, with minimum harm to either side. "Everybody was delighted, and nobody really wanted to have a beef with the old man."

Zander's agreement in hand, Wurf and Schut met later that day with Leo Kramer and Tom Morgan, the director of organization, to work out specific details. Wurf even sketched out a map delineating the regions from which the vice presidents would be elected.

The next day, rumors circulated that Zander was backing away from the deal. That evening, both Wurf and Schut attended a meeting of the laws committee. "Arnold came in, and he turned on every agreement we had reached the previous day," Wurf said. "I could not believe my ears." Wurf turned to Tom Morgan,

> I put Morgan in a hell of a spot. I turned to all the people there and said, "Now I know Tom Morgan is an honest man. Let's ask him. 'Tom, did we or did we not come to an agreement last night?'"

Morgan, you must realize, was on Arnold's payroll, and his job was on the line. But he said, "We came to an agreement," and he pointed to a map showing the districts, and he said, "and that's what we agreed to."*

But Zander continued to insist nothing had been settled.

"Schut turned to Zander. Schut is not like I am, given to bad language or excitement or losing his temper; he's a cool fish. Schut said to him, 'You bastard, you double-crossed us!' "

Wurf and Schut stormed out of the meeting and met with the other members of the group. Joe Ames looked down at Wurf and wagged his finger. "You led us into this, Jerry, now you lead us out."

One final, futile attempt at reconciliation remained. The mover this time was Al Wurf, Jerry's brother, who was on Zander's staff as director of District Council 50, which represented New York state employees (as opposed to Jerry's New York City jurisdiction). The relationship between the brothers was complex. Given the size of their respective councils, Jerry was the dominant figure. "There was the normal kind of sibling rivalry," Jerry Wurf said. "Here were two brothers, both working for a union. One is moving ahead very rapidly, beginning to get a measure of recognition on the New York scene, and the other guy not getting as much status and recognition. I was so sensitive on the question of nepotism that I think I was very harsh, unreasonable, in my demands of him. Therefore, there was a certain kind of discomfort and unhappiness in our relationship, at least work-wise."

In this instance, the Wurf brothers had caucused their delegates and agreed to support the deal Jerry had supposedly arranged. Now that it appeared off, Jerry Wurf told Ames he could not in good conscience support the increased per capita. He said, "I think I better get my brother and tell him I'm going to tear the caucus up in the morning."

This was at about one in the morning. Al Wurf, when roused

* Zander fired Morgan immediately after the convention ended.

from bed by phone, said, "This could all be straightened out. Let me get Zander down here and we'll straighten it out."

"It's silly," Jerry said. "We can't straighten it out." But Al insisted.

Jerry Wurf finally called Zander and told him, " 'I want you up here, I want you to meet with these guys and me. Because otherwise all these things I have done on the floor in your behalf through the years, I will be doing on behalf of your opposition tomorrow.' That brought him running."

Despite the late hour, Zander arrived clean-shaven and immaculately dressed. ("That was Arnold," Ames said. "Never a hair out of place, never mind that it was in the middle of the night.") The meeting was nasty. Al Wurf tried to persuade Zander to stick to his promise. Zander refused. Jerry Wurf took up the argument. Since the vast majority of AFSCME members paid dues voluntarily, "the voluntarianism, the local input to the decision-making mechanism, has to remain democratic and reasonably responsive. Any union, if it's got any meaningfulness, substantially is an institution in which people pay for the privilege of participating." Zander, conversely, "was apparently convinced that he was *leading* the working class toward the better life." Zander did not deign to argue. "He'd just sit there. He was enjoying this."

The next few days of the convention were acrimonious, with shouted threats and tedious roll call votes. Zander realized he did not have the votes for the increased per capita, so he kept delaying a showdown by roll calls. Zander even called on the respected Walter Reuther, president of the United Auto Workers, for support. Reuther had a professional interest in AFSCME bettering its finances, for the UAW had made substantial loans to AFSCME over the years, both directly and through the AFL-CIO's Industrial Union Department. But not even Reuther could swing the convention: The per capita tax increase lost.

The mood was distinctly that of rebellion. The dissidents wanted local control of their union rather than having "regional directors shoved down our throats," the complaint of a Connecticut delegate. Zander, in response, would argue that the at-large elections protected the rights of small locals.

On the last day of the convention, Wurf flung down a challenge to Zander. His voice shaking with emotion, Wurf declared:

> Mister Chairman, I think you are making an appeal not for democracy, not to preserve the rights of the small locals, but an appeal to make it impossible for unions that want to meld together, to grow, to get proper representation in this convention. . . .
>
> I think the chair is treating the large locals shabbily. . . . You used a demagogic appeal. I don't know what has happened to you. It is not becoming of you, President Zander.

In Wurf's view, Zander could have salvaged his presidency even after the embarrassment of Philadelphia. Ames and other persons made peace overtures: Arrange a quiet meeting once tempers have cooled, they counseled, and we should be able to come to agreement. In Wurf's view, "Arnold did two things that were critically wrong, stupidly wrong," directly after the convention.

He wrote an editorial in the newspaper [*The Public Employee*] calling us "the forces of evil." So we began calling our little group the F.O.E., which made a laughing stock of Zander. Next, Zander made the mistake of letting some pretty heavy-handed operatives run the union for him. Arnold made a speech someplace calling one of these assistants, Leo Kramer, "an extension of his desk." Thereafter we called Leo "the extension." Arnold's statement was about the same as saying that he had turned the union over to some nonelected staff guy. That didn't go down very well with people who had done the hard work in the field.

Another attempted peacemaker was William McEntee, president of the Philadelphia AFSCME council (and father of Gerald McEntee, who would be Wurf's successor as president). McEntee telephoned Wurf and said, "You know, Jerry, it's no good for the union" to have such public disputes. Wurf replied that he was appalled at what was going on in the national union. McEntee agreed that "Arnold is making mistakes." But he suggested that Wurf receive Leo Kramer at a small cottage Wurf had just purchased in Harriman, New York, up the Hudson River from the city.

The meeting was a disaster. "Leo affronted me intellectually. 'You take ten questions,' he said, 'and you'll find you, Arnold, and myself don't have a bit of disagreement.' "

"Yeah," Wurf replied, "we all dislike the China lobby and we all despise the Soviet Union line. Let's stop the shit. We're talking about a union here which is at a turning point. Where do we stand on collective bargaining? Where do we stand on civil service things?"

Kramer suggested a quiet meeting between Wurf and Zander. Wurf refused. He knew that a private session would engender rumors and suspicions. If he were to meet Zander, it would be in public. He suggested that Zander address a meeting of the District Council 37 leadership.

A score of people gathered to hear what they thought would be conciliatory words from Zander. His opening line dashed that illusion. "I forgive you," he said, "for the outrageous things you did in that convention. . . ."

A diminutive woman named Fannie Fine—"She was under five feet tall, but she had the voice and temper of a longshoreman," Wurf said—arose with a roar. "Just a minute," she stormed at Zander. "You acted like Hitler at that convention! We didn't come here to hear you giving us forgiveness! Who the hell do you think you are? God?" Zander never regained his composure, and the meeting broke up within a quarter of an hour. Thus ended any chance of reconciliation.

Now the dissidents began plotting in earnest, first as the "Forces of Evil." But, Wurf said, "we decided the name was not exactly a good public relations gimmick, so we worked out another acronym, COUR, for the Committee on Union Responsibility, pronounced 'core.' Joe Ames, Jim Farmer, and I had helped found the original

CORE, the Congress on Racial Equality, so this made a lot of sense, given the large black membership in AFSCME." The COUR group made several key early decisions:

—The campaign would be run from Robert Hastings's District Council 8 in Columbus, Ohio, to get away from what Wurf called "the anti–New York thing." By doing so, COUR hoped to broaden its appeal to Midwesterners in AFSCME.

—The hard anti-Zander material would be disseminated through a newsletter issued by Hastings's office. The approach would be hard-hitting, muckraking; Zander and his record would be called to account. Simultaneously, the District Council 37 newspaper would take the campaign high road, "talking about the kind of thing that we were capable of achieving in New York that would look good." The District Council 37 editor would play down Wurf's role.

—Finally, Wurf would be the COUR candidate for president, a choice that, while much debated, was nonetheless inevitable.

Wurf spoke candidly about his political shortcomings. The strongest argument against him, he said, was "that the one son of a bitch that could not be [elected president] was me, because I was Jewish and from New York City." But Wurf had other overriding advantages: District Council 37, a "big tough council," with about one-seventh the total AFSCME membership, gave him a secure power base, immune to any retaliation by Zander. "I was well-known in the union. Although I was considered a pro-Zander man, not the most pleasant guy or the guy with the most friends, I was considered competent, mean, strong." The actual choice came at a late-night meeting at a Chinese restaurant in Washington, after hours of on-the-other-hand debate about whether Wurf's New York Jewish origins were an insurmountable problem. Joe Ames, who did not want the job, "because I was basically lazy," suggested that everyone write their preferences on slips of paper. Wurf was the unanimous top choice of the COUR leaders present.

Al Bilik's version is slightly different; that Wurf got the nod because he said "me-or-else."

Hastings and Schut did not want Jerry. Neither one of them liked him at all. Ames was in love with Jerry and Jerry was in love with Jerry. So you had the two and two. It was clear to me that Jerry, if he couldn't be the candidate, was going to pack up his ball and bat and go home, and in fact he said so. "If that's the way it is with you guys, I'll just make a deal with Zander," which he could have done.

Zander, if he had any sense at all, would have made a deal at some point and would still be president today. . . . But Jerry made it clear that unless he was a candidate, he really wouldn't be that interested in the program.

Vic Gotbaum had misgivings about Wurf as the nominee. Although he recognized Wurf's strong sense of trade unionism, "I saw that you really weren't part of a group with Jerry. He called it, he dictated it. If you disagreed, he sort of blew up. It made me terribly nervous.

"In fact, when we decided on who would be the opposition to Zander, I sort of made a lame excuse that 'a New York Jew might not make it.' My honest feeling was that I didn't know if I wanted Jerry to be the national president. The misgivings began to set in even then."

Why, then, did Gotbaum opt for Wurf?

"Well, he was the power. The rest of us, it was like Stalin asking the pope, 'How many troops do you have?' Jerry really had the troops and the resources. The rest of us didn't.

"Without Jerry, there really was no COUR. No use bullshitting ourselves. He had the money, the piece of action, everything else."

The COUR campaign against Zander—and, indirectly, against his confidante Leo Kramer—was to rage for three heated years. Zander survived one convention in 1962, by a hair's breadth, but learned nothing of political value from the scare. A loud near-majority of AFSCME's elected local officers clamored for more local autonomy and democracy. Kramer responded with a scheme to abolish the office of secretary-treasurer—the union's only other elective position—and replace it with an appointed business manager. At one point Kramer's minions even floated an idea whereby an appointive staff person would assume the presidency in the event Zander died or was incapacitated.

Before the 1962 convention, COUR concentrated on selling reform, not Jerry Wurf. When Wurf went on speaking tours—and he seemed to be all over America during the eighteen months before the convention—he talked about such issues as regional elections of vice presidents, an end to the detested "special arrangements" that meant all reins of power were held by Washington, and a reformed convention voting system that would end domination of AFSCME by small "paper locals" whose credentials were held by international staff people, not rank-and-file members.

Wurf also raised questions about the somewhat murky AFSCME enterprise support of massive low-cost housing projects under union auspices, but with federal financing. "The first I heard of those deals was around 1959, when Zander told the board he wanted to build something called 'The Zander Apartments' out in Milwaukee. The way he explained it, all the union put up was its name, the federal government did the rest. Arnold got into this in a kind of odd fashion. The parking situation around the AFSCME offices was awful, so Arnold had found some local real-estate promoter named Martin Frank to get some more space. Frank not only did that, he also sold Arnold on this no-risk housing deal. It looked harmless at the time, as if Arnold was building a monument to himself."

But the original Milwaukee project quickly spawned other developments, in San Juan, Puerto Rico, St. Paul, Minnesota, and Los Angeles. Joe Ames, with his tenacious eye for financial detail—Ames is a man who double-checks restaurant tabs—was most wary. "You would ask questions, and you would get fuzz in response," Ames complained. "The general representation was that AFSCME assumed no financial liability if these projects went wrong. That was not exactly accurate." The rationale of the program, run by the Federal Housing Administration, was that sponsorship by nonprofit organizations would permit private developers to obtain low-interest loans, and in turn be able to construct low-income housing. What was not generally revealed was that AFSCME and other sponsors could be stuck with the properties if the deals did not pan out.

The financial risks aside, the fact that Zander would devote so much time—union time—to housing appalled Wurf. When Zander claimed that the housing would help organizing drives in San Juan, Tom Morgan, the fired director of organization, visited the project and declared, "I wouldn't let my dog live there." The Zander Apartments in the black ghetto area of Watts, Los Angeles, were priced beyond the reach of AFSCME members living in the neighborhood. Nonetheless, Zander pressed on with zeal, provoking a bitter comment by Wurf, "You will find that there is more energy and activity spent on the Zander Apartments in Los Angeles, the Zander Apartments in Milwaukee and the contemplated Zander Apartments in St. Paul, than there is in building this union." When Zander loyalists chided Wurf for questioning the president's right to "leave a concrete memorial of his tenure in office," Wurf snapped, "Who the _____ does he think he is—a pharaoh? If Arnold needs a pyramid, let him go to Egypt. Maybe he can rent some space."

COUR went into the 1962 Milwaukee convention expecting rough treatment by the incumbent Zanderites. They got worse. Key committees were packed with Zander loyalists, the aisles were patrolled by burly sergeants at arms carrying walkie-talkies, and the floor was stocked with lavish signs for Zander delegates to wave during frequent "spontaneous" demonstrations. Of the 2,600 votes at the convention, from five hundred to six hundred were cast by international representatives. "The Zander people were blatant about getting these credentials," Wurf said. "An international rep would go into some small little local out in the West and remark how expensive it would be to send a delegate all the way to Milwaukee. He would make this big generous offer: If they gave him the credential, he would go to the convention at international expense. If they griped, he would work up some sort of instant 'trusteeship' and take the credential anyway."

Realizing that Zander had a locked-in majority, COUR looked for an issue that could give them the leverage to pry away delegates. Rather than rally behind one of their own reform proposals, they decided to go after Zander on the issue of the per capita tax increase.

On the basis of the ledger book alone, Zander had a strong case. AFSCME skittered along the ledge of bankruptcy, its books kept black only by loans from the AFL-CIO's Industrial Union Department, the United Steel Workers, and the United Auto Workers. Indeed, AFSCME on its own had operated in the red five of the six years ending with 1962.

To Zander, the only alternative to a per capita tax increase was to "pull down the shades, turn off the air conditioner, and go into semiretirement." By the time fixed expenses were deducted, only fifteen cents of the then sixty-five cents per capita was left for organizing, a piddling sum.

But given the disarray of AFSCME, was the membership compelled to send it more money? The problem seemed circular: Without more money, the international could provide no additional services; without additional services, the membership would provide no more money. Such was the situation COUR exploited at the convention.

First on the agenda, however, was the nomination of officers. Zander, the incumbent, was placed into nomination first, by James McCormack, the secretary-treasurer, with a speech that was quietly laudatory.

Then it was Wurf's turn. The Rev. Albert Blatz of Minnesota made his speech both a celebration of Wurf and an indictment of Zander. That no one had contested the presidency since 1948, Father Blatz said, was "perhaps indicative of a sick organization," and a reason that members felt disagreement was "forbidden either by the constitution or the Ten Commandments." Wurf's records of "bread-and-butter unionism" demonstrated his talents for higher office. Father Blatz did not think Wurf or anyone else would "single-handedly solve all of our problems." There had been attempts to portray Wurf as "evil." Perhaps. "I am sure that, like all of us, he

has his share of the faults and foibles which have plagued mankind
ever since Adam and Eve roamed in the Garden of Paradise. Beyond that, I don't think I am in a position to judge, or I don't think
any of us is in a position to judge. If he is evil, perhaps I am evil."
Father Blatz concluded with a summation of what Wurf hoped to
accomplish in the unlikely event he was elected president:

> I nominate him because he has been speaking out con-
> stantly and courageously and clearly in support of a program
> . . . to change the course of our union, a program designed to
> halt the slow but relentless trend toward one-man rule, a pro-
> gram aimed at broadening and strengthening our executive
> board. . . .
>
> It is a program to strengthen local autonomy and to bring
> back democracy to our union. It is a program which I think,
> with all my heart, is sincerely and absolutely vital to the sal-
> vation of our union.
>
> I nominate a man who is regarded, I know, as a rebel by
> some people. If he is a rebel, he is a rebel with noble cause.
> Without any reservation, I think we need him and I place in
> nomination the name Jerry Wurf, and I ask for no demonstra-
> tions or circuses, please.

These nominations came on Tuesday. COUR nominated Tom
Morgan as its candidate for secretary-treasurer; Zander went with
George Lima, who agreed the office should be abolished. A third
candidate was Gordon Chapman, who had held the office off-and-
on since the 1930s, left AFSCME in 1961 to become a special
labor advisor to Secretary of State Dean Rusk, and had broken with
Zander.

Although nominated, Wurf made no active effort at campaigning, feeling the numerical odds were too strongly against him: "We
didn't think we had a prayer to get more than 10 or 20 percent of
the vote." To Wurf, his candidacy was "sort of serving notice. We
took no precautions. The election committee was Arnold's staff;
most of those bastards weren't even eligible to be members of the
union." To the astonishment of everyone present, Zander was re-

elected by the surprisingly tight margin of 1,490 to 1,085. In a run-off election for secretary-treasurer, Tom Morgan withdrew in favor of Gordon Chapman, who beat Zander's man, Lima, handily. Since Chapman had declared his sympathy for COUR's reforms, the insurgents now had a man high in the AFSCME regime. Further, four of the eleven vice presidents elected ran on Wurf's slate, meaning COUR now had a strong minority on the AFSCME international executive board.

In the postmortems, Zander's survival was clearly attributable to two facts. The one hundred-odd international union officers present as delegates controlled around five hundred votes from some three hundred local unions and councils. Each of these people owed their livelihood to Arnold Zander, and they constituted the margin by which Zander won. Voting procedures giving disproportionate weight to small locals also favored Zander. As Wurf computed later, the twenty-five thousand members of his District Council 37 cast fewer convention votes than delegates representing six thousand members in Michigan. Clearly vote reform would be stressed in the COUR platform thereafter.

Congratulating Zander, Wurf was politely conciliatory. If his group felt it did not agree with the administration it would continue to work for change. "And on the other hand, if we feel the administration is right, I assure you that we will give the utmost support to the efforts of the administration to make this the best possible of all unions."

Whereupon Zander challenged him: "If Brother Wurf wants to give substance to his remarks," Zander said, let him do so by supporting the increase in per capita tax to one dollar. "That is the issue," Zander said. "It is the point of cooperation." COUR supporters interrupted him with cries of "point of order, point of order." To Wurf, this appeal was "an incredible piece of stupidity, because he was obviously bleeding over the fact that he had almost lost the election after twenty-odd years in the union."

When discussion began, Wurf's people had to fight for microphones, but they got them. They would not support the per capita increase, they said, unless it would help local unions. Wesley Solomon of Local 312 in Michigan pleaded for defeat of the increase "until we are shown that the monies that are going into the International coffers are properly spent and are properly handled. Not in housing. Not in housing, but to raise the level of education and the level of working conditions for the people that we represent. . . ." Herb Vander Bloeman, a rotund game warden from Local 1215 in Wisconsin, got chuckles when he declared, "I am the fattest warden in Wisconsin, but I am not a fathead or they wouldn't have me here. . . . I think the books should be straightened out first."

Zander, realizing he was losing the convention's last fight, yielded the gavel to William McEntee and passionately attacked enemies of the increase, and especially Wurf's District Council 37. Leaders there, he charged, without naming anyone, preferred a weak international union so they could build up their "lordships" with dues money. "They talk cooperation from that district council," Zander said. "Let them cooperate where it counts. . . . The lines are drawn. The lines of support and the lines of undercut." As Zander continued, his voice rose almost to a shout, and boos and cries of "Vote! Vote! Vote!" interrupted him. Zander needed a two-thirds vote to obtain approval; he did not even receive a majority.

In the next hour, Zander effectively lost control both of the convention and AFSCME. He offered a substitute motion increasing the per capita tax to ninety cents; his allies pleaded with Wurf and allies for support; none was offered. Realizing Zander had no chance, McEntee offered a substitute motion dropping the increase another dime, to eighty cents. As restated by Zander, a "yes" vote on the amendment would set the per capita tax at eighty cents; a "no" vote at ninety cents. The parliamentary sleight-of-hand did not work. Delegates shouted "No, no, no," and Zander backed away: A separate vote would be taken on each amount. The eighty cents lost, overwhelmingly. Zander was now a futile figure, mired in confusion, attacking opponents as disloyal to AFSCME, accusing them of voting personal feelings rather than common sense. He had no effect. The ninety cents also lost. But Zander would not desist. Steve Clark, a vice president friendly to Zander, proposed seventy-five cents. Victor Gotbaum arose in protest. "Really, Mister Chairman, this kind of reverse auction, I think, hurts not only the dignity of the chair but the dignity of the entire organization. I think we . . . might even go down to sixty-six cents if we stay here until midnight. . . . It is most undignified, and I ask, can't we please get over with it?"

Zander stormed that not increasing the tax "would satisfy those who have the International on the cross and [are] anxious to drive in the nails. . . ." To Wurf, this statement was staggering. "When you compare yourself to Christ and you talk about nails being hammered into you, and you're running against a Jewish candidate, whom you had beaten with less than all the proprieties attendant to a democratic election, you really turn off a lot of people." A leather-lunged heckler cut through the hubbub with a shout, "Who's the other thief, Arnold?"

The runaway convention now disturbed even Wurf. He thought, "It is only a matter of time and we will own this union. I figure we need the money." So he gathered his key supporters—Father Blatz, Ames, Bilik, and Schut—and led them into the corridor. To his surprise, perhaps half the convention followed him out. In the confusion of the crowd, Wurf tried to issue orders: The union could not survive if the per capita tax was cut below sixty-five cents. Persons in the fringe of the mob, apparently feeling that Wurf was suggesting a compromised increase, started shouting, "Don't sell us out, Jerry, don't sell us out."

Wurf hushed the audience. He told the crowd, "I think Arnold Zander is immoral, I think there's every possibility that the election was stolen." Under the federal Landrum-Griffin Act, which regulated union affairs, he had the right to contest the outcome. He would not, because "I think this institution is too fragile to stand it." A change was coming; the best course now was to end the convention as swiftly as possible.

Elation surged within Wurf when he returned to the floor and made his way to the microphone. "It was clear to me that I obviously had the overwhelming convention with me, that they had been convinced by this time that our concerns were legitimate. . . ." Scores of delegates stood and cheered as Wurf asked adjournment. Zander whacked the gavel and strode off the platform in gloomy silence.

When Wurf left Milwaukee late that night, he sensed that AFSCME was now his for the taking. But he also knew Arnold Zander would not surrender without a final, savage resistance. The rebellion that had begun in 1958 with Jerry Wurf as a Zander loyalist now moved into its final stage.

The ultimate weapon for a beleaguered labor president—roughly akin to a nuclear bomb—is to try to throw his opponents out of the union, through disciplinary procedures rigged in favor of the incumbent.

Zander moved quickly along this route immediately after the convention. Charges were filed against Victor Gotbaum of Illinois for allegedly interfering in another council's elections. Gotbaum's close ally, Lillian Roberts, officer of both a Chicago hospital workers local and the district council, was ordered fired, retroactive to the day the convention had opened. Al Wurf was accused of fiscal mismanagement.

These moves—all of which ultimately aborted because of their lack of substance—served as a prelude to Zander's major counteroffensive: an attempt to push Jerry Wurf out of AFSCME. As his vehicle, Zander chose the complaint of a disgruntled fired employee of District Council 37, one "Roberto M____." M____ had gone to work for one of District Council 37's locals in early 1962 as part of Wurf's effort to bring Hispanic-Americans into staff jobs. He was a mistake. Cantankerous, young and strong, M____ used his fists rather than his tongue in arguments. "There was a disagreement at a small meeting in Brooklyn and he badly beat up a middle-aged man," Wurf said. Wurf checked the man's record and found he had been arrested for rape and had served a prison term. Under the Landrum-Griffin Act, he was ineligible to work for a union, so Wurf fired him in November 1962.

M____ filed an appeal, not with District Council 37, as provided by the AFSCME constitution, but directly with the AFSCME international executive board. Next, Zander and Kramer gave wide distribution to a letter M_____ wrote attacking Wurf, with what the latter said were "slanderous charges in an effort to create an impression that threats, coercion and physical violence" were accepted operating procedure in District Council 37.

Wurf knew the charges were phony, and that the IEB would never uphold them. He also recognized exactly what Zander was doing. "He was building a fire in my backyard; he thought I'd have to stay around New York and mess with this crap and not be able to campaign against him. Well, he was wrong. The IEB would not take jurisdiction over the case, and threw it back to District Council 37, where it died a decent death." But Zander was playing with fire in going after Wurf personally. District Council 37 represented about one-seventh of the total AFSCME membership. Wurf felt—although he acknowledged that he could not prove—that Zander was willing to drive the entire council out of AFSCME to preserve his presidency. Wurf those days heard frequent entreaties from the Teamsters and other unions to take his membership out of AFSCME. "I don't think Arnold would have fought all that hard to keep us," he said. "He was willing to give up that big a chunk of the union to save his own hide."

Zander also fought back with a renewed flurry of trusteeships and "special arrangements," attempting to sway the insurgents' bases of power. Because of Wurf's convention showing, however, the locals and councils no longer cowered at the sight of an international representative. Given the stakes, the tussling understandably became nasty at times.

One particularly nasty bit of business took place in Michigan, where District Council 55 had been under special arrangements since 1961, with an agreement that it could regain autonomy at its October 1963 convention. Zander resisted any change: He flooded the convention with international representatives who carried proxy votes for captive locals. Even so, Clarence DeShano, the council president, defied Zander and gave a platform to the COUR leaders. As Wurf worked the convention floor, he got into a shoving match with an international representative and, during the ensuing melee, ripped the shirt from his back. Although DeShano was reelected District Council 55 president, immediately after the convention ended, Zander reimposed the "special arrangement." *The Public Employee*, edited by Zander publicist Ross Thomas, devoted much of its coverage to Wurf's skirmish, rather than to the vote in favor of anti-Zander candidates. Wurf angrily responded to this attack in the COUR newsletter: "Apparently Zander's only hope for continued power is to maliciously attack Wurf and paint him as a bad-tempered ogre. It's as if Zander had published a 'Wurf Coloring Book' for the members and ordered them to color Wurf 'black, red, purple, and bad-tempered.' "

Those were not the only words used in relation to Wurf and COUR. Here are more, taken from a single issue of *Public Employee:* "gang," "destroy," "mob," "invade," "capture control," "unconstitutional," "joke-of-democracy," "tricks," "henchmen," "loudmouth," "bribes-for-votes," "hoodlumism." There were more; the sampling makes the point.

One distinct advantage possessed by Zander was control of the AFSCME mailing list. Each month every member of the union received a copy of *The Public Employee*, which was their only regular link to the international union. Union newspapers do not come into the household with the inherent credibility of the *New York Times* or the *Wall Street Journal*. (As Wurf himself said of *The Public Employee* in 1981, "Fundamentally, it is not a newspaper. We never kid ourselves; it's a house organ.") But even by the loose journalistic standards of an in-house newspaper, Wurf felt *The Public Employee* under Zander played unfair. Any news items submitted by District Council 37's public affairs director, Charles Svenson, were either ignored or distorted beyond comprehension.

Nor could COUR obtain a copy of the AFSCME membership list, essential if COUR were to send mailings to rank-and-file members. Wurf offered to pay the expense of copying the list, and sent letter after letter to Zander; he was either rebuffed or ignored.

The grim campaign was broken by a single sparkle of levity. The

Center for the Study of Democratic Institutions, at the University of California at Berkeley, one of many grantees of the Fund for the Republic, commissioned a series of books on "the degree to which democracy actually prevails within the American labor movement." The project attracted respected authors, chiefly from academia, who studied perhaps a score of unions. The AFSCME volume, somewhat surprisingly to Wurf, was done by Leo Kramer, who, although still Zander's executive assistant, wrote with the brevet rank of "senior research assistant, Graduate School of Public Administration, Harvard University." The book, *Labor's Paradox*, although ostensibly scholarly, was essentially a brief for Zander in his ongoing fight with COUR. Given its sponsorship, *Labor's Paradox* could be of incalculable help to Zander.

However, the commercial publisher, John Wiley & Sons, Inc., seemed oblivious to the politics of the book. When a young art designer there cast about for cover photographs, she looked up AFSCME in the telephone directory and found herself speaking to Charles Svenson. She outlined the book to an incredulous Svenson, and asked if he could help her. Come on down, Svenson invited.

Previous books in the series had had a single representative cover photograph. Svenson explained that AFSCME members worked in hundreds of jobs, so why not a montage? The woman thought this a great idea, but where could she get the pictures? "Well, my dear, come with me," Svenson said.

They rummaged in the District Council 37 photographic files and put together a circular montage of AFSCME activities. Smack in the center was a photograph of a bargaining session, with Jerry Wurf's face in the foreground. The woman was so grateful she gave Svenson a credit line on the back cover.

The first copies arrived at AFSCME, and Zander and Kramer eagerly opened the package—to find Jerry Wurf staring at them from the cover. By one account, "Zander went absolutely wild and began ripping off the covers and shouting, 'That Jerry Wurf, that Jerry Wurf, he's evil, he's EVIL!'" AFSCME paid several thousands of dollars to have the books rebound with a revised montage. A prancing elephant, tended by a zookeeper, replaced Wurf. Joe

Ames kidded Wurf for years, "They replaced your face with an elephant's ass." (Actually, the view of the elephant was frontal.)

In the midst of the COUR campaign, Wurf made another and most important personal decision. He and Sylvia had finally divorced in 1954, their marriage at a dead end, the fault—in Sylvia's estimate—of neither party. Thereafter Wurf dated many women; somehow, however, he seemed to return to Mildred Kiefer. The relationship was off-again, on-again many times, and especially when the talk turned to marriage. Mildred had not been able to work for Wurf; could she live with him? "He was exciting, but he was damned difficult," she said. Finally Wurf forced the issue. He would hear no further talk about "man's relationship to woman, man's relationship to God." As he put it, "We're not going to bargain. We're either going to marry or not. Now, yes or no?" Mildred said yes.

"Well," he said, "let me make two things very clear. I want fresh-squeezed orange juice at breakfast, not that canned or frozen stuff. And *no* paper napkins."

Mildred looked square at Jerry and laughed. He shook his head and said, "OK, OK, I hear you. No bargaining. But no paper napkins, OK?"

Friends who watched Mildred and Jerry over the next twenty years had differing but consistent interpretations of why the marriage flourished. Mildred, strong-willed and intelligent, insisted on her own identity; she was loyal but not subservient. Through silence she rode our Wurf's frequent emotional firestorms. A subtle shake of her head could tell him he had gone too far. But no one to whom I spoke remembered Mildred ever taking serious issue with him in public. "Living with Jerry must have been like camping on the slopes of an active volcano," said one woman who frequently saw the Wurfs socially. "The beauty of how Mildred 'handled' him is that Jerry did not realize he was being 'handled.' Jerry needed a base, an anchor, someone who believed in him. Mildred was that, and more." Another positive quality Mildred brought to the marriage was her network of National Student Association friends, who by the 1960s were moving into positions of influence in government, academia, and the media. Wurf of course had built his own contacts, but Mildred gave him easy connections with people of importance outside the labor movement.

Mildred realized early in the marriage that she had linked her life with an extraordinary man. One summer weekend she went with Wurf to a board meeting of the Committee on a Sane Nuclear Policy, held at the Connecticut estate of Norman Cousins. Enjoying the lush greenery of New England, she paused under a large tree, and overheard a conversation. Norman Thomas, the venerable socialist, and David Reisman, the sociologist, were in earnest discussion on the theology of Reinhold Niebuhr.

The next Saturday's surroundings were totally different: a dinner at the home of Anthony Anastasia, the Mafia figure who long dominated the New York waterfront. Wurf's friend Paul Hall had recently lost an attempt to take the waterfront unions away from Anastasia; the dinner was a peace overture, and a lavish one. Mildred remembered an elegant dinner setting; a restaurant-sized kitchen, with a chef from one of Anastasia's restaurants; and pleasant between-course interludes in a garden with trays of succulent melons.

The talk turned to the Bay of Pigs, and Walter Reuther's attempt to raise money for tractors to give to Cuba to obtain the release of American-sponsored mercenaries seized during the abortive invasion. The debate centered on the morality of Reuther's efforts—whether it was proper to ransom such prisoners. Anastasia cut the debate down to its essentials in several terse sentences.

"This Walter Reuther, who does he think he is? Whether he gets the money or doesn't get the money, no tractors move."

Since Anastasia controlled the nation's docks, that could be considered a definitive statement. But not to Jerry Wurf.

"Well, I think you're wrong about that, Tony," Wurf said.

Forks froze in midair, as did the conversation. "Anastasia clearly was not used to having people argue with him in his own home," Mildred said later. Anastasia stared down the table.

"What do you mean, I'm wrong, Jerry?" he asked.

Wurf did not flinch. For fifteen minutes he and Anastasia

quietly argued a tractors-for-prisoners swap. Should Western nations have given Hitler tractors in exchange for Jews? Anastasia asked.

"I would have been outraged," Wurf replied.

Finally, Anastasia cut off the debate. "All right, Jerry, I'll have to think about it."*

In the context of the challenge to Zander, Wurf's marriage to Mildred was important in that he gained a soulmate who was at once wife, confidante, adviser, and critic. Wurf now had a friend who could both listen and argue, and as an equal.

To Jerry Wurf, the chief memory of the months before the convention was of grinding travel, a campaign in which he sought out prospective votes wherever he could find them. "I learned a hell of a lot about AFSCME outside of New York City those months," he would later remark. An example: One key AFSCME figure in Wisconsin, Tom Gerber, worked for the highways department. As a blue-collar worker, he could not take time off from his job to meet the touring Wurf, who would be in his area only briefly. But he did say, "I'll have my truck parked along Route so-and-so, X miles from town at noon on the 12th," by Mildred Wurf's recollection. "If you come along at that time, I could talk to you on my lunch break." Wurf found Gerber, they shared sandwiches, and Gerber later voted for the COUR slate. (He remains both an AFSCME regional vice president and a highways worker.)

Some of the votes Wurf found by accident. At a Columbia University dinner party one evening, Mildred Wurf casually mentioned to a black graduate student, a specialist in African affairs, that Jerry was attempting to win the public employees union presidency. The man asked a few questions, then volunteered, "You know, I just might be able to help you."

Mildred looked up in surprise. How could this Columbia academician be of any use in an AFSCME internal election?

The man smiled. "I come from Philadelphia," he said, "and my

---

* Events mooted the issue. Reuther could not raise the money, and the Bay of Pigs prisoners finally went free in an exchange for pharmaceutical supplies arranged by Washington superlawyer Lloyd Cutler.

uncles and my cousins and a lot other of my people work for the sanitation department."

So a week later Jerry and Mildred drove to Philadelphia and met a dozen or so activists from the sanitation union in a North Philadelphia row house. Some of the men wore work clothes, others old but neat suits that smacked of "Sunday-best." After listening to Wurf, a spokesman for the workers told him, "We can't vote the entire council, because it's run by one of Zander's men. But we'll give you enough so that Philadelphia can't vote solid for Zander." One of the supporters was a man named Earl Stout, then a rank-and-filer. Later he was to gain control of District Council 33 and win election as an international vice president. "Jerry talked the right stuff," Stout was to remember of the 1964 meeting. "You could tell he was a no bullshit guy. Jerry wanted something out of our union other than a salary and a big office. He wanted to do something for folks like me who knew what it was to pick up a trash can and pitch it on the back of a truck."

Each of these personal contacts illuminated to Wurf the grievances of rank-and-filers. In Contra Costa County, California, for instance, he spoke with members of an AFSCME local that until recently had been in a "civil service employees association." One of their leaders, an earnest and articulate young black engineer named William Lucy, told Wurf of the problems inherent in a civil service group: The "court house crows," the politically-oriented supervisors, looked out for their own interests and ignored the blue-collar workers. Lucy did not like a system whereby a supposedly objective "civil service commission" was in fact appointed by, and answerable to, political authorities. "Jerry impressed me," Lucy said years later. "We became part of that growing group that felt his ideas made more sense than what had gone on in the past." Lucy became active in the so-called Bear Flag Caucus, the pro-Wurf faction in a divided California delegation to the 1964 convention. (Lucy was to join the AFSCME international staff in 1966; six years later he was elected secretary-treasurer.)

A Wisconsin roadside. A Philadelphia row house. A union hall in the San Francisco Bay area. Jack Merkel, head of a New Jersey council, now an international vice president, remembers being bemused when asked to come to New York to meet Wurf on a houseboat in the Hudson River. "A *houseboat?*" Merkel exclaimed. Yes, one of Wurf's District Council 37 staff members lived in a moored boat, and it was used for COUR meetings. Merkel went, he liked what he heard, and supported Wurf.

Wurf's COUR colleagues also campaigned hard. Lacking an AFSCME mailing list, winning the presidency would have to come from personal delivery of the COUR message. Joe Ames, in one marathon push, drove five thousand miles through the West— from his home in St. Louis into Washington state, and back again. "Each guy had a few telephone numbers that he'd gotten from somebody at a convention. I'd call a few guys that I knew and say, 'Look, I'm going to be out there, I'd like to talk with you.' "

With Wurf's drive gaining momentum, the campaign took several decidedly nasty turns. Through confidential Justice Department sources, the COUR group turned up evidence that some of the persons involved in the AFSCME housing projects had unsavory backgrounds. In mid-1963 even Zander had to admit that the projects were causing problems: At his direction, AFSCME sued one of the housing development companies to recover $30,000 the union had put into a Puerto Rican housing venture. "The whole thing smelled Mob," Wurf later said, "although I don't believe Zander knew it."

According to Al Wurf, the COUR grapevine picked up information that nonunion persons connected with the housing program had decided to silence Jerry Wurf. The threat was taken seriously: the car of James Broyle, a pro-COUR district council leader in Massachusetts, had just been dynamited under suspicious circumstances. COUR even learned the name of an underworld goon who was "going to bust Jerry," in Al Wurf's words. Wurf knew exactly where to turn for muscle: his old sailor friend Paul Hall. "Paul Hall then sends his guys to protect Jerry for a while, and then they go to the waterfront and in effect say, 'You touch [Jerry Wurf], we touch you.' So for Jerry, it stopped." And when Al Wurf heard that pro-Zander forces intended to flood his District Council 50 meeting convention, and seize control by force, again he asked Paul Hall for help. A contingent of burly sailors stood around the convention floor. There was no disorder.

Although he now openly sided with his brother, Al Wurf remained on the international payroll through mid-1963. But Zander became more suspicious of him, telling aides, "Blood is thicker than water." The inevitable confrontation came when Zander attempted to do what Al Wurf called a "political audit" of the books of District Council 37. "I wouldn't let them come in," Al Wurf said. "I told Zander, 'If I'm in the state, you're not going to set up Jerry; you're not going to set up anyone in the state.' " Zander demanded a meeting and brought along an aide.

Al Wurf noticed the man was standing rather stiffly, with a suspicious bulge under his suit coat, and that both he and Zander acted nervous. Zander began asking "why I opposed his auditing Jerry's books. What they were doing was setting me up on tape. So I scream, 'Open your jacket before I talk to Arnold here.' " Wurf quit the international staff on the spot and went to work for District Council 50 directly.

As the convention neared, personal attacks on Wurf intensified. He was accused of being a chronic womanizer, a charge to which he entered a limited plea of guilty. "When I was single, I dated lots of girls. . . . I chased girls until I married Mildred in 1960. That marriage was the most important thing that ever happened to me, and Zander distressed Mildred and me very much by saying it was merely an attempt by me to achieve respectability." Other stuff was nastier. Leaflets distributed in New England emphasized Wurf's nose, "an amateurish appeal to anti-Semitism." Other drawings "depicted great ugliness in Joe Ames's face, which was badly chopped up in the war."

The Zander forces set the tone of the convention the first day. COUR stretched a huge banner across the lobby of the headquarters' Denver Hilton Hotel. Zanderites cut it down within the hour, leaving tatters hanging from a string. "Don't try to straighten her out, just leave the fucking sign up there, people will understand," Wurf ordered.

For two years the issues had been defined: COUR wanted decentralization of union power away from Washington, regional election of vice presidents, a lessening of emphasis on Public Service International and withdrawal from the housing program. Zander still hoped to abolish the office of secretary-treasurer; however, he made no serious attempt to push through this change, and he chose William McEntee of Philadelphia, a much-respected member, as his running mate. In what Wurf candidly called "an alliance of expediency," COUR ran the peripatetic Gordon Chapman for secretary-treasurer.

One handicap facing COUR was a large number of delegates from previously-unknown locals who suddenly appeared at the convention. "Obviously they had cranked out the paper for these locals in return for their votes," Wurf said. "We never saw some of those locals or those people ever again; they just disappeared from sight after the convention." COUR circulated leaflets charging that Zander had brought more than one hundred international staff members to Denver at a cost to the union of $40,000.

Wurf and Zander were nominated on Tuesday; the balloting was set for Wednesday, so COUR would have little time for substantive discussion of its reforms before delegates chose the president. Joe Ames worried about slippage. "They were the ins, they were the ones that could make promises or threats," Ames said. "All our promises had to be couched in, 'If we win . . .' and that's not very convincing to a guy that needs, right now, assurances that he's going to have an organizer helping him next week."

Ames prowled the corridors, running a vote total as individual delegations caucused, and he realized that COUR had made a tactical error that threatened Wurf's election. The COUR slate omitted a woman named Rena Ainsworth, a leader of Oregon District Council 75. Upset, the Oregonians threatened to vote for Zander unless Ainsworth was nominated for vice president. Ames withdrew as a candidate in her favor; he persuaded John Zinos of Detroit to do the same to secure the votes of another council. Wurf, meanwhile, deliberately kept a low profile, as he joked later, COUR did not want to risk a public outbreak of his "Donald Duck streak"—his words for a temper tantrum.

Wednesday night the ballots were counted under the auspices of the Honest Ballot Association, and one of the Zander poll watchers walked out and said to Bob Hastings, "Well, you elected Gordon Chapman again, but we croaked Wurf." Hastings telephoned the room where Wurf, Mildred, and supporters awaited the news.

There were tears and shouts of rage and protest. Vic Gotbaum stood at an open window, staring out into the darkness (Al Bilik fleetingly thought he was going to jump). Someone else lamented loudly, "The hell with this, I'm going to go out and join management and make some money." Wurf quieted a group of laborers from his home Local 924, who murmured ominously about "going downstairs and unstealing the election."

Wurf hushed the crowd. "Tough luck," he said, "we've tried. I've done my bit. If you guys are going to fuck around with this anymore, you'd better get someone else." He and Mildred left to go downstairs where the annual AFSCME banquet was just getting underway, with the intention of congratulating Zander. Mildred did not want to go; she had no desire to congratulate Zander. Father Blatz took her by the arm. "You must," he said.

Moments after they left the suite the phone rang again. The Honest Ballot Association had just announced a revised final count: Wurf had won by twenty-one votes. With a magnificent whoop, Tom Morgan, all two-hundred-fifty pounds of him, snatched up the tiny Fannie Fine and raced after the Wurfs. They caught up with them in the lobby, where news of the victory had spread quickly—to everyone except Jerry Wurf. "A group of our people are screaming, 'We win! We win!' and they're trying to grab me and put me on their shoulders.

" 'What the fuck are you doing?' " I yelled. 'I can't stand this kind of shit, so knock it off.' " Finally convinced he had won, Wurf swept into the hotel ballroom at the head of a swirling entourage.

Arnold Zander had been on the dais, making perfunctory remarks. He broke off, looked down at Wurf, and said nothing more.

But Wurf's victory, while at hand, faced one last hurdle: Its formal ratification by a convention bureaucracy loyal to Zander. The chairman of the elections committee, E. John Murphy of Wisconsin, sent word to Wurf that Zander's people were trying to force him to "turn over the ballots to them." Wurf quickly recruited some bodyguards from Laborers Local 924 and elsewhere, and stationed them outside Murphy's door. "We promised him that when he walked out of his room, nobody would assault either him or his wife."

Rumors of plots and counterplots raced through the hotel. At a Zander strategy meeting, his wife, Lola, mounted a chair and declared, "We will not be defeated by these people. We know we're right and we've just got to see to it that Arnold Zander is the president of this union tomorrow. You all know what you have to do, and if you don't know you must figure out what to do."

But one factor worked in Wurf's favor. The Honest Ballot Association had counted the votes openly, in the presence of reporters from the Denver newspapers. Tampering with the results would be exposed as a blatant steal. Wurf took no chances. At one point that evening, he turned to Mildred and said, "Go find me three large people, the larger the better." She went to the hotel bar, surveyed three of the most physically imposing Wurf supporters, and asked them upstairs. Wurf told them, "I want you to get to Washington immediately, tonight, and change the locks on every door and every file cabinet in the headquarters building." They flew out of Denver within the hour. Wurf, meanwhile, telephoned a lawyer in Washington and gave him a power of attorney and told him to meet the men the next morning at AFSCME's headquarters on Mount Vernon Place.

Among the well-wishers crowding the Wurfs' hotel suite that night was Jerry McEntee, the twenty-nine-year-old son of William McEntee. Jerry McEntee had worked briefly for Wurf in District Council 37 when he had first joined the AFSCME staff, and they felt at ease with one another. "Run this union right," McEntee

said, slapping Wurf's shoulder. "Otherwise, I'm coming after you."
Recounting this conversation years later, McEntee said, "I must
have been a pretty brash young man at that time."

Although the official convention schedule called for the elections
committee to report at 9:30 A.M. Thursday, Zander gave the item
no notice; he simply began calling up routine resolutions for approval. His demeanor worried Wurf; did Zander have yet one more
trick to play? Joe Ames sent someone out to buy several hundred
copies of the *Denver Post*, which contained a front-page story
about Wurf's victory, and passed them around the floor. Delegates
began chanting, "We want Wurf! We want Wurf!" Zander ignored them. Norm Schut tried to push the issue, moving that the
elections committee be directed to report at 11:30 A.M. He warned
against any "hanky panky." Zander retorted that the committee
had not finished its business.

So not until shortly after 2 P.M. was E. John Murphy permitted
to announce the final results: Wurf 1,450 votes, Zander 1,429.
Gordon Chapman beat William McEntee for secretary-treasurer,
1,566 to 1,302 votes. And COUR candidates won ten of the eleven
seats on the international executive board.

Accepting victory, Wurf described himself as "overwhelmed,
pleased, and breathless." The "long, arduous, and sometimes unpleasant campaign" was now over, he wanted unity. He praised
Zander. "You will forgive me if I say in a somewhat emotional way
that he and I were as close as two people could be. We disagreed,
and perhaps the closeness of our previous relationship made the disagreement that much harder. But let me say to you that the history
of public union employee unionism owes much to his foresight, his
wisdom, and his judgment."

In a concrete peace gesture, Wurf moved that Zander be ac-
claimed "president emeritus" and continue to draw full salary and
expenses until he reached retirement age.

At Wurf's suggestion, the convention did not take up any of the
substantive reforms that formed the heart of COUR's program. He
wished to avoid the time pressures inherent in trying to rush important issues through the closing hours of a convention. So he

suggested that a commission be appointed to make a thorough study of the AFSCME constitution, and suggest changes. Wurf's idea was pragmatic as well as practical: He knew COUR did not have the two-thirds majority necessary for constitutional amendments.

Jerry Wurf had achieved the nigh-impossible. He had unseated the incumbent and founding president of a major union. He was now to move onto the national stage.

CHAPTER FOUR

Rebuilding a Union

Jerry and Mildred Wurf flew into Washington on Saturday, May 2, 1964, had a post-victory celebration dinner with friends at the Jockey Club, and the next morning drove over to look at the AFSCME offices at 815 Mount Vernon Place.

"Ouch!" exclaimed Mildred. The lawn on the side of the building was littered with garbage and broken glass. Lighting fixtures were shattered. Conditions inside were not much better. Someone had leased a floor of the building to a pizza bakery. "When you came in in the morning, all you smelled was garlic and stale oil," Wurf said. "The building stank so that I knew we couldn't keep staff there." He sought out the pizza proprietor and ordered him to vacate. The man began shouting about a lease—"I think he paid about a hundred dollars a month for it, some absurdly low figure"—but Wurf would not listen: Either leave voluntarily, or we evict you bodily.

But AFSCME's problems extended far beyond broken glass on the lawn and garlic smells in the corridors. In his first weeks, Wurf faced several distinct sets of problems:

—Putting AFSCME on a sound financial basis, so that the union could give meaningful help to its people in the field;

—Disengaging the union from the housing program, which Wurf considered an albatross;

—Rooting out the highly suspect "international affairs staff," which to Wurf appeared to be "spookier than Halloween";

—Bringing to fruition the constitutional reforms that COUR had promised during the campaign that won him the presidency;

—And, most importantly, building the sort of organizing staff that would enable the national union to gain the momentum Wurf had achieved with District Council 37 in New York City.

Wurf's first discovery, and a sobering one, was that AFSCME was effectively bankrupt. To maintain the appearance of solvency, the Zander administration had kept two sets of books. "There's an old trick in how to balance books," Wurf said. "You just don't take the accounts payable and list them. You put them in a drawer." The books were a "total mess." Contrary to assurances Zander had given the convention and the international executive board, AFSCME had a two hundred thousand dollar liability on the housing projects, in the form of letters of credit to the Federal Housing Administration in the event units were not completed.

The huge size of AFSCME's debts stunned Wurf. Zander's final financial report he described as "pure fiction," as Wurf told the 1966 convention. "We owed hundreds and hundreds of thousands of dollars. Bills came in that were fantastic. We owed one hundred and fifty thousand dollars or two hundred thousand dollars in affiliation fees to the AFL-CIO and the Industrial Union Department. We owed money to—you name it—we owed it."

Wurf was acutely embarrassed one morning when he went to the AFL-CIO to pay a courtesy call on the president, George Meany. As he and an aide sat in the outer office, the AFL-CIO director of organizing, Richard Livingston, sauntered by, paused to congratulate him on the election, and said, "You got the same tin cup?"

The implication was clear. Livingston thought Wurf was there to beg yet another loan for AFSCME. This he did not intend to do. So he ordered that the Mount Vernon Place building be put on the block. After paying off the mortgage, AFSCME cleared $437,628, cash that enabled payment of many of the outstanding loans and bills. AFSCME moved into rented offices at 1155 Fifteenth Street, Northwest, under a lease that cut the union's monthly expenses by three thousand dollars.

Wurf next turned to the housing projects. "We found this housing thing a disaster. Our title to it was obscure, we didn't need it, we were losing money. . . . It gets to a point where you don't even know where the hell it goes." Wurf set up an investigating committee chaired by Father Albert Blatz which tried to find exactly what was happening. "When the facts started coming out," Father Blatz said, "it was worse and worse. I became anxious. I was not willing to stir up any water unnecessarily, because it would hurt the union." Meetings were arranged with Robert Weaver, the head of the Federal Housing Administration, which had played a major role in the projects. Weaver, in bureaucratic fashion, suggested that AFSCME rid itself of the mess as quickly, cleanly, and quietly as possible. "I heard him," Wurf said. "He wanted to sweep the whole mess under the carpet. His ass was on the line, too."

Clearly the only person who could help the new AFSCME administration make sense of the housing deals was Zander. Wurf felt the union had a hold on him. AFSCME had guaranteed him full pay until retirement; he also drove a union car. Father Blatz called Zander before his committee, outlined what he had found, and said, "These are the concerns we have, and I would like to know your response." To Father Blatz's astonishment, and outrage, Zander replied, "I plead the Fifth Amendment, because there's the possibility of criminal prosecution."

This episode effectively ended any relationship between Zander and AFSCME. After some shopping, Father Blatz found a religious group willing to buy the housing projects; the union escaped with no serious financial losses.

Another relic proved more ticklish. Wurf noticed "some real cloak and dagger types" working out of offices on the fourth floor, the international affairs department. Several times he asked the department head, Harold Gray* to explain what happened there. Gray would reply "with some kind of mumbo jumbo about drafting a full report. I didn't push him, because I had other things. But I was suspicious as hell." Eventually Wurf received a phone call from an acquaintance at the White House, who asked that he be at a certain house in the Maryland suburbs at a certain time. "It was a

* A pseudonym

meet with the CIA, at a safe house," Wurf said. Wurf listened to whatever was said, and told the CIA it could no longer have a role in the union.

Essentially, that is all Wurf has ever said about AFSCME's involvement with the CIA. He would not even tell Mildred the name of the White House aide who acted as an intermediary, although he did say "he is known to both of us." By ending the association, AFSCME managed to avoid the publicity that linked other unions and many philanthropic foundations with the CIA in 1967, when *Ramparts* magazine deciphered the rather thin cover shielding the operations.

What Wurf heard was this: beginning in mid-1957, AFSCME had acted as a conduit for $878,000 in CIA funds passed to foreign public employee unions, chiefly in Latin America. The Soviet Union and its client states were funding leftist unions; the CIA could not openly finance non-Communist labor groups, hence its reliance upon AFSCME and other receptive unions. As an anti-Communist, Wurf could accept the CIA's rationale. He knew the perfidious nature of Communist covert operations. But he abhorred hypocrisy. Whatever stand AFSCME would make against Communism would be public; he would not play in the shadows with the CIA. He told the CIA contact that AFSCME would no longer handle covert funds, but that he would make no public disclosure of what he had learned. As Wurf stated later, "I'm an American. I disagreed with the way they were doing their business, but when they told me it had to be kept quiet, I agreed."

The CIA and the housing projects were sideline events. Wurf would be judged not on them, but on how he carried out the reforms promised by COUR, and how he stimulated AFSCME organizing.

As chairman of the committee on constitutional revision, Wurf chose Joseph Ames, a valued ally, and one with the intellectual ability to think in concepts. "A goddamned frustrated nonlawyer," Wurf would rage at Ames in later years, when their alliance soured; but in 1964, Ames was the craftsman Wurf needed to fashion a new AFSCME constitution. With eight other members, Ames held hearings around the country, eliciting ideas from AFSCME rank-and-filers and officers on what changes were needed. As consultants, he took along Eric Polisar, from the faculty of the Cornell University School of Labor Industrial Relations, an authority on labor union organization; and Ronald Rosenberg, a labor lawyer whose firm had become counsel for AFSCME. "We wrote a complete new constitution, literally from scratch," Ames said. It was presented to a special AFSCME constitutional convention in Washington in the spring of 1965.

"Our old constitution seemed to be pretty much of a mess structurally," Ames related. "It was difficult to read, except by the attorneys. It was difficult to locate full information on any one item. It required, for example, if an individual wanted to . . . determine how votes were cast in convention, he had to read . . . four different articles to find out. If he wanted even the most general description of the duties of the international president, he had to read twenty of the twenty-five existing articles." The new constitution attempted to describe, in a single article, "as full coverage as possible of some one subject," Ames said.

In the political sense, the major innovation of the new constitution was a change in convention voting strengths. Under the old constitution, locals were permitted one delegate for each one hundred members or fraction thereof, with a maximum of five delegates. In practical terms, this meant any membership strength above 401 was irrelevant, for regardless of how large a local might grow beyond that point, it could have no more than five convention votes. The result was demonstrably lopsided voting strength for the small locals.

This was no accident, as has been seen. Arnold Zander and the men around him had carefully nurtured a union with its roots deep in middle America. By design, they had kept AFSCME's center of power in the small towns of the Middle West and the Middle Atlantic states, among people who accepted the status quo and were content to argue with quiet voices.

The allocation recommended by the Ames commission was a

compromise, for it was not one-man-one-vote. It allocated one delegate for each one hundred members, or fraction thereof, up to five delegates. Thereafter, a local gained one extra delegate for each thousand members. As Ames told the constitutional convention, the change "has nothing to do with voting strength, but it would permit locals of exceptional size to send a few extra people for participation in the convention."

The delegates who would vote on the Ames proposal were the very persons who would lose power by its approval. Wurf had so captivated AFSCME, however, that the opposition was cursory. The major opponent was a man from Washington state who had spoken so often and so poorly on previous issues that delegates moaned when he took the floor. His argument, an odd one, was that city delegates should be kept to a minimum because they were smarter than their country cousins. "The delegate from the large local union . . . is probably a little more capable than the guy . . . from the small local union."

Rebutting the few scattered critics, Ames said the change was not all that drastic. Even with the new system, he explained, the 3,600 small-local members who previously could outvote 41,000 large-local members could still outvote 25,000. "We cut the odds down to something like seven to one, instead of twelve to one," Ames said. But he insisted that the large locals needed "some degree of equity, some degree of relief."

Further, as Ames pointed out, changing the voting strengths would encourage small locals to merge into more viable units. Under the old system, small locals often fought such a merger in order to preserve their voting strength, although combining with other locals would improve services to members. The delegate allocation provision passed by overwhelming vote.

The Ames commission constitution dealt with abuses that COUR had attacked during Wurf's campaign. No paid employee of AFSCME could serve as a vice president, a proviso aimed at the "porkchoppers" who converted union office into a comfortable sinecure.

No longer would the international office dictate the composition of the international executive board. Vice presidents would be elected from sixteen separate regions. Here the Ames commission had had to draw districts from scratch, for none had existed previously. One guideline, according to Ames, was that "we must not, under any circumstances, put part of one state in one district and part in another." Some decisions were easy. New York, Michigan, and Wisconsin, the three largest states in terms of AFSCME membership, were each considered a single district. The committee then attempted to divide the remaining forty-seven states "on the basis of as nearly equal memberships as possible," with a minimum of two states in each district, and a maximum of five. (In actuality, one district, the southeastern, wound up with eight states; in three of these, however—Alabama, Mississippi, and Louisiana— AFSCME had not a single member.) The districts ranged in size from 4,821 to a shade over 16,000, close enough to the desired mean of 10,781 to satisfy the committee, and ultimately the convention.

Another COUR platform plank dealt with trusteeships of local unions and district councils. Wurf and his supporters had charged Zander with indiscriminate imposition of trusteeships. The old constitution had had what Ames called "exceedingly broad and exceedingly vague" grounds to permit the international's taking control of local unions. The new constitution had specific safeguards aimed at preventing abuses:

—The president must have "reasonable cause" to believe that a subordinate body or its officers or members were engaged in financial malpractice or corruption; violating a collective bargaining agreement or the AFSCME constitution; threatening secession or dissolution; or (the catchall clause) "conducting the affairs of the subordinate body in such a manner as directly and seriously to jeopardize the fundamental rights and interests of the membership. . . ."

—A hearing should be held within thirty days of imposition of the trusteeship, with due process guaranteed the officers involved.

—The persons judging the case would be a three-member panel drawn from the Judicial Panel, not presidential appointees; for, as

Ames noted, the president in all likelihood would be the person preferring the charges.

—If the panel voted to lift the trusteeship, the president could appeal to the international executive board.

—If the panel voted to withdraw the trusteeship, the matter ended there; the president had no right of appeal.

Creation of such an independent internal review board was a landmark for American labor unions. A panel not answerable to the AFSCME president would have the authority to review his decisions. Wurf accepted the concept at the time. In later years, as shall be seen, he turned on it.

The result of these changes was to give the general membership a strong voice in AFSCME—a democratization that left heads of other AFL-CIO unions shaking their heads in wonderment at "this damned guy Wurf." As is true in any enterprise of a political nature, the first obligation of a person in power is survival. Wurf certainly enhanced his position by the constitutional change increasing the voting strength of large locals. But the regional election of board members was a definite risk. Was Jerry Wurf as popular in the midlands of America as he was in New York? And if an unfriendly board resulted, could he control AFSCME?

The constitution provision on the powers of the president left no doubt about who would run the union on a day-to-day basis. That would be Jerry Wurf, or whoever else held the position of president. This only recognized reality. The international executive board met every three months, the convention every two years. The first principle of management is, "Find the right man and leave him alone," and this AFSCME clearly intended to do.

Subject to "policies established by the international executive board," the president was authorized to "employ, terminate, fix the compensation and expenses, and direct the activities of such office staff, administrative assistants, technical and professional assistants, field staff, organizers, and representatives as are required to carry out effectively the functions of his office." The broadness of this language meant Wurf had almost total autonomy over AFSCME's internal operations, as long as he stayed within the equally broad language of the constitution. Board control, on an operational basis, required only that the president "report regularly . . . on his actions." Another article gave the president the authority—"notwithstanding any other provision of this constitution"—to "order the immediate suspension, pending full investigation, of officers and staff employees of any subordinate body who in his opinion are engaging in conduct imminently dangerous to the welfare of the international union or a subordinate body." The international executive board, however, must be notified immediately, and the suspension was subject to automatic review and approval or disapproval; the person remained a member all the while. The suspension could be for no more than thirty days, and if the president did not file formal changes within that period, the suspension would end and could not be renewed.

That the convention was solidly behind Wurf in his attempt to reshape AFSCME was demonstrated by an incident during ratification of the article pertaining to the presidency. The constitution set the president's annual salary at $21,000, plus expenses, a low figure by the standards of other large international unions. Delegate John H. Tittle, of Columbus, Ohio, objected, "You are trying to keep us down in the lower levels. There isn't a president of any international union of the United States reaches a salary that low. I amend that to reach $25,000." There were scattered shouts of approval from the floor.

Wurf, embarrassed, abandoned the chair, went to the floor as "Jerry Wurf, delegate from Local 924, New York" and vigorously objected to the raise. The call for the convention had stated that the per capita tax issue would not be raised, which Wurf said was a "clear implication that we would not be dealing with the internal fiscal affairs of the union." Wurf felt the amendment illegal, and opposed it on practical grounds as well. "I think it would be the height of irresponsibility to deal with a matter of this kind without dealing with the basic finances of the union." He asked that the motion be either voted down or withdrawn.

Tittle, however, refused to withdraw the amendment. Thomas Crenshaw of Detroit, a school employee, finally rescued the flus-

tered Wurf by moving that the raise be put over to the next convention; his motion carried by voice vote, to Wurf's relief.

The constitution contained other important words. In talks with
Eric Polisar, the academician helping the Ames commission, Wurf
said he wanted a "statement of purpose" that transcended trade
unionism. AFSCME first and foremost was a labor organization,
but Wurf also saw it as serving a broader mission. Polisar wrote several drafts, he and Wurf worked them over, and the result was the
preamble to the new AFSCME constitution:

> Workers organize labor unions primarily to secure better
> wages and better working conditions.
>
> We hold that they also organize in order to participate in
> the decisions which affect them at work. One of the funda-
> mental tenets of democratic government is the consent of the
> governed. Unions are an extension of that idea.
>
> Union members are both workers and citizens.
>
> Collective bargaining is the expression of citizenship in em-
> ployment. Participation in the political life of the nation is
> but another aspect of that citizenship.
>
> In the same way that unions are dedicated to improvement
> of the terms and conditions of employment, we are equally
> dedicated to exert ourselves, individually and collectively, to
> fulfill the promise of American life. Amidst unparalleled
> abundance, there should be no want. Surrounded by agricul-
> tural surpluses of all descriptions, there should be no hunger.
> With advanced science and medical research, sickness should
> not go untreated. A country that can shoot rockets to the
> moon can provide adequate education for all its children.
>
> For unions, the work place and the polling place are insepa-
> rable, and the exercise of the awesome rights and responsibil-
> ities of citizenship are equally required at both.
>
> Unions are under a solemn obligation: to represent mem-
> bers forcefully and effectively in negotiations with manage-
> ment and to conduct internal union affairs according to dem-
> ocratic standards.

The new constitution was a reaffirmation of the victory Wurf had won ten months earlier. He now had the tools to reshape AFSCME. He had gained the presidency by a razor-thin majority; he was now the unchallenged strong man of AFSCME.

But AFSCME elected Wurf not to write a new constitution, nor to rid the union of CIA encrustations and ill-conceived housing programs. His professed strength was as an organizer and agitator; and his immediate priority was to bring into AFSCME the people who could use his District Council 37 tactics to organize public employees throughout the country.

Several factors worked in Wurf's favor. The United States Supreme Court's "one-man, one-vote" decision on legislative districting meant enhanced big-city influences in state legislatures. This liberalization meant that AFSCME found generally friendlier forums in asking for collective bargaining rights and in negotiating contracts.

Another important gain for public employees was an executive order issued by President Kennedy in 1961 giving federal workers the right to organize and bargain with their employer agencies. Although the executive order did not extend to state, county and municipal employees, it served as a model that AFSCME lobbyists could cite in their dealings with legislators and councilmen.

An even more important factor was the massive infusion of federal monies into state and city governments under President Lyndon Johnson's Great Society programs. Federal funds were a minimal slice of city general revenues in the 1950s. A report issued in late 1978 by the Advisory Commission on Intergovernmental Relations has documented the change. In 1967, the forty-seven largest cities received nine cents from the federal government for each dollar of own-source revenue. In 1978 they received fifty cents for every dollar of own-source revenue. Given the availability of these funds, cities became more amenable to public employees seeking better pay and benefits.

This is not to suggest that states and cities suddenly began handing out money to their employees. AFSCME grew to power through literally hundreds of bargaining situations throughout the country, with governments of all sizes and political predilections.

As his shock troops, Wurf assembled a diverse band of individuals from within AFSCME itself, from other unions, and even from nonlabor areas. Despite the intense rivalries among individual unions, the professional organizer is adaptable. He can organize steel workers one year, rubber workers the next, and truck drivers the next, for the techniques and the goals are not all that different. Professional organizers are a nomadic lot, given to long hours at the job site and long days on the road (and longer nights in motels). Susan Wurf, Jerry's eldest daughter, was startled when she went to work for AFSCME as a field representative in the 1970s. Although she was to live in upstate New York, her assignment was in Baltimore. "I knew Mister Howard Johnson better than I knew my own apartment," she said. Given the volatility of union politics, many organizers work with an eye cocked for whatever position might be open elsewhere; a failed campaign, or a slighted superior, can put an organizer on the street within the hour. Oddly, as employers, the major unions in America get away with labor practices that would often be considered intolerable in corporations. Organizers exchange trade gossip, as do other professionals, and in the mid-1960s the word went out on their circuit: *AFSCME is going to be the "hot" union the next few years. The president, this guy Wurf, is somewhat of a hothead, but if you can take his yelling, he's the best thing that has happened to labor since the 1930s.*

One person who heard of Wurf was P. J. Ciampa, a stocky, balding man who had come up from the bear pits of organized labor. "Champ," a second-generation Italo-American, was born in the soft-coal fields of Pennsylvania, near Altoona. During the 1920s his father, a miner, had held office in the United Mine Workers of America, and he had taught his family to revere the UMW president, John L. Lewis. Then there was a strike, and the elder Ciampa was assigned to a "flying squad" to ensure that no men crossed picket lines. Goons hired by the mine owners caught Ciampa, rolled over his car, and set to work with truncheons. "They gouged out one of his eyes," Ciampa said. "People sent for me—I was a very small child—and I remember that was the first time I was inside a hospital. I remember the whiteness, that's all."

Ciampa managed to get out of the mine fields. He worked in a steel mill in Pittsburgh, where he became involved with the United Steel Workers as a shop steward and organizer. Then he drifted to Baltimore, and the Glenn L. Martin Company, an aircraft manufacturer, and the United Auto Workers. Here Ciampa made a misjudgment. Through his own abilities, he rose through the UAW ranks from voluntary organizer to shop steward, plant chairman, and international representative. He chose to run for regional vice president, opposing a candidate backed by UAW president Walter Reuther. Ciampa won, "I had a little difference of opinion, and Walter had the marbles." When Ciampa's term expired, he was out of the UAW, and out of a job.

Ciampa heard that the new AFSCME president needed field organizers, so he sought out Wurf. They liked one another, and he took the job, with responsibility for the states around the District of Columbia. Ciampa was a disarming individual even to persons who thought they knew him well. He could speak the dem-and-dose jargon of the Baltimore blue-collar worker, then shift to the clipped sentences of a negotiator who knew exactly what he wanted, and on what terms. The ability to summon trust from the hearts of suspicious workers is essential to a good organizer, and such a facility was perhaps Ciampa's strongest point.

Ciampa proved himself as a persuader in June 1966, during a strike by drivers and trash collectors in Montgomery County, Maryland, a Washington suburb. The men had no union, but they did not like their pay or working conditions. They struck and asked their employer, the Washington Suburban Sanitary Commission (WSSC), a governmental agency, for a fifty-cent-an-hour raise (they earned from $2.04 to $2.56, depending upon the job). The WSSC offered ten cents to nineteen cents an hour, which the men rejected as inadequate; whereupon the WSSC broke off talks, withdrew the offer, and said no more negotiations would be held unless the men returned to work. When the strike continued, the WSSC declared it "illegal" and summarily fired all 280 workers and hired a private firm to take over the trash collections.

Calling a strike under such circumstances ran counter to union common sense. The workers had no union. Maryland law did not require the WSSC to even nod at them. Yet this strike, in the immediate outskirts of Washington, was the target of opportunity that Wurf and AFSCME could put to advantage. Ciampa showed up at the main WSSC garage the morning of June 10, stood in the back of the crowd and listened as the newly-hired private contractor told the workers the "strike was over," that they no longer were public employees, but that he was willing to permit them to return to work "on his own terms."

Ciampa took over the crowd. He climbed onto the hood of a trash truck and in stentorian tones told the trashmen that "it would be absurd for you to take the deal these new bosses are offering you. They are selling you a bunch of nonsense! They run in here offering you what was a bum deal yesterday, when the government offered it. Why is it any better today, when this private bunch offers it?" Ciampa asked the workers to put their trust in AFSCME. "We're a union, a national union, and we're here to stay. You go with us, and we're with you to the wall." Within an hour, 245 of the 280 workers had signed AFSCME membership cards. They also remained on strike.

Ciampa walked through the crowd and found the foreman of the private contracting company. He displayed the cards, riffling through the stack like a riverboat gambler. "I think," Ciampa said, "that we have some business to discuss."

The private contractor knew reality when he saw it. He agreed to meet with Ciampa and an *ad hoc* committee of strikers in a nearby hotel. The company accepted AFSCME as a bargaining agent, and Ciampa started negotiating on the contract. By four in the afternoon they had an agreement providing pay raises of fifteen cents to thirty-one cents an hour, company-supplied foul weather gear, union security, a grievance procedure, and other technical benefits.

The workers, meanwhile, had milled around the yard, awaiting the outcome. Ciampa realized a technical defect: No local union had been formally organized.

Ciampa telephoned Wurf. "This sanitary commission thing," he said. "I got a contract."

"Contract? I didn't even know you had a union," Wurf said.

"Get on out here and see for yourself," Ciampa said.

Wurf hurried to Maryland for a unique ceremony: the chartering of a new AFSCME local, and the simultaneous signing of a contract giving increased benefits. In the space of twelve hours, P. J. Ciampa had increased AFSCME membership by some 245 people.

"Give me a dozen like him," Wurf said, "and I'll organize the goddamned United States Congress." Some other effective organizers came from within AFSCME's own ranks. This was deliberate. Soon after his election, Wurf directed that the union create a Staff Intern Training Program (SITP) in which candidates suggested by locals would be brought to Washington for intensive schooling, then assigned to the field under experienced organizers. The training program, under Betty Miller of the AFSCME education department, drew some three hundred applicants from AFSCME locals. Of these, fourteen were selected to come to Washington. The first phase was classroom work, with simulated situations organizers were apt to encounter in the field. Class members took the roles of employees who disliked unions, or who preferred other unions to AFSCME, or thought membership in a civil service association was preferable to a union. In one class a student actor portrayed a worker who was about to be fired for drinking on the job. He stumbled to the front of the room with glass in hand, mumbled a few words, and collapsed on a chair. "OK," asked Ms. Miller, "what do you do?"

These classes attracted serious unionists. Not untypical was Leamon Hood, who had gone to work for the city of Atlanta as a school custodian in the early 1960s. Hood managed to obtain a better job in the water department, despite blatant promotion discrimination, and he also played a key role in organizing the first Atlanta local for AFSCME workers. When AFSCME offered Hood a position in the staff training program, he accepted.

Another member of the first class was Ernest Rewolinski, a muscular Polish-American from Milwaukee, a sometime football center and baseball catcher, "all those positions you get killed on," with a solid union background. As a high school student holding a full-time job, Rewolinski served as a shop steward for the International Association of Machinists; after Korean War service, he was a member of the United Auto Workers. Then he went to work for the Milwaukee sewage treatment plant, which, although offering little money, did give security. After thirty days on the job a shop steward asked if Rewolinski would join AFSCME. "I told him I didn't even know what AFSCME was." After a short history, "I told him I believed in unions, and I would sign the card, although there were no contracts in place, there were no grievance procedures—it was just that you joined an organization that tried to represent you with the employer." At his first union meeting, Rewolinski asked the president of the local about an unsafe condition in his sector of the sewage treatment plant.

The president replied, "Well, if I'm not mistaken, you just joined the union today. There's many of us who have been here for years, have all kinds of problems, and I don't know where you're coming off with your complaints."

This response irked Rewolinski, who had joined AFSCME because he felt it would represent him. "The president was telling me, 'whether you're a member or not, you have to have fifteen years in here before you say something.'" Rewolinski did not accept this. He involved himself in union politics, and eventually became president of Local 366.*

Rewolinski had no union aspirations beyond Local 366; he was content to remain a city employee for thirty years and retire. Jerry Wurf put some fire into his ambitions, however.

* In December 1981 Rewolinski became executive assistant to AFSCME president Jerry McEntee.

Jerry Wurf came onto the scene and began talking about the trade union concept, the rights of public employees, the rights to collective bargaining. It was the incentive for me to get involved because I was young, I was married, I had three children, I was struggling, and he was just kind of my hero at the time.

Based on these impressions, Rewolinski took a leave of absence from his city job, persuaded his wife he was doing the right thing, and went to Washington for the AFSCME training program. Fourteen people eventually graduated. Coupled with organizers it had hired from other unions, AFSCME was now ready to assert itself as a viable union.

What Wurf intended, from the first days of his presidency, was a two-pronged strategy. In the first instance, he would campaign for changes in the law that would give public workers bargaining rights, including the right to strike. To do that, he knew he had to overcome public antipathy toward public employees. Public support was all important, because increased pay benefits inevitably had to be supported by higher taxes; hence Wurf faced an obvious challenge. Persuasion was the carrot. The second phase of Wurf's approach was the stick—the strike. The result was an organizing blitz not seen in the United States since the unionization of the auto industry in the 1930s, when the United Auto Workers literally seized physical control of plants with sit-down strikes. In the next few years, Wurf was to be at once one of the most reviled, and admired, men in America, to be depicted as an ogre by many of the nation's politicians, but as something of a saint by the people who followed him.

In his many speeches on public-employee bargaining rights, Wurf went through several recurring themes. He acknowledged that during its early years AFSCME was a "supplicant," content to improve civil service procedures. The first law permitting public workers to join a union—passed in Utah in 1953—did not require governmental bodies to recognize and negotiate with unions. "This is like giving a kid an ice cream cone and telling him he can't lick it," Wurf said. Although isolated states and cities—Wisconsin and Philadelphia, to name two—did have intelligent bargaining procedures, most governments conducted themselves like medieval monarchs. Speaking to the International Association of City Managers in 1966 (Wurf tartly called it "your union"), he asserted that workers deserved a say in their economic and social fates:

> They are outraged by the idea that you sit there in your infinite mercy and in your infinite wisdom dispense largess like the kings of old . . . and that they just must be happy and grateful for that which you give them, whether it's a piece of meat or a crumb of bread.
>
> I say to you that this day has come to an end, and the reason our union is growing, and the teacher's union is growing, and the National Education Association is changing, and the federal employees are joining unions in the tens of thousands, is because workers are essentially tired of being patronized. . . .

A second theme Wurf sounded was that government managers were notoriously inefficient. He would not apologize for the inconvenience of hospital strikes. "For some thirty years now, the people that work in hospitals have been exploited in a way second only to the way people have been exploited in agriculture. Those of you that have the authority to make decisions to prevent this kind of exploitation have not exercised your power intelligently." At one state hospital in Delaware—which AFSCME was to unionize by overwhelming vote—some workers made as little as two hundred dollars monthly; they survived through food stamps and other relief programs. In Ohio, more than a thousand state employees received welfare. As a result, "We are confronted, across the nation, with chronic shortages of policemen, hospital aides, nurses, welfare workers, and technicians." Given higher salaries in the private sector, and inefficiency in government, "many vital public services have been transformed into . . . employment turnstiles, inducing, simultaneously, administrative inefficiency and excessive operating costs."

Elaborating on this theme to the National Conference of Mayors in June 1967, Wurf had his audience sitting in tight-lipped anger as it heard his indictment:

> Public employee efforts to improve wages and working conditions have been regarded as arrogant and unbridled self-interest and treated in a manner more appropriate to major insurrections.

> This disparity, ironically enough, operates largely at lower levels and in what we term social services. Executive assistants, administrative heads, and top level staff are recruited and retained by salaries in the fifteen thousand dollar to thirty thousand dollar bracket. We appear to have little difficulty in rationalizing this; given market realities and the need for talent, such compensation appears unavoidable. It is at the four thousand dollar to ten thousand dollar level that we balk and resort to pious and passionate declarations of the requirement of a sense of dedication to public service.

> We have been governed since the 1930s by a public policy which specifically repudiates unilateralism in labor relations. We declared, by statute, that employees had a right to form organizations of their own and that employers were obligated to bargain in good faith. Yet this fundamental, and sound, public policy applied only to private industry. Government officials appeared curiously reluctant to adhere to the rules they imposed on others.

> Government representatives who regularly negotiated, directly or indirectly, with private sector unions for the construction of schools, highways, hospitals, and government office buildings found similar negotiations with their own employees to operate these facilities an unacceptable intrusion.

> Officials who, in pursuit of their duties, unhesitatingly executed contracts involving fiscal commitments far into the future, suddenly discovered an implacable inability to negotiate

the terms and conditions of employment beyond the current
legislative session or administrative term. . . .

Even now, a public employee union harried or frustrated in
genuine collective bargaining which turns to legislators to
correct inequities is condemned as irresponsible, denounced
for flexing political muscle, and regarded with the jaundice
conventionally reserved for extortion.

Wurf did not accept the "thesis of cruciality" as applicable to
every public worker's appearance at the job:

> Reasonable men cannot really be expected to accept the
> thesis that all public services are equally crucial. The parks
> attendant is performing an important function, but social ca-
> tastrophe is not imminent in his temporary absence. That
> decorative secretary in a government agency is really not per-
> forming differently from her sister in her private world. [But
> the thesis] has simply been repeated so frequently that is has
> gained unwarranted stature and credibility. In our society
> where are the critical functions concentrated? Our farms and
> factories are private. The facilities which transport their prod-
> ucts are private. We are dependent for medical research and
> care upon a profession which is ferociously private in orienta-
> tion. In war we rely on private enterprise and stake our na-
> tional survival on its successful performance.

Such were the words of the tough Wurf. He needed the right to
strike in those early years because he needed a lever. But he also
advocated a less Draconian alternative: fact-finding by an impartial
outside body, which he termed a "sound and useful way to avoid
strikes." And here he could point to the record of Wisconsin,
which in 1962, largely at AFSCME's urging, had adopted an insti-
tutionalized system of fact-finding.

Under the act establishing collective bargaining for unions in
Wisconsin counties and cities, either labor or management could
ask the Wisconsin Employment Relations Board to name a fact-
finder when negotiations deadlocked or one of the parties refused to

bargain in good faith. The fact-finder held hearings to determine the merits of each side's case and then recommended a settlement. The decision was advisory, rather than final and binding.

Nonetheless, the voluntary system seemed to work well. James L. Stern, a professor of economics and labor education at the University of Wisconsin, studied the state's first three years experience with the law. He found that seventy-three disputes were submitted for fact-finding between June 1962 and June 1965. Of these, thirty-five were settled by mediators without formal hearings. Ten cases were consolidated, one was withdrawn, leaving twenty-seven for fact-finders to investigate. The recommended settlements were fully acceptable in fifteen cases, substantially accepted in five, substantially rejected in two, and fully rejected in five. The rejections, Stern found, occurred in rural areas where "unions are weak and managements do not recognize collective bargaining."

Stern concluded that all the winners praised the fact-finding process and that only a few losers criticized it. Local unions generally accepted the fact-finders' terms even when they lost. Stern felt fact-finding could reduce unions' tendencies to strike "if it is viewed as a special alternative developed for public employees to compensate them for the loss of the right to strike."

In a talk to one mayors' conference, Wurf could not resist a jibe. His finger jutting at the audience an accusatory jab, he told the mayors:

> You represent our best organizers, our most persuasive reason for existence, our defense against membership apathy and indifference, our perpetual prod to militancy, and our assurance of continued growth. . . .
>
> Unions would be unable to sign up a single employee if he were satisfied, if his dignity were not offended, if he were treated with justice. What is important is not the motives of union officials in organizing public employees, but the astonishing rapidity and success of their efforts.
>
> Barren ground yields poor crops. But here, the ground was fertile beyond belief.

Such was the reasonable Wurf, the unionist stating his organizing philosophy and goals to the officials with whom he had to bargain. Wurf had no illusions that he would win over governors and mayors through logic and oratory. "Nothing attracts a politician's attention more than a good kick in the ass, or a picket line, or demonstrators raising hell outside his testimonial dinner," Wurf once said. Wurf had to establish AFSCME's credibility: If he or local officials threatened a strike, they were prepared to carry it off, regardless of threats of jail. The *mal'ach hamaves*—angel of death— who had harried Brooklyn cafeterias in the 1940s was now to hover over much of the United States.

There is a play in football called the red dog, in which the defending team ignores potential pass receivers and sends both its linemen and linebackers in hot pursuit of the quarterback. The play has understandable shock value, and it often results in the quarterback giving serious thought to a change of professions. What AFSCME did the first two years of Jerry Wurf's presidency was the union equivalent of a red dog. Everywhere city, state and county officials looked those months, they seemed to see an AFSCME organizer huffing after them, Wurf often as not storming along in support. Wurf did not intend to be a chair-bound administrator; when a tough situation developed, he wanted to be in the field "with my people." Given his abrasive confrontational techniques of bargaining, mayors, county administrators, and seasoned state officials found themselves recoiling before a personal onslaught the likes of which few had ever experienced.

Consider Lansing, Michigan, where Wurf flew to bolster the morale of city workers who had struck for a pay increase. During his first meeting with the mayor, Wurf discovered a tape recorder. He stormed out. "Get rid of the damned bugs," he told the mayor, "or we're staying out forever." The recording devices disappeared. When Wurf resumed bargaining, he saw that police around city hall carried shotguns and bayonets. "Get the damned storm troopers out of here!" Wurf yelled. The mayor did, and a settlement was reached. "See you again sometime," Wurf told him with a handshake when the last session ended. "That statement gives me a reason not to seek reelection," the mayor replied.

In Massachusetts, the legislature had passed laws permitting collective bargaining for state and city employees, chiefly at AFSCME's urging. Wurf sought to transmit his organizing fire at a massive Boston rally kicking off "Operation First Class." Here he sounded a theme that was to run through his public speeches the first years of his presidency:

> With the new law you no longer have to go hat in hand to beg politicians for a raise. The new law in Massachusetts should mean you will now be able to bargain with your employers across the table.
>
> I would advise any politician who cannot take the responsibility of being a good employer to stay out of politics.

In states where local officials pleaded lack of authority to negotiate, Wurf threw the law back into their faces. As a laboratory demonstration, he chose Ohio, where the Ferguson Act forbade strikes by public workers. Wurf persuaded a pro-labor administration in Cleveland to negotiate with AFSCME—where major units of city workers chose the union to bargain for them—and then used this experience as a bludgeon against other cities. Wurf did a media blitz of Cincinnati to coincide with a conference of thirteen Midwestern governors. Of the states represented, he noted, only three had any modern collective bargaining laws for public employees. "While the governors grapple with broad questions such as education, taxes and urban needs, too few have troubled to tidy up their own housekeeping and set up sound labor relations policies, which are needed to boost employee efficiency and morale, without which the best of programs must suffer." Ohio, despite its ranking as one of America's wealthiest states, was thirty-fifth on a list of average monthly earnings for state employees.

As Wurf accurately noted, the Ferguson Act did not deter workers from striking. In four major Ohio cities in 1965 and 1966, AFSCME members struck their jobs to press contract demands. Each time, city officials noticed, AFSCME picked up more members. These walkouts, in Dayton, Warren, Youngstown, and Toledo, proved the inefficacy of the Ferguson Act. As Mayor Raymond Schryver of Warren lamented, after losing a strike, "All the law does is declare the strike illegal and allow us to fire the employees. It doesn't force them to go back to work, which is the thing we're after." None of these four struck cities sought to invoke the law. Politicians, in media interviews, suggested the net effect would be the repeal of the law—which the Ohio legislature eventually did.

AFSCME during those years resembled a string of firecrackers exploding across the nation. During one stretch AFSCME—in this instance led by the redoubtable P. J. Ciampa—won no less than fourteen consecutive elections in Delaware, including one where the vote was 100 percent. When Governor John Chafee of Rhode Island vetoed a bill giving collective bargaining rights to public employees, AFSCME prodded the legislature into overriding him; District Council 70 immediately began an organizing drive. Other governors were more receptive. In Maine, Governor John H. Reed was a keynote speaker at the founding convention of Pine Tree Council 74. "There is a need," he said, "there is room, for a public employees union. I have no reservations but that you are developing a responsible organization." Wurf responded with his first-class-citizen speech. Maine public employees, he said, are "among the worst paid in the nation." Although their needs were as great as those of workers in private industry, "I don't think that when you go into a store and display your state employee card that they allow you to pay a little less."

But to Wurf, the sweetest victory of his first months as president related to some unfinished business of his District Council 37 years: an election establishing AFSCME as the single bargaining agent for New York City municipal hospitals. And here some background is in order.

The hospital workers' election was important to AFSCME for several reasons. Local 420 was one of the early AFSCME organizations in New York City, and potentially one of the largest, with some seventeen thousand prospective members. But it also had some of the gravest problems. Most of the workers were poorly-paid, ill-trained blacks and Hispanics who lived a hand-to-mouth existence, subject to arbitrary changes of working rules and capricious supervisors who were quick to replace them if they "talked out of turn." Unions were considered anathema by administrators. Rudy Mitaritonna, one of the early stalwarts of Local 420, first went to work at Morrisania Hospital in 1937: seven days a week, from seven in the morning until seven in the evening, for thirty dollars a month and a room, with an occasional two hours off in the afternoon at the whim of a supervisor. Three times the hospital fired Mitaritonna for organizing activities; three times he complained so loudly that he was put back on the job. After one firing Mitaritonna had co-workers flood the mayor's office with telephone calls. "A hundred dollars worth of nickels later, they gave up; the lines were all tied up and they couldn't get any work done. So they had to take me back."

The workers affiliated with AFSCME in 1944 as the Joint Board of Hospital Locals, under District Council 37. But conditions did not visibly improve. Many employees worked eight or twelve days without a day off, few enjoyed the eight-hour day, work rules varied from hospital to hospital, and salaries were among the lowest paid any city employees. John Boer, a one-time hospital worker who became an organizer for, and then president of, District Council 37, felt overwhelmed at times with the futility of trying to get a decent contract. "We wrote letters protesting working conditions, but we had no political strength." This was in the late 1940s. "Just about that time one Jerome Wurf arrived on the scene. He was a new international representative for AFSCME."

To Wurf, the city hospitals were part of broader overall problems facing municipal employees—low pay, unstructured working conditions, no union recognition that meant anything, lack of status. As noted earlier, Wurf set about trying to get a toehold in various city departments. It was not until 1954 that he felt in a position to give serious attention to the hospitals. The first step was to consolidate the Joint Board of Hospitals into a single unit, Local 420. Hospital workers, Wurf and District Council 37 leaders decided upon special goals: decent treatment of employees, a genuine forty-hour week, and a wage differential for night duty and work on contagious wards.

One early organizer hired by Wurf was James Farmer. "Jerry hired me to help organize hospital workers," Farmer said. "I said, 'OK, where do you want me—Harlem or Bedford-Stuyvesant?' " "Jerry stared at me. 'Neither,' he said, 'Get out to Staten Island.' Man, that was the *whitest* borough in all of New York."

Farmer, already a national civil rights leader, quickly identified with the hospital workers. "The major issue at that time," he related,

> was not money, though the hospital workers were among the lowest paid in New York. The grievances were seldom built around money. They were built around two words: "decency" and "dignity"—the desire to feel that you were somebody of importance. Hospital workers were looked upon as the dregs of society. They were considered to be floaters by the city [of New York], the politicians, and by people of status in the hospital.
>
> They hadn't worked long. Many had come up from the South fairly recently, looking for any kind of a job. They were expected to have a poor attendance record and everything else. They were looked upon as dirt, literally. So the major issue in Local 420 was dignity, human dignity—to be addressed as a human being, to be called Mister or Miss. That was the key thing.

But the organizing work was done *sub rosa*. According to Victor Thompson, long-time chapel chairman at Lincoln Hospital, the local had only twenty to thirty members when he came to work there in 1952. "Nobody knew who to go to or which way to turn," he said. "Maybe once a week or once every two weeks someone would come from the union office to collect dues, or hold a meeting in a backroom or a basement. There was no set place. You couldn't 'talk union' and allow yourself to be heard by some people, otherwise you might lose your job. But I joined the union anyway, because I had gotten filled up with aggravation from these people, the nurses and other supervisors. So I looked around." One friend he found was Jean Conturier, a Local 420 organizer. Conturier agreed the local was weak, with only about one hundred eighty members, "no growth, no staff for the local, with very few shop stewards." Conturier and other organizers worked the lunch lines and locker rooms, asking what grievances the workers had, and trying to handle them with management; but given the lack of a checkoff system, whereby dues could be deducted from members' paychecks and passed on to the union, "we had to spend a lot of time collecting dues by hand."

Because of Wurf's work elsewhere in New York, the city Board of Estimate in 1956 did agree to provide for the automatic checkoff of dues. This decision meant that union representatives could spend their time handling grievances and other important business; also that membership could be continuous—and not dependent on whether a business agency could find each member every month and collect the dues. (Once workers fell behind in dues payment, they lost their membership.)

AFSCME was first challenged for control of the hospitals in 1956, when the Teamsters started a drive to gain a majority of the employees. Had the drive succeeded, AFSCME would have lost its beachhead. AFSCME, with its meager resources, faced the challenge with less than total confidence. As Conturier stated, "We found out after the drive that the Teamsters had started the campaign with about five thousand members; we had about one thousand five hundred. By the end of the six weeks, we came out . . . with about five thousand six hundred members and the Teamsters had about six thousand, and that was when the big struggle started over which union would represent the hospital workers."

Given the closeness of the split, neither AFSCME nor the Teamsters was anxious for a definitive election over which union would be certified as the bargaining agent. As Conturier said, "There was the fear that if the Teamsters were way ahead, they might win recognition from the city as the only union for hospital workers, and they feared the same thing. We knew it wouldn't come within a week or even a year—but we all knew that one day the test would come, and one union would represent all hospital workers."

Given the performance of blacks among hospital workers, AFSCME organizers had the good political sense to forge a close alliance between unionism and civil rights. Consciously or not, black ward workers in New York hospitals suffered many of the racial jibes and discrimination endemic to the South. Projecting the union and civil rights as a valid common cause meant that the hospital workers could equate their own situation with the plight of other blacks elsewhere. When AFSCME spoke strictly in economic terms, admitted Rudy Mitaritonna, "when there was nothing extraordinary to present to the membership . . . attendance was very slack." Mitaritonna credited Jerry Wurf with the idea for the merger of causes—as has already been shown, Wurf believed strongly in it. "The leadership showed interest in all kinds of social activities. We sent contributions to Negro colleges and various charitable organizations," Mitaritonna stated. "We gave support to all the major civil rights programs, beginning with the demonstrations for Emmet Till* at Madison Square Garden. Every time an African nation went on its own, we participated in celebrations here."

By 1959, Local 420 had a network of three hundred shop stewards in nineteen city hospitals—a picket line of defenders for workers' rights. But there was an anomaly. Although such high city officials as Mayor Robert F. Wagner, Jr. recognized the importance of stewards' functions, actual day-to-day recognition by the supervisors on the job existed only on paper. Lower-level administrators treated AFSCME with disdain; nursing supervisors, long accustomed to complete autonomy over their wards, would not deal with a union steward.

James Butler, a chapter chairman at Fordham Hospital, and later to become the president of Local 420, was disgusted that "some of

---

* Till, a black teenager, was murdered in Mississippi in the early 1950s for allegedly speaking with familiarity to a white woman. His killers were never punished. The murder became a civil rights *cause célèbre*.

the supervisors were treating the workers like they were animals. My co-workers were regular human beings. They lived in the city, they had families, they took part in the community like everyone else. So who gave a supervisor the right to talk to them as if they were prisoners? The workers were taxpayers, too, so they were part owners of the hospitals."

By 1965 AFSCME was ready to go head-to-head with the Teamsters for control of the hospitals, in a winner-take-all election. There had been changes in District Council 37. Wurf's immediate successor as executive director there, Charles Tabia, was ill, and Victor Gotbaum had been brought in from Chicago as his replacement. Gotbaum had had qualms about Wurf's temperament even during the COUR campaign; now that he was working directly for Wurf, and going into the "largest AFSCME election that had taken place," he did not want any interference. Wurf watched the campaign from a distance, then phoned Gotbaum. "I got to come in, I got to work with you, I won't do anything," Gotbaum quoted Wurf as saying. Gotbaum replied, "Jerry, you're full of shit. You can't come in. There can be only one guy in charge."

"Victor, it's my baby," Wurf said.

"The only one who can save your baby right now is me," Gotbaum said. "Just stay out."

Later that day Gotbaum received a phone call from Mildred Wurf, who asked, "Victor, Jerry is so nervous. Why don't you let him come in?"

"I said, 'Fine, let him come in. Let me know when his plane arrives so I can take a plane and get out. It can't be done and you know it and I know it.' He didn't come in."

As Gotbaum was to reason later, his firmness in keeping Wurf away from New York and District Council 37 during that important election was important to their future relationship. "I tried to let him know that I wanted to work on my own. I recognized what he had done in building the council. But what the hell—it's like a parent raising a kid. Eventually you've got to let the kid out of the house. If I had let Jerry take over the hospital election, I would have been a flunky the rest of my time here. And that, friend, I wouldn't have liked." For the next twelve years Gotbaum was to be Wurf's closest friend and ally in AFSCME.

The day-to-day direction of the campaign fell to Gotbaum and his associate director, Lillian Roberts, who had worked as a nurses' aide before joining AFSCME in Chicago. She became an international vice president, then resigned to come East for family reasons, where she joined Gotbaum. Roberts immediately saw some serious problems facing AFSCME in competing with the vastly richer Teamsters.

"We just didn't have enough staff to wage a drive throughout all of the hospitals," she explained. "The Teamsters were by far the stronger local, and it seemed almost certain that they would win the election. We had only six months to organize an all-out campaign."

Roberts reviewed the campaign material the council had distributed and found it mostly negative, attacks on the Teamsters. "I knew people would soon get tired of reading negative things. We had to come up with positive programs which would give the local a new image, a new sense of purpose."

From her experiences as a nurses' aide, Roberts knew the frustration of being locked into a dead-end job. "Although many of us wanted to go to school to become nurses, the salaries were so low that it was impossible." This situation worked to the disadvantage of the hospitals as well as the aides, for most institutions were chronically short of trained staff. Training programs, then could both help the workers and improve the quality of health care.

"Antipoverty money seemed to me a good place to start looking for help," Roberts said. "I contacted friends in Chicago and got encouragement from them on our chances of getting money for training programs." The first request was for money for a program to train nurses' aides to become licensed practical nurses. "We then outlined a career ladder for each job title in the hospitals. In the kitchens, in the craftshops, on the wards, within every job title throughout the hospital, aides performed work at different levels of skill. Our program called for formal recognition of each level, with training and a salary which rewarded that skill." For instance, experienced dietary aides could become senior dietary aides, and with additional training move up to the position of food supervisor. Nurses' aides who worked in a particular department of the hospital and acquired skills would get "technical licenses" in their respective fields, and salary increases.

"We sent out seven thousand applications offering aides the opportunity to go to school to become licensed practical nurses. Four thousand came back," Roberts said. "That was really encouraging, and it reassured me that the members would take advantage of the opportunity if it came."

So Roberts and other AFSCME officers sold a positive program to workers. They held meetings, they distributed literature, they explained the collective bargaining process, a subject completely foreign to many of the workers. The message was strong: Vote for AFSCME representation, and "we could push for training programs, promotions, health benefits, and other improvements," Roberts said. "We offered the workers a whole new brand of unionism."

To John Staten, an oxygen therapist and later a Local 420 representative, the campaign meant almost daily physical confrontations with Teamster organizers, and the omnipresent threat of violence. "The other union [the Teamsters] had some little bitty dudes with big knives and some were big dudes with whatever they had, and some were just ugly dudes, but they had plenty dudes. A lot of our people were afraid to come out to night meetings. It was really rough."

When Staten woke up on election day, "I really had to get myself prepared for war—it was that bad. I wasn't in a very jubilant mood when people from the other side told me that if I showed up I was going to get my tail whipped." So Staten, a broad-shouldered man not easily frightened, decided to use some psychological scare tactics of his own. "All during the day I made myself quite obvious around the hospital. I let certain people know that if I was going to wind up in the morgue as a result of all the competition, that I was going to have some company." No one bothered John Staten on election day.

Another Local 420 representative in the trenches during the bitter campaign was Lester Wright, later to become District Council 37's division director for hospitals. "Competition with the Teamsters was so tight that people would join 420 one day and then quit and join the Teamsters the next day. A worker might lose a grievance with one union and then join the other union for the same grievance. You were never certain of your membership."

On election day, Wright worked at a polling place at Bellevue Hospital, passing out leaflets and giving a last-minute word of encouragement to workers arriving to vote. "As the people walked past me, they would make a 'V' sign or wink and smile at me. The trouble was that they did it on the sly, so that the Teamsters or a supervisor wouldn't see them. So I couldn't tell if they were sincerely with me and planning to vote for 420, or if they were planning to vote for the Teamsters and were just making fun of me. That's when I started to worry, and with everyone who went by, I felt worse and worse."

When the balloting finally ended at seven o'clock that evening, "I couldn't face going over to watch the count, the tension was too great." So Wright walked out onto First Avenue, and sat in his car for four hours, stomach churning. Had he done everything possible to win the election? What would his future be at the hospital should the Teamsters win? Was it time to search for a new job?

"Then around eleven o'clock, this hospital worker, a 420 member, stepped out of the door where they were counting the votes. Now this man was sometimes quite a foul-mouthed individual, especially when he got excited. I saw him in my rearview mirror. He jumped way up in the air and shouted some choice words. When I heard him I thought, 'Oh, no, we've lost the election.' Then I heard him shout, 'We took 'em, we took 'em!' "

Indeed AFSCME had "took 'em." Through appeals, the Teamsters managed to delay certification of the election for nine months. At one point the Teamsters even threatened to cut off deliveries of medical supplies to the hospitals. "This really compounded the crime," said Victor Gotbaum. "Not only were they now hurting the lower economic workers, but they were now threatening the helpless sick. It was stupid, it was disgraceful." In the end, District Council 37 won and became the exclusive bargaining agent for some thirty-five thousand hospital workers. Jerry Wurf, by obtaining the "little Wagner Act" order from Mayor Wagner, had caused AFSCME membership to make a quantum jump.

Another New York strike of the same period, although involving fewer workers, also had significant long-range implications for AFSCME and other unions. On January 1, 1965, about seven thousand AFSCME welfare workers, members of Local 371, struck when the city refused to negotiate a new contract. They were joined by members of the independent Social Service Employees Union, whom Wurf termed "way-out radicals" who saw the union as a "playground for their revolutionary class war." The city invoked the Condlin-Wadlin Act, and nineteen officials from Local 371 were fined $250 and sentenced to thirty-day jail terms.

With the local leadership in jail, Wurf assumed personal command of the strike, which was a tough one, with pickets marching in subfreezing temperatures. Although Wurf claimed that "the entire labor movement in New York City" supported the strike, this was by no means true. Paul Hall of the Seafarers International Union, Wurf's old chum from District Council 37 days, was the only leader of note to help AFSCME. The Central Labor Council, which Wurf said "liked AFSCME about as much as a bone in the throat," did nothing. But Hall supplied sailors to supplement Wurf's pickets, who were predominantly women. As Wurf joked years later, "There's many a child walking around the streets of New York who is the son or daughter of a social worker who got impregnated during that strike by a sailor! There were literally hundreds of sailors on the picket lines, passing somebody a cup of coffee, relieving pickets so they could warm up in the cold snowy weather."

The strike dragged for twenty-eight days, then the longest by public employees in New York's history. Eventually it was settled when the city agreed to submit contested issues to an impartial fact-finding panel. The city agreed to establish an Office of Collective Bargaining, a chief AFSCME goal. Wage gains were from five hundred to nine hundred dollars a year, along with a reduction in workloads. Finally, the fines and jail terms were thrown out, although that was little solace to the AFSCME leaders who had already spent time behind bars. And as lagniappe, the Social Service Employees Union, convinced Wurf was satisfactorily militant, rejoined AFSCME.

To Wurf, the welfare strike had added significance because it pointed up the absurdity of laws banning public employee strikes. Until public workers were able to bargain freely and fairly, he told a strike rally, there was no real alternative to a strike—even if work stoppages were illegal. "What we are fighting against is the same 'take it or leave it' bargaining policy which the National Labor Relations Board recently said was illegal in private industry."

That the existing Condlin-Wadlin Act was inadequate was brought vividly to public attention in yet another New York strike almost exactly a year later. Beginning New Year's Day, 1966, the Transport Workers Union shut down city subways for three weeks, to the distress of commuters and businesses alike. Clearly both the city and the state needed more effective labor-management mechanisms. The state's two ranking Republican politicians, Governor Nelson A. Rockefeller and Mayor John V. Lindsay, proposed diametrically opposite solutions.

The Lindsay panel, appointed after the welfare strike, had structured an impartial and independent Office of Collective Bargaining. The office would oversee bargaining procedures, including impasse situations, and determine and certify bargaining units. If bargaining broke down, the office would appoint a fact-finding panel to intervene. Two members would be appointed by the mayor, two by public employee unions involved, and three by agreement of the mayor and the union representatives. Strict timetables were established for bargaining.

To Wurf, this format was highly acceptable, and he agreed with Lindsay that it was the "best hope for the peaceful solution of disputes affecting city employees."

But Governor Rockefeller supported a law of a drastically different nature—"bidding for the most horrible kind of right-wing Republican support for his idiotic presidential ambitions," in Wurf's angry words. As a vehicle, Rockefeller used a study commission headed by Dr. George Taylor, a labor specialist at the University of Pennsylvania. The Taylor Act,* as eventually passed by the legislature, created a labor board, the Public Employee Relations Board (PERB). But unlike Lindsay's balanced board, PERB's three members were appointed by the governor alone, for six-year terms, with no requirement of a balance between labor or management, nor indeed even of impartiality. From labor's viewpoint, the only positive feature of the Taylor Act was that it guaranteed unions the right to organize and bargain for state, county, and municipal employees. The PERB would resolve representational disputes and provide mediation and fact-finding aid. The state and each of its political subdivisions were required to bargain collectively with employees.

But despite Rockefeller's depiction of the Taylor Act as "reform" legislation, it actually extended what labor considered to be the worst features of the Condlin-Wadlin Act, which it was ostensibly supposed to replace. Any public employee who struck would be subject to penalties ranging from reprimand to dismissal. The union itself, if the PERB so decided, would lose its right to representation, including dues checkoff, and be fined $10,000 or the loss of a week's dues, whichever was greater, for each strike day.

That such legislation would be passed in his home state infuriated Jerry Wurf. Working with the Transport Workers Union and the United Teachers Federation, Wurf arranged a rally of some twenty-five thousand unionists in Madison Square Garden to protest the "RAT Act." He predicted accurately that the law was unenforceable and would lead to even more strikes.

> Jails are no answer to militancy; fines don't stop unions from protecting their members from injustice and unfair practices; and the repeal of checkoff provisions—while it may

---

* The bill first went before the legislature as the Rockefeller-Travia Act, Travia being the Democratic speaker of the house. AFSCME publications immediately began calling it the "RAT Act," for Rockefeller And Travia, and sponsors decided to put Taylor's name on it for obvious reasons.

cripple some unions—does not contribute to the stability of labor-management relationships in government.

He objected that the Taylor Act was to be "administered by a board appointed by, and beholden to, the governor. The board's budget is developed by the governor's budget director. And the governor is the boss, so far as New York state employees are concerned." The board by its very origins "lacks independent authority. It is not a separate, neutral agency counterposed between labor and management; it is, I repeat, an agency of the state government, an adjunct of the office of the governor."

The Taylor Act alone was enough to sour Wurf on Nelson Rockefeller—and on politicians in general. He scorned the governor as a politician who "can be a liberal on Monday, a moderate on Wednesday, and a reactionary on Friday. Thanks be that on the seventh day, he rests." But even as Wurf raged against the Taylor Act, Rockefeller did something AFSCME considered even more reprehensible. He certified, as the bargaining agent for state employees, the Civil Service Employees Association, (CSEA), with which AFSCME at that very time was contesting elections.

CSEA for some forty years had been the largest state employees group in New York. Wurf refused to call it a union or even a bargaining agency. "It is, in fact, a loose association held together by an insurance sales operation," he charged. An Albany insurance company with links to the then top officers of CSEA offered low-cost insurance to state employees ranging from blue-collar workers to judges of the New York State Court of Appeals. "Joining this association was the only way they could get the insurance," Wurf said.*

For whatever reason, state workers did join CSEA, some one hundred forty thousand of them. AFSCME's District Council 50, the unit for state employees, had something less than fifteen thousand, chiefly in state hospitals. Numerous other unions also competed for members.

---

* Under new leadership in 1979, CSEA agreed to merge with AFSCME, an overnight gain of 215,000 in membership. See Chapter Ten.

Recognizing that the Taylor Act offered organizing opportunities, despite its defects, Wurf in late 1967 ordered a major drive in New York state, to be directed by his brother, Al, then the director of District Council 50. Wurf sent in reinforcements from the outside, including Ernest Rewolinski, who had just completed the staff training program.

Rewolinski sensed immediately that AFSCME had serious problems in organizing New York State. "It was an incumbent organization that was in place, people felt complacent and comfortable with it; state employees at that time really didn't look at themselves as being second-class citizens," Rewolinski said. Logistics were another problem. "Pilgrim State Hospital, with a potential membership of five thousand, was a city in itself. It had so many buildings and maintenance facilities and boiler plants and psychiatric wards and treatment centers that you'd have to spend a lifetime just to get around the buildings." And Pilgrim was but one of many.

Nonetheless, Al Wurf, Rewolinski, and other AFSCME organizers such as Vincent O'Brien, tried spreading themselves all over the state. Hundreds of prospective members began to sign cards. AFSCME was slowly—very slowly—moving into position to challenge CSEA in specific areas.

Then, to the astonishment of Jerry Wurf and others in AFSCME, Rockefeller in November 1967 announced he was designating CSEA as the exclusive bargaining agent for one hundred twenty-four thousand state employees. Although the designation was to last only one year, Rockefeller's action gave CSEA a clear advantage in organizing, for by the time AFSCME had a chance to contest for members again, many would be signed. Both Wurf brothers denounced the move, Al calling it "disheartening and vulgar," Jerry terming it "arsenic under the sugar coating" of the Taylor Act. Al said that Rockefeller acted "without a scintilla of proof that these employees wanted this organization to negotiate for them. . . ." Al continued:

The decision was based on insurance checkoff cards which employees had to sign if they wished the low-cost CSEA insurance. Using this criterion, actually, the governor should have recognized Blue Cross. . . . To top the denial of free choice required the mind of an autocrat; and it appears that this administration wasn't lacking one.

AFSCME challenged Rockefeller's certification of CSEA in court, lost, and continued organizing in state hospitals. Once CSEA's one-year certification ended, Wurf felt AFSCME had a fair chance of winning a majority of the hospital workers. Rockefeller double-crossed him again. In October 1968 he repudiated his one-year agreement, and his administration began negotiations with CSEA to represent the hospital workers. This decision was repugnant even to Rockefeller's own PERB, which urged that the CSEA negotiations halt until representational elections could be held for mental health workers in hospitals, the key test group. Rockefeller refused, even after Wurf warned him that his breach of promise would bring "drastic action" by AFSCME.

Wurf, Rockefeller learned, was not a man of idle threats. In October 1968, AFSCME struck for a day at four state hospitals—Creedmore, Manhattan, Brooklyn, and Buffalo. Rockefeller telegraphed Wurf that the strike was illegal, and urged him to "direct the members of your union to return to work." "Fuck you," Wurf shouted, crumpling the telegram and hurling it to the floor. In more polite language, he said in a return wire that his powers as AFSCME president did not include directing members of affiliated unions to return to work.

Rockefeller broke at that point. All right, he said, if you return to work, you can have your election. The strike ended, and AFSCME won bargaining rights. But Rockefeller exacted his revenge. Lillian Roberts, the District Council 30 organizing director, and Robert Fuller, the president of Local 69, received thirty and twenty day jail terms, respectively, for violating the Taylor Act with the strike.

Roberts and Fuller considered the sentences badges of honor. The day they surrendered, thousands of pickets jammed the street in front of the New York City jail on West 37th Street. (Wurf later said, "I was probably filled with more rage that day than at any other time in my life.") Megaphone in hand, he called the jailings a "disgrace. It is unbelievable that in this day and age, somebody would have to go to jail simply because they wanted the right to choose a bargaining unit." Demonstrators carried signs reading, "Jail Rocky, Not Roberts."

Roberts replied quietly, "As long as there are public employees who do not make adequate salaries . . . and do not have the right to vote, there will be people like me who do not mind spending thirty days in jail." Then she put her arms across the shoulders of Jerry Wurf and Vic Gotbaum and walked across the street and entered the dingy ninety-eight-year-old jail.

The initial public reaction to the strike was strongly condemnatory of AFSCME. Sanitation workers and teachers had also struck in New York that year (through unions other than AFSCME) and the press took the general line that public comforts were more important than labor rights. A good example of the press hostility came in a television interview show. Martin Tolchin of the *New York Times*, asked, "Mr. Wurf, how do you justify a strike that increases the anguish and the agony of mental patients?" Wurf agreed that the strike was "tragic" but pointed out that AFSCME had tried for a year to persuade Rockefeller to permit the workers to choose their own union, rather than have one imposed upon them.

Six months later, after the tumult had died, an impartial arbitrator appointed by Rockefeller's own PERB agreed with Wurf that the governor and other state officials bore responsibility for the strike. The arbitrator, Robert F. Koretz, a labor relations professor, listed a number of legitimate grievances claimed by the workers that had not been corrected. He concluded that the AFSCME international office, District Council 50 and four local unions had violated the Taylor Act. In addition, Koretz wrote:

> I also conclude and find that the public employer and its representatives engaged in such acts of extreme provocation as to detract from or mitigate the responsibility of the employee organization for the strike.

Jerry Wurf at his *bar mitzvah*.

As a New York AFSCME leader, Wurf was effective in direct confrontation with city officials.

In 1962 Wurf walked a picket line at Beth-El Hospital, just behind daughter Susan, who wears a District Council 37 poster.

For years Wurf was the "fair-haired boy" of AFSCME president,
Arnold Zander, right.

When Zander called Wurf and other opponents the "Forces of Evil,"
they turned the phrase to their own advantage.
From left: Robert Hastings, Wurf, and Al Bilik.

The Wurf brothers, Jerry and Al, had their rough periods,
but never lost a deep affection for one another.

When the Memphis City Council refused to hear the testimony
of sanitationmen during their 1968 strike,
the impromptu sit-in turned into a "sandwich-in."

P. J. Ciampa (right) was
one of Wurf's key operatives
at Memphis and elsewhere.

Ciampa paid a price in Memphis, however,
when police doused him with Mace during a protest march.

The Rev. Dr. Martin Luther King, Jr.,
put his prestige behind the Memphis strikers;
he was killed the night before he was to march on their behalf.

The Memphis issue was not so much money as the slogan
stated on marchers' placards: They wanted dignity.

An attentive William F. Buckley, Jr.,
listens to a guest who held his own.

The calm before the internal storm:
at the 1976 AFSCME convention, center stage is shared by Joseph L. Ames,
Victor Gotbaum, William Lucy, and Wurf.
(Photo by Diana Walker)

George Meany, with omnipresent cigar, had rowdy fights
with Wurf, but they also enjoyed a mutual respect.

William Lucy, AFSCME secretary-treasurer since 1972,
said of Wurf, "We were brothers."

Wurf was an early backer of Jimmy Carter for president,
but soon realized he had made a mistake.
Bringing the AFSCME executive board
to the White House did not patch differences.

Jerry McEntee, who succeeded Wurf,
built his career on successful Pennsylvania organizing drives.

Wurf enjoys a moment of repose with Mildred,
Nicholas, and Abigail.

Further, the PERB ordered Rockefeller to halt any further negotiations with CSEA. It split the state's labor force into five units for
representation elections instead of lumping all one hundred
twenty-four thousand eligible employees under CSEA. And PERB
directed that the state negotiating committee "remain neutral in its
treatment of competing employee organizations until the board
certifies employees' organizations in the units deemed appropriate."

As it turned out, AFSCME lost most of the elections anyway, although it did manage to maintain a toehold in the state hospitals
and other outposts. In retrospect, Ernie Rewolinski, for one,
thought that AFSCME overreached; "that maybe we were better
off in New York not to pursue a collective bargaining law at that
time; that it was just too big and too complex and maybe we didn't
have enough sophisticated staff." Rewolinski thought Al Wurf had
performed a minor miracle even in having fifteen thousand members. "If it wasn't Al Wurf, who could ever put together fifteen
thousand people . . . without a collective bargaining law and without a contract in place, but just by indicating that they will service
them on grievances. . . ." Nonetheless, when the elections were
held, "We really got beat. Al Wurf went into shock. . . . We dis-
mantled the whole operation in New York."

The failure to become the dominant public employee union in
his home state irked Wurf. But even in defeat he was not a man to
lose his momentum. Soon after the elections, he contacted Rewolinski and others and said, in effect, "Get your asses down to Pennsylvania. What we couldn't do in New York, maybe we can bring
off there."

Pausing for breath, more or less, at the 1966 AFSCME convention in the Shoreham Hotel in Washington, D.C., Jerry Wurf
summarized impressive membership gains. AFSCME's average
membership in 1964 was two hundred thirty-four thousand. Two
years later, it was up to two hundred eighty-eight thousand, a
growth of 16.5 percent. As Wurf told the convention, "That is four
times the rate of growth of all the unions in the labor movement,

and it is substantially larger than the growth rate of many big and important unions." But he was not satisfied. AFSCME had only begun to touch its potential membership of five million. AFSCME's growth rate was not comfortably ahead of the 11 percent annual increase in the number of public employees. "The only numbers game that counts," he said, "is the one that adds large numbers of members to the roster of AFSCME."

For reporters at the convention, one thing was obvious. Wurf in two years had consolidated his hold on the presidency. In dramatic contrast with his razor-thin win of only two years earlier, this time he was elected by acclamation.

In another form of tribute, the convention raised Wurf's salary from $21,000 to $27,500, and that of secretary-treasurer Gordon Chapman from $16,000 to $22,500, the first pay raises for AFSCME's top officers in eight years. As Joseph Ames, acting as chairman of the laws committee, explained, salaries in the twenty largest unions in the United States ranged from $75,000 to a low of $24,500, with the average around $38,000. Since labor tradition was that no staff person could earn more than the second-highest elected officer, AFSCME was finding what Ames called a "substantial problem" in recruiting top-level technicians. And, finally, the delegates raised the per capita tax to one dollar per member, accepting without serious opposition the proposal that had played such a large role in Arnold Zander's downfall.

In these months Wurf also moved to stengthen the international hierarchy. Robert Hastings, his colleague from COUR, had served Wurf for two years as executive assistant; for a number of reasons, he now wished to do other things. Wurf persuaded Joe Ames to leave St. Louis and come to Washington as his executive assistant; Al Bilik followed in a key organizing role. And William Lucy of the San Francisco Bay area was brought in to help direct the legislative and political department.

One person who fell by the wayside was Gordon Chapman, the secretary-treasurer. He suffered from angina, and he and Wurf had had more bad moments than good ones. Soon after the 1966 convention, Wurf asked Ames to act as the intermediary in persuading Chapman to resign on health grounds. Ames agreed to do so, but stalled, reluctant to do such a painful chore. As it turned out, Chapman came to Ames on his own to discuss resignation: He was having further heart problems, he was ready to leave, but wanted financial protection. A suitable retirement package was arranged, and on July 26, 1966, the international executive board elected Ames as secretary-treasurer.

AFSCME had come very far very fast. But these years, it turned out, were but a prelude. Events elsewhere were to make AFSCME the most conspicuous union in America. Wurf's next major challenge was to come in Memphis, Tennessee.

CHAPTER FIVE

A Tragedy in Memphis

In the late 1960s Memphis was a Southern city that had long taken quiet pride in doing things more or less as it pleased. A Mississippi River trading port, Memphis thrived during the 1800s by catering to the commercial and physical needs of Southern plantation owners—buying their cotton, selling them whiskey and women, entertaining them with a distinct variant of jazz. Early on, Memphis established its racial and economic mores: The city's commercial overlords were tantamount to plantation overseers, and they intended to rule with a benign if firm hand. Memphis never had the hard-core racial meanness of Birmingham or Jackson, Mississippi, or Shreveport, Louisiana. Its prejudice took the form of a seemingly unconscious indifference. The whites had one place, the blacks another; the rich one place, the poor another. Historically, blacks had always done the dirty, hard, and ill-paid work; why should Memphis tamper with time-proven historical imperatives? Besides, who cared, and who noticed?

Although the sight of a robust black man singing "Ol' Man River" might excite audiences in a Broadway theater, the actualities of Memphis day labor were somewhat less glamorous. Garbagemen, for instance. Beginning at seven o'clock in the morning, they went into the backyards of Memphis and sought out the cans into which citizens had dumped their trash, cans that were smelly, heavy, wet, and usually overflowing onto the ground. You picked up the can and dumped it into a heavy leather tub, which the garbageman then slung over his shoulder. If a few stray cans and egg shells fell out, you'd best stop and pick them up, otherwise the housewife would be on the phone to City Hall about "that nigger who messed up my driveway." Then you'd run to catch the truck, which was now halfway up the block. The leather tubs leaked, and during the course of the day the caustic flow from the garbage caused huge welts on the men's shoulders, arms, and torsos. Maybe you snatched up a piece of plastic, even a dry-cleaner's bag, in the hopes of shielding your body.

The working day was measured not by hours but by blocks. Between seven in the morning and three in the afternoon, the garbage trucks had to cover a specified number of blocks. What if the truck broke down? What if a Southern summer rainstorm obliterated the streets with sheets of water? What if every householder in South Memphis decided this was the day to dispose of the accumulated rubbish of the past six months? The answer was: *Keep driving, nigger; keep picking up trash, we don't pay overtime on this job. You want overtime, go up to Detroit and work for Mister Ford and make cars. You quit ahead of time, though, your pay gonna be docked.*

In 1968 the average pay of the men who did this work was $3,-746 a year, or a bit above $70 a week. No vacation pay. No holidays. No health insurance. You showed up for work and lifted the leaky leather tubs and finished the shift, otherwise you packed up and got out.

The first of many men who tried to do something about these degrading working conditions was a rotund black man named T. O. Jones. A native of Memphis, a navy veteran, a onetime shipyard worker in Oregon, Jones returned home in 1959 to work for the Memphis Public Works Department. Disgusted with the plight of sanitationmen, he busied himself organizing a union, Local 1733 of AFSCME. For his pains, Jones was fired in 1963, along with some thirty other workers. Jones did not give up. He begged office space from a retail clerks union, and supported himself with odd-dollar contributions from sympathetic labor officials. But the answer from the city was always the same: Under Tennessee law, it was illegal for a city to recognize a labor union, hence AFSCME would get nowhere.

Actually, the Tennessee legislature had never said any such thing. One state court ruling, in an aside remark, had termed municipal unions "contrary to public policy." Labor lawyers called this "precedent" meaningless; nonetheless, Memphis officials were to cling to it tenaciously.

Besides, Jones was told time and again, "grievance procedures" did exist. The Memphis mayor traditionally held an open house each Thursday, where he entertained complaints or other comments from any citizen. If the sanitationmen had gripes, he should take them up with him. Jones noted the absurdity of this procedure:

> After a man has worked eight hours on a garbage truck, and he's got a grievance, he has to go up to the mayor's office, and he hasn't had a chance to change clothes, he hasn't had a chance to properly clothe himself. Now here he is—he's gotta get in line and he's gotta wait to see the mayor. He discusses his problem with the mayor, and the mayor tells him, says, "Well, I'll take care of this for you."
>
> All right. This gripe or this grievance continues to linger on, linger on, linger on. It steadily builds up. The foreman is still possibly doing the same thing he was doing at first. No relief from the mayor. So we were not able to get the proper things that the men needed.

Despite many setbacks, T. O. Jones continued trying. Other city workers might have snickered at the busy little man behind his back, but a respect began to grow for Oliver Jones, the man determined to build a union.

Jones saw a possible breakthrough in 1966, with the election of T. E. Sisson as public works commissioner. Sisson, during his campaign, had told the sanitationmen he would work out an understanding with them, and, according to Jones, a tentative agreement was even put onto paper. "Somewhere, somehow," Jones said, "someone got to him and put the arm on him, and he was unable to keep the agreement." Sisson told one AFSCME field representative—Pete Brown, who was sent to Memphis by Wurf—that if he recognized the union, "he would be impeached." So he refused to sign the tentative agreement.

Memphis having been only one of many problems he inherited when he took the AFSCME presidency, Jerry Wurf did not pay close attention to the situation there. He knew that Tom Morgan was giving Jones several hundred dollars monthly "to keep the flag flying in Memphis." To Wurf, the paramount issue in Memphis was obtaining a dues-checkoff system.

By Wurf's account, "There was all kinds of diddling and daddling to get some checkoff in some back door fashion from [Mayor William] Ingram, because without checkoff, we couldn't have a viable union."

But AFSCME failed. Divergent accounts exist of what happened thereafter. According to T. O. Jones, rank-and-file workers were so angered that they went out on strike. According to Wurf, "the workers were stirred up and had been persuaded to go out on strike." Regardless of the cause, the strike suffered from a lack of advance planning. Wurf, with his experience, was irked.

> Now a strike is a big thing whether it's a small group, a large group, anything; any experienced guy knows the matter has to be studied, and preparation has to be taken.
>
> You must never strike in anger. You must never strike in frustration. You must only strike if you can win.
>
> It's generally the workers who instigate these things. They're generally not instigated by leaders. What happens to the leaders [is] that they become trapped. They're afraid they'll lose credibility with the workers. So they agree to things that they know are beyond the possibility of winning.

In Memphis in 1966, Wurf asserted, the workers were "steamed into a strike." Ill conceived or not, Wurf felt AFSCME had no choice but to "find a dignified way" to settle the dispute.

To his dismay, city lawyers obtained an injunction ordering the strikers to return to work, and Pete Brown told the workers to obey it. Wurf blew his stack: "It was intolerable that the strike was called without setting up some way of dealing with it, and it was equally intolerable to fold in the middle of the night on that crappy injunction." Although Wurf had no direct role in this strike, "I was outraged that the thing had been handled with such ineptness." The fact that Brown and the local were under a court injunction did not justify abandonment of the strike, in Wurf's estimate:

> I have never been impressed with injunctions. The point is, if you got the power to win the strike, it's academic. If you ain't got the power, they're going to knock your head off anyway. Now that's super-simplistic, but the real truth is this. I've been around this thing; I've participated in literally hundreds of [public] employee strikes.

Despite his displeasure, Wurf did nothing to displace Jones as head of the AFSCME local. (Technically, Jones had autonomy as an elected official; practically, AFSCME sent him his paycheck.) But Wurf now realized that although Jones was a spirited fighter, his concept left much to be desired.

Memphis went onto AFSCME's backburner until early 1968, when a change in the city government offered an opening. The new mayor, Henry Loeb, had been neutral toward the sanitationmen's union several years earlier, when he had served as head of the public works department. Son of a prosperous Memphis family, Loeb had been educated at Eastern preparatory schools and Brown University, served as a PT-boat commander in the navy, and come home to run the family businesses (with a brother) and dabble in politics. Loeb carried the self-assurance—arrogance, Wurf would term it—of a man secure of his position in a supportive business and political community. This trait was to make him a difficult adversary for AFSCME in the weeks ahead. Even Loeb's admirers called him "stubborn" and "hard-headed as a mule" when he had decided on a position. Loeb also apparently felt a familial mandate to oppose unions. One city councilman remembered Loeb saying, "My daddy would turn over in his grave" if he recognized a union. Nonetheless, AFSCME field representative P. J. Ciampa thought that the change of administration was a good time to ask for recognition and a dues checkoff. Get what you can during the transition, before policies are set, Ciampa reasoned. He flew to Memphis and talked with Charles Blackburn, head of the public works department. Blackburn turned him down flatly; Loeb would not recognize a union, he told Ciampa, so there was nothing to discuss. Ciampa left disappointed, and with no further plans for Memphis. Given AFSCME's limited resources, neither he nor Wurf intended to get bogged down in an organizing drive in an off-the-track Southern city. But as Wurf was to recount later, Memphis "was one of those situations where strategy was made by events, instead of events resulting from strategy."

The events were two, each tragic in its own context, each directly attributable to insensitivity by the persons running the Memphis government. For weeks, workers had warned supervisors about defective "off-on" switches on trash compactor trucks, but nothing had been done. On January 30, two black men were crushed to death in one of these trucks. The next day, sanitationmen came to work in sour moods. A heavy rain was falling, and supervisors told twenty-two of the men—all black—to go home, there could be no work that day. Nor pay either, the men realized. As they left the garage, they noticed that the white employees were standing around talking and smoking. An hour or so later, the rain slackened, and the whites went out on the job and received a full day's wage.

When T. O. Jones complained on behalf of the black workers, all AFSCME members, a supervisor said, "We'll take care of it." But the next pay envelopes contained only two hours "call-up pay." At a local 1733 meeting a few days later, the consensus was that the city's actions had been racist, and that the sanitationmen had had enough of it. The membership authorized a strike unless the city recognized Local 1733 as a bargaining agent.

Jones sought to bargain with Loeb, but the mayor bridled at the mention of the word "strike." Such an act was illegal, Loeb said, and he would not bargain under a threat. Whereupon Jones arose, removed his suit, and began donning a set of old clothes he pulled from a paper bag.

"What's that?" Loeb asked.

"These are my going-to-jail clothes," Jones replied. He marched out of the office. The next day all but two hundred of the one thousand three hundred sanitationmen were off the job.

AFSCME's international staff first learned of the walkout on Monday morning, February 12, when reporters for Memphis newspapers called to ask for information. Neither John Blair, the union public affairs director, nor P. J. Ciampa knew anything. When T. O. Jones finally got around to calling Ciampa, his supervisor, Ciampa thought, "My God! What in the blank am I going to do with a strike in the South? Where do I go from here? This is the end." Wurf, profanely unhappy, ordered Ciampa to go to Memphis immediately to "assist" the local strike leaders, meaning to take charge. Another call went out to Bill Lucy, who was on assignment in Detroit. "How long should I expect to stay?" Lucy asked. "A couple of days," Ciampa said. So Lucy drove to the Detroit airport, left his car in the parking lot, and flew to Memphis. He was not to return to Detroit for 67 days.

The fact that the black sanitationmen would be so audacious as to call a strike outraged much of white Memphis; that "outsiders" would come to their assistance was even more threatening. (That Bill Lucy was a Memphis native went unnoted in the press.) Memphis took an immediate and deep dislike to the gruff, brash Ciampa. Downing Pryor, the city council chairman, lamented that Ciampa "acted like a Sicilian anarchist or a hood." Other council members were convinced AFSCME international officers had singled out Memphis for attack. Robert James felt that the union "had several feelers out. . . . This happened to be the one that came in on Monday morning when they didn't have any others to push. So they said, 'Let's go. Memphis is ready.' " Gwen Awsumb, who described herself as a "moderate to liberal" council member, felt that the "ultimate destruction of the country could come through the municipal unions. . . . It was time somebody dug their heels in and said, 'This has gone far enough.' "

By any objective reading of the evidence—real and circumstantial—James and the other plot-theorists were wrong. The parallel stories of AFSCME officials about their surprise at the strike admittedly is challengeable evidence; if a common explanation was to be adopted, Wurf assuredly could have ordered it. No matter. In the early months of 1968 Wurf was far more concerned with organizing in such states as Pennsylvania, which was about to adopt a collective bargaining law that would give AFSCME the chance to organize upward of one hundred thousand state workers. Diverting such organizers as Ciampa to Memphis defied logic. Wurf's own explanations were totally consistent, in public and private statements while the strike was in progress, and in interviews afterward. As Wurf saw the situation:

> I've been in the business for twenty-one years, and that was a hell of a thing to do. First of all, you are stupid if you have a garbage strike in January or February. It doesn't stink as much as if you have it in the middle of summer.
>
> The second situation is, you don't go after a politician the moment he gets into office. You haven't had time to get people mad at him and you have to develop this.
>
> The third reason is that the guy can cry—and [Loeb's] been doing it so successfully—"I hadn't had time to be in here six weeks, and this is what they're going to do. This is this other guy Ingram's mess [meaning his predecessor] and I've inherited it."
>
> For those three reasons, you are a fool to do it, and I'm not a fool. I didn't call the strike, and I would have advised anybody against it; but now they're out, it's got to be. We are faced with available alternatives, and sending them back to work without settling it is not one of them. If I get them back to work, we'll never get them out again.

Wurf's reasoning, based on two decades of running strikes, was that a work stoppage develops a psychological momentum of its own. The strikers worry about money for food and rent and other bills; for them to go back to work without victory, or a satisfactory settlement, saps their resolve and makes them less receptive to calls for a renewed strike. And the Memphis strikers hurt financially from the first day off the job. When Mayor Loeb continued to accuse Wurf of "singling out Memphis" for the strike, Wurf shot back at him, "You silly son of a bitch, if I'd of singled you out I'd picked July to do you in. If I'd planned this thing, we'd have done this altogether different, and I'd have you begging for mercy. I'm confident the fools who set this up just have good hearts and weak minds."

But Wurf did admit to one mistake in his initial handling of the strike: his choice of Ciampa as the AFSCME field marshal. Ciampa had learned strike tactics around Baltimore, where as Wurf said, "the first thing you do is call your boss four letter words because you're rallying your workers." What were needed in Memphis, given AFSCME's weak position, Loeb's intransigence, and lack of other labor support, were "diplomacy, sensitivity." As Wurf said, "Maybe we eventually will have to scream and holler, but that should be last, not first."

That Ciampa and Loeb were ill fitted to negotiate with one another was obvious the moment they stepped into a room together. Ciampa, despite his penchant for noisy bluster, was a most skilled negotiator, and he knew the importance of adversaries taking realistic positions if they wished to accomplish anything. Loeb insisted that any negotiations had to be conducted with the press present— an absurd condition in the view of Ciampa. But the AFSCME representatives had no choice but to negotiate in what Bill Lucy called "a fishbowl of publicity." Loeb used the newsmen to his advantage. As Lucy said, "We'd be sitting there just talking, and all of a sudden the TV lights would go on and the mayor would leap up and say something real militant and then the lights would go off. And he'd sit back down."

Lucy finally suggested to Loeb that talks be conducted by a four-man subcommittee—he and Joe Paisley for AFSCME, any two men Loeb named for the city. Loeb agreed, and Lucy and Paisley withdrew to an anteroom with Frank Gianotti, the city attorney, and Myron Halle, his assistant. The guidelines were that if "we can come up with something that's agreeable to the mayor and to the union, then it would be implemented," Lucy said. If nothing concrete resulted, nothing would be said to the press.

To Lucy's suprise, the subcommittee reached fairly swift agreement on the major issues: recognition, a grievance procedure, and a tentative format for dues checkoff. As Lucy stated, "It was about at that point that the mayor came in to see where we were, I guess, and he just came apart at the seams. He just literally went apart, because apparently he did not believe it [the agreement]." This was after midnight, and Lucy told Loeb, "OK, fine, nothing's won or lost. Under the guidelines that we set down we will simply say to the press that nothing was accomplished." When Loeb balked, Lucy told him, "OK, you can make the statement." So Loeb went before the TV cameras and reporters and said nothing had progressed.

A few hours later Loeb double-crossed the union. Lucy said, "He went to the news media and he said that the only thing that the union was concerned about was the deduction of union dues. He didn't mention the other items that had been resolved."

Ciampa and Lucy heard news reports of this statement in astonishment. Not only had Loeb broken his agreement about publicity, he had given a grossly distorted version. The AFSCME representatives bearded him in his office later that morning. Loeb said there was nothing further to discuss, that the strike was illegal, that the city was breaking off negotiations, and that new sanitationmen would be hired.

Ciampa exploded. "If I'm violating the law, arrest me; if you don't want to arrest me, then you're violating the law, your oath of office. And shut your big fat mouth." Memphis citizens did not like their mayor being addressed in such fashion. Within twenty-four hours, bumper-stickers abounded in the city, "CIAMPA GO HOME." Hate mail flooded Ciampa's hotel room.

Frank Miles, an experienced labor mediator who had worked both for unions and industry, and who was to play a key neutral role in the final settlement, felt that at this stage of the bargaining, Loeb and Ciampa simply were not talking with the same frames of reference. When Ciampa told Loeb that AFSCME insisted on a dues checkoff, and that other issues were secondary, the Mayor interpreted this as meaning, "See, all he wanted was the money." In Miles's opinion, "What they were really saying was 'Give us union security, and then we can go from there.' " Later when Loeb continued to insist that AFSCME's main concern was dues money, Wurf replied, "If you believe that, I'll tell you what I'll do. I'll give all the dues for one year to a charity that you name." Wurf made this offer both in television and newspaper interviews; Loeb did not accept it.

It was at this point that Wurf decided to intervene personally. John Blair, the AFSCME public affairs director, telephoned Wurf and said, "For goodness sake, the whole thing has gotten out of hand. Ciampa has gotten to the point where the mere sound of his name sends tremors, not only through the white community, but even through responsible elements in the black community. We need something strong in here, perhaps your presence."

Wurf said that at the outset he was "determined to take a reasonable posture," then came to realize that Memphis was bent on "trying to save the day for Dixie"—that is, to become the Southern city that stood up to "outside labor agitators." His first days there he realized how deeply Ciampa had offended the power structure.

> He had apparently touched nerve endings in his public confrontations with that mayor that were really unbelievable. What I didn't understand was that Loeb was wallowing in the confrontation. The strike was not seriously inconveniencing the city. Loeb was sort of imitating John Lindsay* with much more success than Lindsay had in standing up to the union. We had allowed the bitterness of the quarrel—the

---

* A few days earlier New York sanitation workers—not AFSCME—had ended a strike through negotiations with Mayor Lindsay.

outsider issue, the black issue, and so on—to obscure the very fundamental problems that were involved here.

Wurf went to Memphis reluctantly: His wife, Mildred, was in the latter stages of a difficult pregnancy (she was ultimately to deliver daughter Abigail by Caesarean birth) and AFSCME organizing activities elsewhere were so brisk he hated to leave his desk. But given the likelihood of the strike failing, and the resultant loss of AFSCME momentum, Wurf had no real choice.

Wurf arrived late the evening of Sunday, February 18, and immediately saw Mayor Loeb in operation at firsthand. The forum was a "conciliation meeting" sponsored by a biracial, multidenominational group of ministers at St. Mary's Cathedral. The ministers, sincerely but naïvely, felt that such an outside forum would give the adversaries an opportunity to settle their differences quickly.

Loeb, though outwardly civil to Wurf when they met, showed no enthusiasm for the meeting. At first he insisted that he would not speak directly to the union people; the strike was illegal, he claimed, and any form of negotiations could be termed a violation of the law. With mock propriety, he would look away from Wurf and make a statement supposedly intended for one of the ministers. Wurf shook his head and muttered, "Ridiculous! Ridiculous!" But as the meeting droned on—it did not end until almost dawn— Loeb and Wurf finally began speaking directly to one another without the sham intermediary of the preachers.

Wurf and Loeb first sparred over the availability of money to pay higher wages, the mayor claiming that Memphis was in "an intoler able, impossible situation. My administration has inherited problems; we're attempting to come to grips with something bigger than we are. When we come to a final solution of it, it isn't going to be satisfactory for all concerned but it's going to be the best way that we can devise from what we took over." Wurf was unimpressed. "Sir, let me say this. I have represented public employees almost all of my adult life and I have never found a public budget that was not on the verge of going out of balance. I also never found that when there was adequate need, adequate necessity, some unforeseen circumstances, that somehow or other the administration, without terribly disrupting the municipality, couldn't find a way to stretch out and meet that need."

Then Wurf put forth a proposal to settle the dues-checkoff issue: The sanitation department had its own credit union, and deductions were routinely made from workers' paychecks for a variety of purposes, including pledges to the United Fund and repayment of loans. The credit union was not a city agency, although some city officials did serve as officers *ex officio*. AFSCME, Wurf said, would be willing to use the credit union as a mechanism for collecting dues, provided the members agreed.

Loeb objected. The union could hire an armored truck to go to job sites to pick up dues money, the union could send around shop stewards at job sites, but collecting dues was not the city's business. "This is the union's business," Loeb said. "The city's affair is to be above taking part in something that's not the city's affair."

"Perhaps we ought to wipe out the American labor movement to satisfy the mayor," Wurf rejoined. "Well, I'm not willing to do that." Credit unions in many other jurisdictions collected dues from willing union members, Wurf said, and dues would be deducted only for workers who gave signed authorizations.* But Loeb was not to be moved. When the meeting finally ended, in the early morning hours, he and Wurf had stated their positions, and solidified them.

Although Loeb still insisted any bargaining was illegal, he did agree to informal talks the next few days. Admit defeat and get out of town, the mayor told Wurf; I'm not going to yield on recognition and checkoff. Wurf, angered, told Loeb in no uncertain terms that AFSCME was in the fight to stay. As he reconstructed what he told the mayor:

> Look, you silly son of a bitch, I'm not getting out of town, I'm going to fight you. You've won a few battles, but you

---

* Wurf later said he erred by proposing the credit union checkoff so early. The better strategy, he said, would have been to save it as a bargaining chip to be used later.

know, in the long run you can't win. And in the long run you've got to live with us. Why don't you knock it off? Understand that this is the end of the line? I am not going to leave Memphis; the union is not going to leave Memphis, and you can beat us on Monday, Tuesday, Wednesday, Thursday—we'll come back on Friday. I've mobilized the total union. If we spend money on nothing else, I'm bringing in anything that I have.

You've got to understand that we cannot walk away from these men. We just can't. I can tell you it's a moral issue, I could tell you it's a pragmatic political issue; I'm just telling you this is it.

Loeb apparently sensed that Wurf was serious, for he immediately became conciliatory—as a tactical move, Wurf was to discover. "Son of a bitch," Loeb told Wurf, "you're getting to me." He suggested that they break off the negotiations for the day, and go to the annual dinner of the Memphis chapter of the National Conference of Christians and Jews. Loeb chose to sit in the general audience, rather than at the dais, which as mayor he could have done. "He sat with me because he wanted to be the 'humble guy.' And he was showing me that although he was *gashmat* [the Yiddish word for a Jew converted to Christianity], he had busted loose from the Jewish community in his own way—that this joint crawling with the Jewish community approved of what he was doing." Predictably, Loeb received tremendous applause when introduced; the ovation for Wurf was much more restrained. Wurf chided Loeb as the mayor drove him to his hotel. "So what? This had nothing to do with it [the strike]. I am not running for mayor. I don't care if I have community approval and I don't care if I have establishment approval." Wurf also gave Loeb a prophetic warning: "that these people would grow to hate him, because the price he had to pay to win would hit these people where they lived"—that is, in the pocketbook.

Wurf ultimately concluded that talks with Loeb were fruitless; so in conference with Lucy, Ciampa, Jones, and other advisers, he agreed to a two-prong strategy: to use the city council as a bypass around Loeb, and to mobilize broad community support behind the strikers. Involving the council could enable Loeb to save face, for he could always claim that settlement was "forced" upon him. Identifying the strike with the civil rights movement, with respected black ministers at the forefront, would put it beyond traditional trade unionism, and also hit at Memphis's collective conscience.

Key to this strategy was Wurf's deep conviction that Loeb was talking nonsense in claiming he was legally powerless to deal with a public employee union. Loeb had an "ongoing relationship" with building trades union members who worked for the city; the public transit system had a union; the teachers had a union. Yet the sanitationmen were turned away when they asked for equal treatment. "It was clear," Wurf stated, "that one of the reasons that these men were being treated this way was the contempt that men like Loeb had for black people. Loeb understood the portion of his constituency that was redneck, and he thought it was good politics to exploit these men, to treat them viciously, to fight this union."

One group conspicuously absent from the community coalition supporting the strikers was Memphis labor. Bill Ross, executive secretary of the Memphis AFL-CIO Council, which had thirty-five thousand members, felt it was a carry-over from the days when Ed (Boss) Crump ruled Memphis and surrounding Shelby County with an iron fist. Crump gave the building trades city construction jobs and ensured that labor had a representative on the county legislative delegation. "That is the way Papa Crump satisfied the labor movement," Ross said. So when Wurf looked around Memphis for labor support in the fight with Loeb, he found only one friend, Taylor Blair, a field representative of the International Brotherhood of Electrical Workers (IBEW).

With Blair as an escort, Wurf went to a meeting of the Memphis Building Trades Council. The accepted procedure when an international union president enters such a meeting is for the proceedings to be interrupted while he speaks. But the Memphis tradesmen gave Wurf no such courtesy. They continued what Wurf called a "rather nondescript discussion" while he sat in the back of the hall. Blair finally whispered to the chairman, and Wurf was given the floor. He asked for assistance in trying to persuade Loeb and the council to recognize the AFSCME local. He did not speak to racial injustices: "To these guys, being antiblack was apparently a feather in their cap with their members." What he expected was a perfunctory resolution and a check for perhaps fifty dollars.

But there was one rotten son of a bitch who when I got done said, "President Wurf, I would like to say. . . ." He was saying "President Wurf" the way Southerners sometimes say "Reverend" when talking to preachers to avoid calling them "Mister." In any event, he told me that there had been some frost on the ground that morning and driving to work he'd seen a car skid a few feet, and he really thought our union ought to take a few dollars and buy an ad in the newspapers to apologize to the good people of Memphis, how we were inconveniencing them, that there was nobody to clean off those crosswalks that morning, sweep the water off and put the salt and so on.

Everybody nodded their heads in sage agreement with this rotten bastard and I uttered a few words about the tragedy of the situation and agreed it might be good to buy an ad, thanked them, and left.

With Loeb on the sidelines, the talks with the councilmen went smoothly. As a contact point, AFSCME used Fred Davis, a black insuranceman who headed the council's public works committee. Through intensive talks, Davis was persuaded to support a resolution calling for union recognition and dues checkoff. At this stage, such council figures as Downing Pryor, the chairman, and Louis Donelson appeared ready to end the strike, which they considered a civic nuisance. Trash was beginning to pile up on the curbs, and such expediencies as the use of Boy Scouts to collect garbage and "central pickup points" were fast losing their public appeal. By Donelson's account, he called Loeb and said, "Henry, we are perfectly willing to have you publicly disagree with us and even denounce us for settling the strike. We'll take the full blame for it if you would just tell these people [who supported the resolution] that you don't care." Loeb remained adamant. As he told Donelson, "His reasons were that we were going to beat this thing, that there wasn't gonna be any problem, that it was his responsibility, and not ours, that he didn't want us to get involved in it." Nonetheless, the councilmen readied a resolution on recognition.

Concurrently, Wurf and others worked nightly to rally support from black churchmen. For a Brooklyn-born Jew, exposure to the evangelical style of black Southern Protestantism, with its emphasis on stirring hymns and sonorous oratory, was a moving experience. Wurf easily picked up its unique cadence. "I brought down my fist on so many Protestant Bibles," he said, "I almost became converted. I understood we couldn't win this fight under the narrow issue of one thousand three hundred men in a confrontation with this man Loeb. The only way we could win this thing was by mobilizing the black community to understand that what these men were going through was what the community was struggling for. If these black workers with the power of the black community could win this beef, then that black community had achieved a measure of freedom that did not exist before."

Almost everyone involved in the strike, on both sides, recognized that the ministers' support was crucial to AFSCME. As labor mediator Frank Miles put it, "If the ministers walked out and said, 'We're not going to have a thing to do with it,' the union would have been done for." Miles knew the ministers' support had soft spots because of the historic hostility toward civil rights by the building trades. He heard one key minister say, "I hadn't given one dad-gum about the unions before. They didn't mean a thing to me." So Wurf had to walk a thin line: He had to find a way to keep the ministers' support, but to keep the militants among them from getting out of hand.

The labor-civil rights alliance was cemented in vivid fashion at the council hearing on Thursday, February 22, at which Fred Davis's resolution on union recognition and dues checkoff was to be presented. Unbeknownst to Wurf, Loeb had persuaded the council majority—including Davis—to continue their support of his position, their earlier agreements notwithstanding. That the deal had fallen apart was soon apparent when the hearing opened. Davis, the chairman, began by hinting that Wurf and other union officers did not necessarily speak for the strikers. "We are going to pay particular attention to what the men themselves have to say on the issues," Davis declared. "We are concerned that the men as individuals have not been able to bring out their views."

Wurf, in what even outside observers called "conciliatory words," tried to persuade Davis and other council members to "stand up to Loeb" and reverse the anti-union policy. Davis kept insisting that the "workers should speak for themselves." Wurf, Jesse Epps, an AFSCME field representative working in Memphis, and others insisted they were the proper spokesmen, not some unlettered member chosen at random; the presence of the workers was proof enough of their support of the union. But as Wurf realized, "Davis was grimly determined to support the concept that we were a bunch of out-of-town troublemakers and that the workers were repudiating us and he didn't want to hear from the people outside of town. I'm making a decision. 'Let's stall the goddamned thing and ask the people to come over.' "

Someone called the Rubber Workers Hall, a few blocks distant, where strikers were to begin their daily rally at noon. Soon strikers dressed in work clothes filed into the chamber, more than seven hundred of them cramming a room with a seating capacity of four hundred seven. "We could have packed the chamber over and over again," Wurf stated. Davis, seeing his challenge had backfired, began yelling about violations of the fire code, and demanded that some of the men leave, or go into the balcony. When several of the men instinctively obeyed, the Rev. Ezekiel Bell, a black Presbyterian minister, yelled up at them, "Get the hell out of the balcony! They've been putting us in the balcony all these years! Come on down here on the floor!" From the podium Davis kept babbling about fire codes and overcrowding; until the auditorium was cleared, he said, he would hear no one.

To break the tension, the Rev. Baxton Bryant, director of the

Tennessee Council on Human Relations, hurriedly scrawled a shopping list (one hundred loaves of bread, thirty pounds of bologna, fifteen pounds of cheese, mustard, and mayonnaise) and dispatched volunteers to a nearby grocery. The table normally reserved for the Memphis city attorney was appropriated as a sandwich bar. The strikers made themselves lunch while various ministers spoke and hymns were sung. The police came, milled around, and left; all they saw was a group of black men eating sandwiches.

Several councilmen, meanwhile, caucused upstairs, then Lewis Donelson called Wurf to the hallway. Donelson said, in effect, that there would be some "reasonable adjustment to the whole thing" if only the entire council could have time for another meeting. Donelson assured Wurf that he "had the votes with us" and that the council would "stand up to the mayor." Given these assurances, Wurf agreed to end what had become a sit-in in the chambers. Davis himself reopened the hearing to agree to recommend union recognition and "some form of dues checkoff." The resolution would go to the full council the next afternoon. Jubilant AFSCME officers felt victory was in hand, and a relieved Wurf planned to leave Memphis late the next day, after the council vote, to attend to other pressing business. What neither AFSCME nor the city council could account for in advance, however, was the studied viciousness of the *Memphis Commercial Appeal,* which killed any chance of settlement with its early Friday morning editions.

First there was the cartoon. In silhouette, a fat Negro man sat atop a garbage can surrounded by mounds of debris and upended trash cans.* The garbage can was marked, "City Hall Sit-in." Undulating lines hinted at odor rising both from the man and the trash; they joined over his head to form the words, "Threat of Anarchy." The caption beneath the cartoon was, "Beyond the Bounds of Tolerance." The accompanying editorial was as harsh in language as the cartoon was in graphics:

* Thirty-six hours before this cartoon was published, the *Commercial Appeal's* editor, Frank R. Ahlgren, had received a "brotherhood" award at the National Conference of Christians and Jews dinner that Wurf attended with Loeb.

Memphis garbage strikers have turned an illegal walkout into anarchy, and Mayor Henry Loeb is exactly right when he says, "We can't submit to this sort of thing. . . ." When the council deals with the problem today it should not be intimidated or stampeded into imprudent decisions by yesterday's belligerent show of force.

Although strike leaders had taken great pains to avoid dirtying the council chambers during the sit-in, the *Commercial Appeal* wrote of the sit-in as if it were a raid by barbaric Visigoths:

The plush, red-carpeted council chamber was jammed with strikers who vaulted across the railing onto the dias reserved for city officials. . . . The usually immaculate carpet of the chamber soon became spotted with bread crumbs and tiny pieces of paper despite the small trash cans placed in each aisle for refuse.

Wurf and others thought the cartoon, editorial, and news coverage outrageous, but perhaps naïvely they saw no reason to believe their deal with the council was in jeopardy. Bill Lucy, for instance, was so confident that once the meeting opened, he hurried back to the Local 1733 office to deal with distribution of welfare benefits to strikers who faced financial crises. Wurf settled in at the chambers with aides and the ministers to await the vote.

So many strikers turned out for the council meeting that it was moved to a municipal auditorium; estimates as to its size ranged from one thousand (the antistrike newspapers) to two thousand (strike leaders). The public works committee resolution was never heard. Instead, the council moved directly to a substitute resolution, prepared in advance, which gave total support to Loeb on the issues of union recognition and dues checkoff. The council chairman, Downing Pryor, announced that citizens would not be heard that day, and the resolution passed nine to four. The opponents were three black councilmen and a white member who thought that some cosmetic compromises went too far. The council adjourned after fifteen minutes.

As the councilmen left their seats, union and black leaders came to their feet in angry protest. T. O. Jones shouted, "We are ready to go to their damned jail." Dr. Vascoe Smith, Jr., a dentist and NAACP official, said, "Don't let them hoodwink you. You are living in a racist town. They don't give a damn about you. . . ."

Wurf, who had been through many tough confrontations over the years, could not believe what he was watching. "That council spit in their eye and treated them with a kind of contempt with which I've never seen public officials treat anybody. There was bitter, bitter anger in the room that day by the men, and even more bitter anger by the leaders—the preachers who were accustomed to having a kind of phony courtesy, which they treasured, given them by the white establishment."

Wurf quickly sensed "how inflammable the situation was." It was important to get the crowd out of the auditorium before the shouted speeches led to violence. Although the normal rallying spot, Clayborn Temple, was only a few blocks distant, he ordered that everyone leave the building and march to Mason Temple, considerably farther away, "feeling that we would walk off some of the anger."

Outside, police insisted that the strikers stay on the sidewalks. Wurf rushed over to protest. "I pleaded for the right to walk in the streets, saying, 'These men have just had an absolutely devastating thing done to their dignity. I plead with you for the sake of the safety of the city, the safety of the men—please let them walk in the street.'" Wurf was worried. Many of the men were shouting angrily they intended to march in the streets, "cops or no cops." He told one police official, "Please, please don't start something that will result in people getting killed." Wurf finally persuaded the police to let the men walk along the west lanes of the street.

Squad cars and foot patrolmen formed a tight, moving fence along the flank of the march. Then one of the squad cars edged close to the crowd, and a wheel rolled over the foot of marcher Gladys Carpenter, secretary to a black councilman. She screamed in pain (fortunately, her discomfort was fleeting, and she did not require medical attention) and other marchers began pushing against the patrol car. According to the Memphis press, an officer later quoted a marcher as saying, "Let's turn this patrol car over." Whatever the sequence, the five officers inside the car jumped out and sprayed the marchers with Mace. Other officers raced to a van and were handed yard-long billy clubs. The peaceful march suddenly became what black Memphibians still refer to as the "mini-riot."*

When P. J. Ciampa saw "all hell break loose" he ran to the marchers and urged calm. He heard shouts from three policemen, "That's him, that's him." Ciampa glanced up. One of the men held a cylinder perhaps the size of a can of shaving cream. "I looked at him and said, 'Just a minute, mister.'"

"Yeah, we'll take care of you," the officer replied. He began spraying Ciampa with Mace.

> The Mace hits me in the face, and I start heading for the curb and I stumble, and grovel, and then I feel awful. I feel this stuff all over me. You can't breathe, you can't see. . . . I was rolling helplessly on the street.

> All I knew was that I was completely disoriented, didn't know where to go. I was just groveling for something to hold onto. And the earth was the best thing I could find. And some hands started grabbing me, and I thought, "My God, they're going to—this is it—this must be the cops."

But the hands belonged to rescuers who led the blinded Ciampa into a bank, where someone washed the Mace out of his eyes. A car was brought to take him to Mason Temple. But as the car began moving, Ciampa saw "the remnants of our line," the few marchers still on the street. He told the driver to halt. "These were the workers that I marched with. I'm going the rest of the way with them." He got out and, ignoring his stinging eyes, marched the last six blocks.

Several days later Ciampa still had raw, peeling skin under his left eye, as well as facial abrasions and bruises. "I've never seen such brutality," he said.

---

* Because of his lameness, Wurf dropped out of the march after several blocks; that no Mace hit him personally did not diminish his rage at the police.

Other persons on the scene also suffered. Jacques Wilmore, staff director of the regional office of the U.S. Civil Rights Commission, saw police pull a man from the crowd; one whacked him in the head with a club. Wilmore stepped forward, credentials displayed; Mace hit his eyes. Gerald Fanion of the Shelby County Community Relations Commission, was helping a woman out of a ruckus when a policeman sprayed Mace into his face. "I told him who I was and that I was acting as liaison for the county. He squirted me again," said Fanion, a black.

The Memphis establishment rallied behind its mayor. The *Press-Scimitar,* the afternoon newspaper, on February 24 lamented that "leaders of the union have shown no respect for Tennessee law. . . ." It continued:

> On the other hand, Memphis can take quiet pride in the prompt and efficient way its law enforcement officers handled the volatile situation. Police were on the job as the strikers and their leaders boiled [sic] out of the meeting and started a march on Main Street.
>
> They [the police] had guns, but they didn't shoot.
>
> They had Mace, the new irritant gas which incapacitates but does not permanently injure—and they used it. They went into action as soon as fired-up marchers attacked a police car.
>
> How much better to do it this way than to be late and soft as were police in Detroit and other places . . . letting disturbances grow into full-scale rioting.

The *Press-Scimitar* editorial did not address the cause of the march, the council's refusal to consider the strike settlement proposal of its own committee.

Wurf, Ciampa, and Loeb had snarled at one another verbally. But now the Memphis police had drawn blood.

The violence of the "mini-riot" prompted Loeb to make what in retrospect proved a bad decision: to obtain a court order to halt the strike. Loeb acted against the advice of his inner circle. City Attorney Frank Gianotti felt an injunction would be "tying his own hands" because he could no longer negotiate if the court ordered the strikers to return to their jobs. Downing Pryor, the city council chairman, reported that "the Mayor thought that he was getting a weapon in his hand that he could walk around with. He could bat people over the head with this injuction."

Loeb did not listen to Gianotti. After the February 23 violence, according to Gianotti, "The newspapers began putting the pressure on, and as a result of that we filed this thing."

What Gianotti did was drag out the old 1966 injunction, update it, and present it to Chancery Court. On February 24, Chancellor Robert Hoffman met city lawyers at his home and issued an injunction prohibiting AFSCME and its leaders from engaging in a strike against the city; causing, authorizing, or inducing employees to strike against the city; picketing city property and coercing the city by striking; picketing or other means to recognize the union as bargaining agent. The injunction named twenty-three individuals: Wurf, Ciampa, Lucy, T. O. Jones, and other local officers.

Wurf paid absolutely no attention to the injunction. Over the weekend he participated in numerous rallies and meetings. Concurrently, the black ministers formed an *ad hoc* Committee On the Move for Equality (COME) to push for an economic boycott of all downtown stores; the two Memphis newspapers; and a chain of chicken and barbecue restaurants and a laundry chain, all owned by the mayor's brother, William.

Wurf's actions brought the city lawyers back to court on Monday, February 26, with a motion that he and others be cited for contempt. Both sides agreed to put off the formal contempt hearing for a week; Wurf, meanwhile, continued his strike activities— which included speaking before the city council for half an hour to explain the union's position. When the contempt hearing was finally held, on March 1, Loeb's chief legal strategist was Sam Weintraub, a Memphis lawyer who had formerly served with the National Labor Relations Board, and then become a corporate labor lawyer. Weintraub's decision was to attempt to prove, not that the AFSCME national office had ordered the strike, but that

Wurf, Ciampa, Lucy, and others had kept it alive through public statements and other acts. This task was made all the easier because Wurf, from the witness stand, cheerily testified as to what he had done in Memphis. To Wurf's suppressed rage, one of the "overt acts" which Weintraub put into evidence was his appearance before the city council.

During a recess Weintraub found himself standing alongside Wurf, with whom he had never spoken privately. "You know," Wurf said, "I don't want to go to jail." Weintraub muttered something about jail not being a nice place, but Wurf continued, "No, it's not that, I got a desk piled high with work, and boy, this strike down here is wrecking my business and I don't want to go to jail."

"Well, I don't think anybody wants to put you in jail," Weintraub said, in attempted sympathy. He immediately knew he had said the wrong thing.

"Well, why'd you file it?" Wurf asked him.

As Weintraub said later, "I mumbled something which must have sounded awful silly to him and hypocritical and everything else, but he took it pleasantly." Wurf simply repeated his question, "But, then why did you file it?" Weintraub made another weak reply.

Wurf said, with a smile, *"Nu, Yoisha?"* [Where is justice?] He walked away, leaving Sam Weintraub a disturbed man.

To no one's surprise, Chancellor Hoffman found the union group guilty of contempt. City lawyers suggested that lower-level officials be dismissed from the citation; as one of them stated, "We entered into the spirit of hitting only those people who were responsible—not some pawns, like stewards who went along." Whereupon Hoffman ordered ten-day jail sentences for Wurf, Lucy, Ciampa, Jesse Epps, T. O. Jones, and Joe Paisley.

Deputy sheriffs strode across the courtroom, took Wurf and others by the arm, and led them out of court, in custody. AFSCME lawyer Anthony Sabella filed an appeal, and they were released on bond. AFSCME's bail bond bill for the strike, for the contempt appeals and other arrests, ultimately totalled $2,544 paid to the M & M Bail Bond Company.

The AFSCME strike was now officially illegal, by court order, a decision that hardened Mayor Loeb's intransigence. Other persons in the Memphis hierarchy were not so confident. Sam Weintraub, for instance, worried that if Wurf used the contempt jail sentence as an excuse for withdrawing from the strike, the black ministers would respond with the charge that "they were going to be sold down a river by the union." If the strike continued, both sides would be frozen. The City of Memphis was left in an ambiguous situation. Part of the "evidence" used to convict Wurf was that he continued to advocate the union position while under injunction. Now that he was under formal sentence for contempt, the city would be "joining in with the conspiracy, more or less," if it negotiated with him.

Actually, Chancellor Hoffman's order contained a loophole, one which Wurf deliberately ignored. The injunction did not cite AFSCME, only individuals. Hence AFSCME could have sent other representatives to Memphis to resume negotiations. But Wurf was determined to keep command.

The contempt finding did cause soul-searching in the AFSCME hierarchy. Wurf had personal worries as well. Mildred was in the last weeks of her difficult pregnancy, and as Wurf said, "It seemed I was always on the phone or on the plane back to Washington." These concerns meant he could not give full attention to the strike. During a staff discussion, one person argued, "We're dead. Let's give it up." Other staff members said such things as "People are paying too big a price." The strikers were facing foreclosures on their houses, on various appliances, on their cars. Wurf, however, would not flinch.

> My position was that we had to go on, there was no way back. Maybe the undertaking was a mistake in the first place. Perhaps we should have treated it as one more wildcat strike and tried to ease our way out of it. But we hadn't done that.
>
> We had decided that we had an obligation, that the obligation in spite of all the suffering, or even because of all the suffering, was such that we couldn't walk away from it. Fur-

ther, I thought that we would ultimately reach some point where we could have an existing, going union.

But Wurf knew he was in a dangerous situation. He had welcomed—even relied upon—the support of the black ministers, but now some of the more strident blacks were publicly calling on the firebrands H. Rap Brown and Stokely Carmichael to come to Memphis. Wurf wished to keep the strike nonviolent. The eruption of emotions during the mini-riots shook him. He did not intend to abandon the strike simply because Loeb was accusing him of fomenting a dangerous situation. But he passed the word to the AFSCME staff members in Memphis: "Cool it, and make the ministers cool it." Meanwhile, Wurf looked for channels through which he could negotiate with Loeb indirectly, the court injunction having blocked any face-to-face communications.

There was no shortage of volunteer mediators. One such interventor was David Caywood, a law partner of attorney Lucius Burch, and at the time Burch's son-in-law. Relatively young, Caywood was free of the political encrustations that might have handicapped another establishment member. As was the case with many sober Memphis citizens, Caywood felt that the time had come to end the nagging strike. Surely no settlement would come through Loeb. So Caywood met privately on Sunday, February 25, with Lucy and Baxton Bryant, the Methodist minister in charge of civil rights for the Tennessee state government.

Caywood shrewdly realized that direct confrontation was no solution; that a formula had to be devised that could let both sides claim victory, even though the reality was something else. Caywood found that the union would not insist upon a written *contract* provided it received the dues checkoff and a fifteen-cent an hour pay increase. To Lucy, the dues checkoff was tantamount to recognition, and thus acceptable to AFSCME. But Loeb could continue to claim, with strictly legalistic truth, that he had not signed a "contract" with the union.

Caywood presented this proposal to councilmen Downing Pryor and Louis Donelson, and they said it was acceptable. Pryor agreed to take the offer to Wurf that night when he returned from Washington (Wurf had made one of his many trips home to be with Mildred). But Wurf refused to see Pryor. As Caywood said, "It wasn't because Mr. Wurf was too busy. He just wasn't going to talk to anybody. He was mad about the injunction." There were telephone calls, and Baxton Bryant finally persuaded Wurf to see the city councilmen and Caywood.

There was hard bargaining that night, for three solid hours. Wurf hinted (in Caywood's estimate) that he was having "problems . . . with some of his own people," especially the undiplomatic Ciampa. "Wurf had Loeb pegged about right," Caywood said. "He was stupid and he was honest." Because of those two things, Wurf told the lawyer, "there was going to be some serious trouble." But in the talks, Wurf and the mediators did strike an agreement, which was reduced to writing: an immediate pay raise of ten cents an hour, with a nickel more July 1; a checkoff through the credit union; a no-strike promise; a grievance procedure by which the worker had the right to be represented either by his own lawyer or the union; health and accident insurance; and participation in the city pension plan. AFSCME would not insist on a written contract.

Loeb, however, would not budge from his opposition to the checkoff. Collecting dues was the union's business, not the city's, and he did not intend to change. Caywood glumly reported this response to Wurf February 27 over breakfast, in the form of a letter from Loeb. "Wurf was very indignant about the letter. He threw it down, said he was tired of dealing with Loeb; that Loeb was not negotiating with him; that he could see absolutely no change in Loeb's position; and that he didn't know why he was even going to spend any time talking with him." (Wurf, it will be remembered, had been in court the preceding day on Loeb's contempt citation.) Caywood called the breakfast "very unpleasant."

But the tenacious Caywood did not give up. He wrote yet another letter for Loeb's signature "that had all of Loeb's stuff in there about the strike being illegal, immoral, and whatever it may be, but at the same time getting all of the union's demands in there." Caywood's idea was for this letter to be sent to the strikers individually, and not to AFSCME because of Loeb's refusal to take any action that might be construed as recognition of the union. Numerous councilmen saw this strategem as a means of ending the impasse. Wurf agreed. "If Loeb sends a letter out to the men," he told David Caywood, "that's enough for me. I'll buy it if he's honest." Such influential Loeb advisers as Frank Ahlgren, editor of the *Commercial Appeal,* and industrialist Edward W. (Ned) Cook also urged acceptance.

Caywood and Cook used their persuasive powers on Loeb for some four hours on March 4, to no avail. Loeb's main objection, on the surface, was that Memphis "was in bad financial condition." But he also said, according to Caywood, "These men don't know what they want, and I'm here to protect them."

Caywood remarked that Loeb was "only elected mayor, not God," which made him "all the madder." Caywood argued that Loeb had no obligation to "protect" the sanitationmen since few if any of them had voted for him. Caywood continued:

> This also made him mad. He then got down to the point where he said, "Well, the people that voted for me want me to take care of them." At which time I told him that he was either a liar or a fool, and it was a toss-up because he was not being honest.
>
> The people that voted for him "didn't like niggers" and they couldn't care less what happened to those folks down there and for him not to believe that. Well, that made him all the madder, and we had a very unpleasant session. It finally got down to the point, he says, "Well, look at all those letters and everything over there. . . ."
>
> Finally I backed him in the corner and I said, "Well, hell, you're just playing politics. Your mail is coming in here from the white people, they're the ones who elected you, and that's what you are going to do. . . ." We really got down to the point where he tacitly admitted that it was strictly political.

Caywood gave up and left. Wurf, meantime, despairing of working with Loeb, had turned to the city council, where a straw vote showed a majority favoring the fifteen-cent pay increase. The council was also willing to let the dues checkoff be done through the credit union. All that was needed was a promise from Loeb that he would not tamper with the checkoff. Caywood particularly wanted Loeb nailed down firmly on this point, so "Loeb or nobody else could say that they have been deceived." Caywood's law partner, Lucius Burch, made the key call to the mayor. "I couldn't hear what went on the other end of the phone," Caywood related, "but all of a sudden Burch, in no uncertain terms, told Loeb what he could go and do. And some violent exchange occurred over the telephone. Burch made some uncomplimentary remarks about the mayor's heritage, and I'm sure it was vice versa, and then the phone was slammed down." Thus ended any semblance of negotiations. The next talks would come under a backdrop of national tragedy.

For weeks the black ministers of Memphis had discussed the feasibility of asking the Rev. Dr. Martin Luther King, Jr., to add his considerable moral stature to the strike. In the winter of 1968 Dr. King was at the apex of his prestige as the nation's foremost civil rights leader, a man capable of commanding enormous compassion among his followers, black and white. Asking Dr. King's support was a logical step, for his movement had long and strong ties with labor—philosophical, economic, and racial. In his first book, *Stride Towards Freedom*, Dr. King wrote, "[T]he Negro . . . has the right to expect the resources of the American trade union movement to be used in assuring him—like all the rest of its members—a proper place in American society. . . . Strong ties must be made between those whites and Negroes who have problems in common. White and Negro workers have mutual aspirations for a fairer share of the products of industries and farms. Both seek job security, old age security, health and welfare protection." Speaking to the AFL-CIO national convention in 1961, Dr. King received a standing ovation when he drew a parallel between the civil rights movement and the labor struggles of the 1930s:

> We are confronted by powerful forces telling us to rely on the good will and understanding of those who profit by exploiting us. . . . They are shocked that action organizations, sit-ins, civil disobedience, and protests are becoming our everyday tools, just as strikes, demonstrations, and union organization became yours to ensure that bargaining power genuinely existed on both sides of the bargaining table. . . .
>
> This unity of purpose is not a historical coincidence. Negroes are almost entirely a working people. Our needs are identical with labor's needs. This is why Negroes support labor's demands and fight laws which curb labor. . . . The identity of interests of labor and Negroes makes any crisis which lacerates you, a crisis in which we bleed.

Nonetheless, Dr. King had misgivings about becoming involved in Memphis. Earlier efforts to build a civil rights infrastructure within the city had gone poorly. Also, Dr. King was spreading his resources very thin the spring of 1968. Civil rights marches in Chicago early in the year were received coolly, with Mayor Richard J. Daley's deft blend of patronage and power keeping local black "leaders" aloof from King's efforts. Dr. King's main concern was organizing a "poor people's march" on Washington in May which he hoped would be the largest nonviolent demonstration in the nation's history.

The Rev. James Lawson, an intellectual black minister and King's theoretician on nonviolent action, made the first overtures and found King sympathetic yet reluctant. Other persons also telephoned him, including AFSCME's Jesse Epps, who had worked in past King campaigns. King expressed fears of "getting bogged down in Memphis" and pleaded the lack of time and staff. "I said to him, 'Well, if no more than to lend some inspiration to the men, to the folk involved, you ought to come,' " Epps said.

So Dr. King came to Memphis and spoke to some fifteen thousand persons at Mason Temple, combining labor, religion, and civil rights in a harmonious blend. Jerry Wurf, a preliminary speaker, talked about the injustices shared by blacks and workers and turned to Dr. King and intoned, "We know, Brother, we've been the same places." A black minister, speaking later, pointed to Wurf and said, "This man's skin is white. But he is a brother. Whatever his skin is, he is a brother underneath." "Amen. Amen," intoned the listeners. King, for his part, lauded the strikers, the striving for justice that embraved them to leave their jobs, the inevitability of their cause. One discordant note was the ring of police cars around the church; the crackle of their car radios often punctuated Dr. King's address.

Jesse Epps felt the rally "rejuvenated Dr. King. He saw his whole movement getting alive again." Although Epps and others knew Dr. King's staff opposed further trips to Memphis, "right there on the stage we sort of . . . pushed him into saying he would come back and lead one march for us." The march was set for Friday, March 22, but a freak storm dumped seventeen inches of snow on the city that day, so the event was postponed until March 28. Neither Dr. King nor his staff took any part in the planning, a bad mistake.

Unbeknownst to King, young black militants calling themselves the Invaders renounced nonviolent tactics. At church rallies they demanded that garbage trucks being driven by nonstrikers be stopped; otherwise, the strike could go on forever. "Preaching and money raising are fine," one youth declared. "Somebody has to do it. But there are some *men* out there, we've got to do some *fighting!* And when you talk about fighting a city with as many cops as this city's got, you better have some guns! You gonna need 'em before it's over." A minister replied, "We have chosen our weapons. These are the weapons of nonviolence." Such was not to be.

The March 28 march went poorly from the start. As is often true of disorder, the exact origins are lost in a welter of scattered and contradictory eyewitness reports; but most accounts agree there was scuffling between teenagers at a black high school. When police arrived, rocks and bottles pelted their cars. A report spread that a policeman had struck a fourteen-year-old girl with his nightstick, cutting her head. Meanwhile, bystanders along the route were drinking heavily, one group looting a liquor store. The march leaders pleaded for order, but the situation rapidly got out of hand, with many youths bolting away from the route agreed upon by strike leaders and the police.

AFSCME had printed hundreds of placards affirming the dignity sought by the bulk of the marchers, the denial of which was the original grievance of the strikers and their community. The signs proclaimed proudly, in block letters six inches tall, "I AM A MAN!" (Bill Lucy had conceived the slogan.) But the militants snatched away many of the signs and scrawled their own crude slogans on the reverse sides. "LOVE MY . . ." began one, the words trailing over to a drawing of a posterior. "DAMN LOEB—BLACK POWER IS HERE" read another. Some others were obscenities.

Such was the scene when Dr. King arrived around 11 A.M. He strode to the head of the procession, and it began marching from Hanley Park along Beale Street, heading for Main Street, Memphis's major downtown thoroughfare. Hundreds of persons stood on the sidewalks, small shops at their backs.

Suddenly there came the frightening sound of shattering glass. The television cameras swung away from Dr. King and picked up the sight of a youth in his late teens, racing along the sidewalk, pounding plate glass windows with a club until they broke. Other youths joined him, their angry blows leaving the sidewalks covered with shards of broken glass; some leaped through the gaping windows to snatch up merchandise and flee.

As this happened a picket line of police wearing gas masks moved into position to block Main Street. The march leaders made a snap decision. With the street jammed with marchers and spectators, sorting out the hooligans from the peaceful demonstrators would be impossible. Dr. King was hurried out of line and returned to his motel. The Rev. James Lawson took up a bull horn and persuaded the bulk of the marchers to return to Clayborn Temple.

There was a calm of about ten minutes during which remnants

of the crowd continued to mill around Beale and Main Streets, their shouts punctuated by the occasional sound of a breaking window. Then the police moved, and in force, firing tear gas grenades before them, chasing the crowd of youths down Beale Street. There was no discrimination: any black caught in the street, regardless of his business, age, or sex, was punched, hit with a club or (for the fortunate) threatened.

Once the melee ended, Memphis congratulated itself on the fact that the casualties were kept to one dead—a sixteen-year-old youth killed by police gunfire—and sixty injured, calling this a "credit to police restraint." The fact that the riot occurred at all must also be credited to obstinancy on the part of Loeb and other officials.

But AFSCME did not intend to let official indifference break the strike. According to Lucy, "Dr. King was concerned about the impact of the violence. He was being blamed for it, and that did him very little good." Wurf and Lucy rode with Dr. King to the airport after the abortive march; they promised him they would consider carefully what had to be done next. But neither doubted that there must be another march, "if for no other reason than to show the city that we had not been driven off," in Lucy's words.

But once out of Memphis, Dr. King showed no enthusiasm for a repeat performance. Jesse Epps, who took over liaison work, reported that Dr. King's staff people were arguing against any further involvement "in a little private fight with a little mayor in Memphis." Epps finally went to Atlanta and spent an entire day in Dr. King's office. "I'd never seen him with as much gloom. Because here was a man of real courage." Playing a devil's advocate, Epps showed Dr. King a compilation of press stories that said, in effect, he had "run" when the violence began. "You are as much stuck in Memphis as we are," Epps told King, "and you can't leave Memphis no more than we can. And if you do, you're doing in a sense what the press says, you're running."

The staff answer was that Andrew Young and Ralph Abernathy would be just as useful. "They talked about how labor had always reneged on its promises and hadn't kept its word . . . in many instances where the civil rights movement is concerned." Ultimately, Dr. King held a small prayer meeting in his office, and he announced his decision: He would return for another march on Friday, April 5.

At about the same time, Mayor Loeb rejected offers from President Johnson and George Meany, president of the AFL-CIO, to help mediate a settlement. "The law's the law, and Memphis is not going to be run by outsider labor leaders," Loeb declared.

Labor and civil rights delegations began gathering in Memphis several days before the scheduled march—Bayard Rustin of the A. Philip Randolph Institute and rank-and-file members from AFSCME and other unions. What had begun weeks earlier as a local strike by several hundred garbage collectors was becoming a national *cause célèbre*.

Memphis officials responded by obtaining a temporary restraining order barring Dr. King and "all nonresidents acting in concert" with him from "organizing or engaging" in any parade. Dr. King called the order a "basic denial of First Amendment privileges"; if his lawyers could not overturn it, he would ignore it. Dr. King came into Memphis April 3 to speak to several thousand people at Mason Temple. The rains fell heavy that night—just as they had the February day when the garbagemen decided to strike—and claps of thunder boomed during Dr. King's eerily fatalistic talk:

> Well, I don't know what will happen now. We've got some difficult days ahead. But it really doesn't matter with me now. Because I've been to the mountaintop. I won't mind.
>
> Like anybody, I would like to live a long life. Longevity has its place. But I'm not concerned about that now. I just want to do God's will.
>
> And He's allowed me to go up to the mountain. And I've looked over, and I've seen the promised land.
>
> I may not get there with you, but I want you to know tonight that we as a people will get to the promised land.
>
> So I'm happy tonight. I'm not worried about anything. I'm

not fearing any man. Mine eyes have seen the glory of the coming of the Lord.

Jerry Wurf was away from Memphis the first days of April on very practical business: to find money to keep the strike alive. "We were paying off refrigerators and secondhand cars to every finance company in Memphis," he said. "The bastard finance companies—they ganged up on the strikers. Get one payment behind, and they'd come around and foreclose." Keeping the strikers in house and home, and fending off their creditors, was a burden AFSCME shouldered to keep the strike going. The cost was an item Wurf never had his accountants pursue. It was enormous. Estimates go above half a million dollars. Whatever the amount, AFSCME clearly could not continue the strike on its own.

So on April 4, Wurf and Joe Ames, the AFSCME secretary-treasurer, called on George Meany of the AFL-CIO. They were no longer the tin-cup supplicants of four years ago but spokesmen for a strong union in trouble. That the two men had ideological differences went unspoken. "I explained the situation to Meany. Meany understood the nature of the beef, and he made a donation of $25,-000. He said he was for us, 'money, marbles, and chalk.' " Meany also agreed to sign a letter to every union local in the country "to give us money."

Dr. King spent the day in staff meetings, where meticulous attention was given to march control. That evening he strolled onto his balcony motel, relaxing before another rally supporting the AFSCME strike. The crack of a rifle broke the stillness, and a bullet cut through Dr. King's neck, smashing the lower part of his face. He died before his body hit the floor.

That evening Wurf had been shopping with Mildred and his son Nicholas. He returned home to ringing phones. Wurf allowed himself only fleeting time for grief. King's killing, he feared, would touch off terrible violence. Ending the strike was essential. But to whom should he turn, and under what terms? Wurf had a philosophical abhorrence about asking government to intervene in his strikes—after all, government was AFSCME's only adversary. But tonight was different. People shouted advice at Wurf, in person and by phone, until he finally said, "Fuck you all, I'm going into my bedroom and shutting the door and making calls." He decided to start with William Welsh, an assistant to Vice President Hubert H. Humphrey.*

"Bill," Wurf said, "I don't know what buttons to press, but, goddamnit, Memphis is going to burn." They decided that the Tennessee governor, Buford Ellington, had to be persuaded to supersede Mayor Loeb.

No one seemed to have a private number for Ellington, which did not deter Wurf. "The hell with all of that," he said, "let me get to the switchboard and tell him who the hell I am and let's get through." Wurf reached the governor immediately. "Ellington understood clearly that we couldn't let Loeb go on with his intransigence and if Loeb wasn't capitulating, he [Ellington] was prepared to move in. I was reassured by the conversation . . . because it seemed to me that only a maniac would allow Loeb to remain in control. I was trying to say, 'I'm not a union advocate now, I'm an American at a very desperate moment in history.' "

Late that night Wurf and Mildred stood on their porch and watched an orange glow in the sky. Entire blocks of Washington burned that night, as they did in dozens of other American cities.

One measure of power in Washington is the quietness with which it can be effectively asserted. In 1968 James Reynolds was undersecretary of labor—the Labor Department's number two position—but a man who kept his name out of the papers. Reynolds was an unusual man. A Columbia graduate, he worked on Wall Street, then decided to go into industry. Reynolds did tough labor relations work for the navy during World War II, served on the National Labor Relations Board, then came into the Labor Department where he specialized in mediating cases involving the national interest. On Friday, April 5, President Johnson called him and asked, "Why aren't you down there settling that garbage strike

* Welsh later served as AFSCME political director.

in Memphis?" Reynolds attempted to explain federal jurisdiction, but Johnson cut him off. "I don't care whether you are asked to do it. I am telling you I want you to go down there. And you may say that you are . . . there at my direction to do everything possible to bring that strike to an end."

In Memphis, Reynolds immediately telephoned Loeb, who pleaded exhaustion and asked that any meeting be put off until Saturday. So Reynolds sought out Wurf, and met with him and Lucy late that Friday evening in his hotel. "Jerry gave me a picture that I felt was a fair appraisal of the situation from his point of view," Reynolds said.

The next morning Reynolds strolled to City Hall—noting the knots of armed guards around and inside the building—to meet Loeb. "Let me get something straight, Mister Mayor," Reynolds told Loeb. "I have been sent here by the President, *but* having said that, let me tell you that I am not going to tell you how to run this city. . . ." Reynolds went on to explain that he was there "to terminate this thing in as quick and as peaceful and as logical and honorable way as we can."

Loeb talked precedent and poverty. He had vowed never to recognize the union, he would not do so. He gestured at the City Hall and mentioned "all of the money that went into building this." Reynolds decided to let everything sit over the weekend, when the memorial service for Dr. King would preoccupy everyone.

Then the serious bargaining began. Reynolds later summarized the ambience of the meetings:

> Here was a group of well-bred, educated Southern gentlemen on the one hand, and here was a tough little Jewish irascible Northerner (in their opinion), Jerry Wurf, backed up by a little group of ignorant black men. With the exception of Lucy, the local leaders were sanitation workers and they were humble black men.
>
> And here they were at the tables with these fellows from Duke and Harvard and Yale and so forth. And it was obvious at the beginning . . . there was a certain condescension on the

part of the spokesmen for the city that they would even sit there and talk to these people. . . .

The one problem that Wurf constantly had was to keep his little group from blowing up. To me this was one of the great contributions he made in this whole thing. Dr. King, their great leader, had been killed. There had been these terribly violent incidents on the street. And here were these men sitting down attempting to discuss the contract, and getting rebuffed at every turn. It had all the ingredients of a disaster. Everybody would walk out and that would be the end of it.

When Reynolds sensed the meetings threatening to erupt into irreparable acrimony, he would shoo out everyone except Wurf and Loeb and say, "Now we are going to have a very frank review of where we are, and why we are here." Reynolds felt that Wurf "conducted himself . . . with great dignity . . . under what I would regard as a very serious strain and provocation. Jerry was going to blow a couple of times, but he didn't. I told him to keep his seat belt on."

The meetings dragged on, and Wurf had nothing to report other than that Loeb continued to say he would not recognize the union. "Two or three times Wurf said to me, 'Jim, there is no point in going on with this. Why don't you stop it?' "

"We're not going to stop it," Reynolds said, "We're going to keep at it day and night if necessary and we are going to settle it."

Wurf complained of an infected tooth. Go get it fixed, Reynolds said, "but you will be right back here."

Unbeknownst to either Loeb or Wurf, Reynolds did some quiet checking on the plight of the strikers. Incognito, he talked with men on the picket lines. What they said impressed Reynolds. "Some of them [had been] working for twenty and twenty-five years and they were getting the absolute minimum wage that one could get," Reynolds said. "I asked them about promotions and supervisors and so on. They told me that only the white men got the supervisors' jobs." Reynolds had his staff compare wages paid for comparable work in Chattanooga, Birmingham, New Orleans, and other Southern communities. "So I had some basis to conclude that these men were being rather unfairly treated," Reynolds said.

Armed with this information, Reynolds went around Loeb to the council, just as previous negotiators had attempted to do. This time, Loeb did not block him. He told Reynolds, "Fine, if they want to do it, that's fine. But I will make it clear that it wasn't the mayor. It was the council." Thus Loeb determined to save face until the very end. But the deal had been made. The council approved the settlement, by a one-vote margin.

At the ratification meeting of Local 1733—held in Clayborn Temple on April 16—Wurf spoke eloquently of Dr. King's contribution to the strike settlement. "Let us never forget," Wurf said, "that Martin Luther King, on a mission for us, was killed in this city. He helped bring us this victory.

"Mayor Loeb and the city council can hardly be blamed because a mad racist assassinated a world-renowned civil rights leader. King's life had been repeatedly threatened in city after city. Yet the fact remains that if he had not gone to Memphis in response to an appeal from the strikers he would not have been murdered, and large areas of Washington, Chicago, Boston, Baltimore, and Pittsburgh would not be in ruins."

The strike had lasted sixty-five days, at tremendous psychic and financial costs; but AFSCME had established a beachhead in Memphis: Local 1733 was now recognized as the exclusive bargaining agents for sanitation workers—laborers, truck drivers, and crew chiefs. Organizers went after workers at other city facilities. Memphis officials continued to play tough. The day before an election covering cafeteria workers, the superintendent of schools called in managers and their assistants and told them if the union won, they would no longer be considered supervisors. AFSCME lost the election. But in a broader vote, this one covering all nonteaching employees of the Memphis Board of Education AFSCME won 1,397 to 143.

Local 1733 was to have problems in the years ahead. T. O. Jones, dissatisfied with what he felt were inadequate services from the international staff, and disgruntled with his own field assignments and lack of contact with Wurf, left within the year to become an organizer for the retail clerks union. Jesse Epps, his successor, fell into disfavor with other local members and Wurf imposed a trusteeship; he, too, left AFSCME. As one person familiar with the local's history said, "You go through that much turmoil, things keep falling off the shelf for years afterwards, regardless of who is involved." Despite these bumps, Local 1733 survives and flourishes.

Wurf grieved over the tragedy of Dr. King's death for days. He asked himself—and others—the same questions time and again. Were we in any way responsible? Should we have done anything differently? The answers always came out the same: No. But the Memphis strike, the tragedy of Dr. King's death notwithstanding, was a seminal event in AFSCME's history. The union now enjoyed a reputation as an organization that would fight for its members, regardless of the cost. Jerry Wurf suddenly had the deserved reputation as the most dynamic man in the mostly moribund American labor movement, due the respect of such titans as Meany and Walter Reuther of the United Auto Workers. He had identified AFSCME, in the public mind, as a union linked to the surging civil rights movement. In sum, Jerry Wurf was now a unionist of national stature.

CHAPTER SIX

The "Outsider" Enters
Labor's Inner Club

The violent denouement of the Memphis strike alarmed Jerry Wurf and brought a distinct change in his approach to organizing public employees. "We cannot organize this nation one Memphis at a time," he told Mildred. "No union in the world has that large a staff, that many resources." Wurf would never dampen his militancy, the inner anger that set him apart from most of the rest of the world; yet reality—and prudence—dictated that he find a viable alternative to direct confrontational tactics.

Thus it was after Memphis that Wurf began a metamorphosis that was to take several years. Wurf was a bifurcated man through the 1970s. In one role he remained the intense, demanding labor organizer, a man whose very existence evoked reflexive tremors in public officials. Simultaneously, he found a role as the maverick of organized labor, the president of a major union who would speak—often and forcefully—on issues his counterparts ignored.

In terms of trade unionism, the most significant change in Wurf's strategy was a stated willingness to surrender the public employee's right to strike in return for fair arbitration by a truly independent body. During the 1960s, at the height of Wurf's first big organizing drives, such a position would have been heresy. Wurf had spent two decades arguing the importance of the *right* to strike. At the same time, however—and this caveat was often not heard— he did not like to strike. Although necessary as labor's ultimate weapon during the 1960s, given the scarcity of public employee bargaining laws, the strike nonetheless was a nuisance to all parties concerned, and especially the workers on the picket line. As Wurf put it in one interview:

> Nobody ever prints this, but I say it to our staff and I say it to our membership. I am opposed to strikes. I don't want strikes. They're bad. They're hard on the city but they're harder on the workers.
>
> I fight bitterly for the right to strike—the *right* to strike. But I don't think there's any principle involved in striking. Striking is a tactic to persuade an employer to deal with us. If it can be avoided, almost any price ought to be paid in order to avoid a strike.

Such was one theme sounded by the "new" Wurf as AFSCME entered the 1970s. To the general public—the newspaper readers whose eyes glaze over when they see a story about compulsory arbitration or mediation—Wurf was most visible as a dissident voice in the labor movement, a unionist who would speak out against the redoubtable George Meany.

The relationships between Wurf and Meany, and AFSCME and the AFL-CIO, were complex. Although AFSCME became one of the federation's largest constituent unions in the 1950s, Meany never gave the necessary blessing for Arnold Zander, then president, to be elected to the AFL-CIO executive council. "George considered AFSCME to be kind of a bastard child," Wurf said. "He had some reasons, I'll admit. AFSCME was so broke Zander was always coming to the executive council and asking for a handout. Putting him on the executive council would have been like inviting some guy to a family dinner when you knew he was going to start hitting people up for money." As Wurf told the 1968 convention, "Our role in the AFL-CIO was that of being the oddballs, the peculiar ones. . . . We were simply lacking in stature or prestige or image or whatever Madison Avenue word you want to use."

There were other, selfish reasons for AFSCME's exclusion. Theoretically, the AFL-CIO forbade one member union from raiding another's territory; once an AFL-CIO affiliate won the right to represent a bargaining unit of employees, it represented it forever. Another affiliate could not come in and take those members even by a majority vote. But in reality, the rule was no stronger than the union trying to use it for protection.

The wide range of workers covered by AFSCME's jurisdiction made it a prime target for raids. The building trades unions, for instance, considered that a worker's job, not his employer, should determine his union. If a carpenter worked for a city, state, or county, they figured he should be in the carpenters union. Additionally, three unions with strong voices on the AFL-CIO executive council gave AFSCME persistent raiding problems during Wurf's first years in office: the Service Employees, the Laborers, and the Communications Workers. The Communications Workers union, primarily telephone company employees, especially irritated Wurf. As he said, "They are even changing the emblem of their union. They are taking off the telephone. I don't know what they are going to substitute—a typewriter or something."

To Wurf, these raiders were rapacious vultures, interested more in dues dollars than in offering any real services to members. "When you had to hand-collect dues for public employees, nobody was really interested," he said. "When you got a checkoff card signed for 10 percent of the people, and you [could] represent 100 percent, a few people began to get interested." When other unions saw the potential, they "decided that they would cut off a little piece of income for themselves."

Wurf did not mind fair organizing competition—although he thought it wasted union assets—but he felt the raiders went after public employees only so "their business agents would have a few bucks to justify their existence." Once the public employees were signed, however, nothing was done for them. As Wurf complained:

> In a couple of instances, they have even entered into agreements with cities that were absolutely unbelievable, where they gave up every right that a public employee was entitled to in exchange for dues income. The danger that we have in

this raiding situation is not only the vast amount of money that is necessary, but that these people in their zeal to get a few per capita units do not seriously injure the well-being of public employees all over this nation.

Wurf raised these problems with Meany privately, with no initial hopes of any sympathy. History certainly suggested the reception would be hostile. Wurf had been a delegate to the 1954 convention that merged the AFL and the CIO, and for several hours "I was quite excited, quite enthralled with the idea that these two great movements were going to come together in America. Instead of diversion, we were going to have unity." Wurf left the convention hall "with great enthusiasm."

The next morning Wurf picked up the *New York Times* at his apartment door and read a long interview in which Meany talked about the future of the labor movement. "The one thing he said, and this took all the wind out of my sails and the breath out of my body, [was] he didn't see the possibility of collective bargaining for public employees in the United States."

In his first talks with Meany about the raiding problems, Wurf found surprising empathy. Document us a strong case, Meany said, and let's see what happens. Within months the AFL-CIO executive council upheld a ruling that the Laborers had violated the constitution in a raiding case and ordered it to desist.

Relations between Meany and Wurf the next few years were correct but guarded. To Meany, Wurf was the antithesis of what he expected in a labor leader. He went public with his arguments, he was abrasive, he reveled in confrontational methods. Much of what Meany knew of Wurf came from hostile buildings tradesmen in New York, his home town. Since these men detested Wurf, Meany obviously heard only the worst. Further, Wurf had unseated an incumbent president of his own union, which Meany found unsettling.

But on the positive side, Meany recognized Wurf as a man of integrity and ability, and one who came from a legitimate power base. To friends, Wurf would rage about Meany's "blind allegiance to those goddamned bums in the building trades," and how "George ought to get off his ass or get out of the presidency." In more reflective moments, Wurf was kinder. "He knew George had no real power in the AFL-CIO other than what he had created for himself," Mildred Wurf said. "As strong men, they came to admire one another, even when they might be yelling at one another." And George Meany, it will be remembered, was ready with the AFL-CIO's checkbook and public support when AFSCME needed help in the Memphis strike.

In public, Wurf assiduously avoided taking any positions that would unnecessarily offend Meany. An issue on which Wurf particularly suffered, in those years of self-imposed silence, was the Vietnam War. He knew Meany's strong pro-war feelings. To Meany Vietnam was a litmus issue—cross him here, and you were blacklisted forever. Wurf avoided discussing the war even at dinner parties, and as Mildred Wurf recollected, "In those years in Washington, especially in our liberal circles, you couldn't go *anywhere* without Vietnam being Topic A. Jerry had deep doubts about the wisdom of the war, but he was not ready to take a public position contrary to Meany. So he refused to talk about the subject, even when a dozen or so people would be debating it at our dinner table."

Wurf even tried to keep AFSCME affiliates from going against Meany. When he heard that a leadership conference of District Council 37 had adopted an anti-war resolution, he telephoned Victor Gotbaum and asked that it be withdrawn. "I won't do that," Gotbaum said, "but if you want to come and try to persuade the people on your own to drop it, come on." Wurf flew to New York and talked the conference into dropping the resolution.

Knowing that Wurf was straining to speak out against the war, Gotbaum baited him constantly. "He told me, 'Don't torture me on this one.' And I was, I was torturing him on it." Wurf, Gotbaum, and Eric Polisar were in Paris once for a Public Services International meeting, and heard of a peace demonstration. Wurf would not go. "You sons of bitches," he told Gotbaum and Polisar, "you go, and you know I want to go, too." As Gotbaum heard

Wurf, "What he was really saying was, 'I agree with you guys and I ought to be there, but I can't face myself.' "

On one occasion, however, Wurf was forced publicly to support the Johnson Administration's Vietnam policies. In September 1967 Wurf attended a meeting of the British Trades Union Congress (TUC) in Brighton, England. Minutes before Wurf spoke, delegates overrode the TUC leadership and passed a resolution calling on the British government to diassociate itself from American policy in Vietnam. Wurf, the next speaker, began by saying the AFL-CIO stood "four square" behind the United States effort to defend freedom in South Vietnam. When he observed, "There is enormous intellectual confusion about the struggle now going on in Vietnam," there was a burst of derisory laughter, and murmurs of "nonsense" and "rubbish."

Wurf glanced up and quipped, "Believe me, I'm not taking part in the present debate of this great Congress. I am merely reading a speech prepared for me beforehand." As a British reporter observed, "Such splendid candor gave him an uninterrupted run after that."

When he returned to Washington, Wurf sent President Johnson British press clippings about his speech and the reaction. "I expected to find a strong resistance to our national policy on Vietnam because the formal vote preceding my speech had, in fact, recommended British disassociation from that policy," Wurf wrote. But after the initial outburst, his "attempt at a reasoned statement . . . was received in a cordial manner by an audience not unaccustomed to expressing its opinion in boos. . . ."

During those anguished days Wurf was forced to use his considerable persuasive powers to keep the biennial AFSCME conventions from taking a stand contrary to Meany. The first such challenge came in 1966, when Sam Slattery, chairman of Local 1489 of the Boston hospital workers, offered an anti-Vietnam resolution. The resolutions committee, controlled by Wurf, recommended its defeat. Slattery, on the floor, argued "that most of the delegates here . . . do not know what is going on in Vietnam." He did not want Great Society monies pulled out of America at the rate of three million dollars a day to "support another dictatorship."

Al Viani, of District Council 37 in New York, the resolutions committee chairman, questioned "whether we should even take a position on something such as the foreign policy of the United States" without either international executive board or convention approval.

Wurf took the floor. As a delegate to the AFL-CIO convention, he said, "I voted to support the position of the AFL-CIO on Vietnam. I also want it known that I took this position on the grounds that I do not recognize what is going on in Vietnam, on the part of the Vietcong, as a war of *liberation.*" Since Communist nations had no free trade unions, Wurf continued, "there is no freedom there."

Wurf said he and other AFL-CIO delegates were "very painfully aware that we need in our country a continuing examination, a continuing study of how to bring to an end that terrible war that is going on there." Decision-making could not be delegated to the government.

"I would be less than fair and honest," he said, "if I did not let you know that our union, like everybody else in the country, has sort of pretended that this thing does not exist. We know it is going on, and it is tragic." He hoped for peace and withdrawal of American troops. But at his urging, the resolution was rejected by voice vote.

Given such loyalty, Wurf certainly had reason to expect election to an AFL-CIO vice presidency, which meant membership on the executive council, in February 1969. It was the first post-Memphis winter meeting, and Wurf assuredly had made a name for himself and his union during the past months. In terms of AFSCME's numerical strength, Wurf deserved the seat. AFSCME had passed the four-hundred-thousand-member mark a few weeks earlier, continuing its thousand-member-a-week growth.

Three seats were vacant that February, and most outside observers felt Wurf had a sure chance for one of them. Given his control of the executive council, Meany could have elevated Wurf with a nod. Only he did not nod. Instead, heads of three smaller unions were elected vice presidents. Wurf clearly remained unacceptable to the old bulls who ran American labor.

Stanley Levey, labor writer for the Scripps-Howard newspaper chain, asked Meany why Wurf had been passed over. Levey noted that no public employee union representative had been on the council since 1961, when William Doherty of the Letter Carriers had departed.

Meany replied, with technical but not total accuracy, that "council members represent the whole labor movement, not individual unions." Yes, Meany was cognizant of the public employee unions' desire for a seat, and he had appointed a committee to see what should be done.

What Meany did the next months was a classic bit of labor politics. Privately, he told Wurf he did not object to putting him on the council, and he felt that Wurf deserved the position. Wurf's selection, however, would risk offending presidents of the three major AFL-CIO unions representing federal workers. These unions had also achieved considerable growth, although admittedly not on AFSCME's scale. Meany promised Wurf that the council would be expanded by three seats, one of which would go to him, and a second to whomever the federal unions decided upon among themselves. Ultimately, the latter chose Joseph Griner, of the American Federation of Government Employees, which had doubled in size the last two years (from one hundred thirty-two thousand to two hundred sixty-three thousand members). As veteran labor journalist John Herling wrote, tongue-in-cheek, "Failure to recognize these two government unions on the executive council would have caused considerable dismay."

Another factor in Meany's politics was that in early 1969, he was being forced to look over his shoulder, with justifiable nervousness. A year earlier some labor backbenchers had formed the National Labor Leadership Assembly for Peace in order to take strong anti-war positions. It had attracted no significant support. However, in June 1969 leaders of the United Auto Workers and the International Brotherhood of Teamsters—two of the nation's largest unions, and both outside the AFL-CIO—met in Washington to form the Alliance for Labor Action, and promptly took the same positions. Despite the Teamsters' notorious corruption, the ALA could not be overlooked, for it meant that the leadership of a sizable portion of the labor movement was on record against the war.

Meany knew that Wurf was disgruntled with the AFL-CIO and its policies; he also must have worried that Wurf would add AFSCME to the UAW-Teamsters coalition. Anyone even vaguely familiar with AFSCME's growth pattern realized it would reach at least a million members. Could Meany risk letting AFSCME slip away from the AFL-CIO?

Wurf made no overt move toward affiliation with the UAW-Teamsters alliance. "Dual unionism" is a cardinal sin in the American labor movement, and Wurf chose to give Meany a signal by another means. At a District Council 37 leadership conference in the Poconos in June 1969, a few days after the UAW-Teamsters Washington rally, Wurf for the first time spoke out against the war. He called for a total and immediate withdrawal of American troops from the war. "Nixon says he is going to withdraw twenty-five thousand troops from Vietnam, but he is four hundred seventy-five thousand short of what it has to be," Wurf said. He wanted America's resources to go to Americans, not to an Asian war. "Seventy percent of the taxes in this country are used to wage war," Wurf said.

Labor reporters do not cover such internal affairs as the District Council 37 conference, but Wurf made sure his remarks were circulated beyond his immediate audience. Bill Schleicher, editor of the *Unionist,* the newspaper of Local 371, the AFSCME social service employees union in New York, was at the conference, and he hurriedly telephoned a story about Wurf's break with the AFL-CIO leadership. Schleicher's article ran on the front page. As he noted, delegates "broke into wild standing applause after the speech, and many ran up to congratulate him for splitting with the AFL-CIO hawks on the war."

Soon after the speech Meany sent word to Wurf: You are going on the executive council in October. If Meany expressed any pique about the anti-war speech, Wurf never revealed it. Thus it was that in October Wurf found himself filling one of six new positions on the executive council. The expansion brought the council to thirty-three members. After twenty-eight years as an "outsider," Wurf now had a seat in the inner councils of the American labor movement and one that he intended to use to the utmost to bring life into an organization that could charitably be described as moribund. (Soon after his election, Wurf, who was fifty years old, did some checking and discovered he was the only one of thirty-three members who had been born after World War I.)

Wurf certainly did not expect that his presence on the executive council would change AFL-CIO policies. He saw the council as a forum in which to ask questions and try to persuade Meany and other members at least to acknowledge problems. Wurf recognized that many of the men with whom he sat in the council were labor *bureaucrats,* rather than labor *leaders.* None were disposed to question Meany, and Meany discouraged dissent. Despite his domination of the council, Meany routinely called each member in advance of meetings to outline the business that would be discussed, and to ascertain whether there would be any opposition. To the outside world, Meany was the gruff, dem-and-dose Bronx plumber with the omnipresent cigar, a strong man who ruled the AFL-CIO by force of intellect and personality. Another view was expressed to me by an executive council member, after I had subtitled a biography of Meany, "the unchallenged strong man of American labor." By this person's testimony, and he had been around Meany long enough to be credible, "George deep down inside was a spoiled kid who wanted things done 'George's way' or not at all. He could not tolerate dissent. If anyone questioned him, he would chew the cigar very fast and get a red tint on his face. His voice would change range. He could not conceal his agitation. The first time Jerry Wurf went after him, I thought George was going to have a coronary."

Wurf's first dissent came at his very first executive council meeting, during which Meany presented a resolution supporting the United States' incursion into Cambodia to destroy Vietcong bases.

The AFL-CIO no longer keeps verbatim transcripts of executive council meetings, and Wurf later acknowledged that he did not remember the exact language he used. However, "I gave the war hell, at length, and then George called for a vote, and there were thirty or so of them, and one of me. I really bugged him. He called me a son of a bitch later, but he slapped me on the shoulder when he did. George realized he didn't have a bunch of yes men anymore. A *majority* of yes men, to be sure, and he wasn't about to lose on any issue. But I could rattle him, and that I did."

Wurf savored his new role in the AFL-CIO for two reasons. It enhanced AFSCME's prestige, and it enabled him to begin whittling away at AFL-CIO policies and procedures that he felt retarded the growth of American trade unionism. Even as he moved upward in the AFL-CIO, however, Wurf continued to press AFSCME's organizing activities. For chronological sense, let us now return to those activities.

For psychological reasons, AFSCME needed an organizing victory of state employees in a major industrial state. As related earlier, AFSCME had tried to win bargaining rights for New York state workers, but had failed for a variety of reasons. Casting about for another organizing target, Wurf hit upon Pennsylvania. Circumstances there certainly seemed to invite unionization. In a speech in 1969, Pennsylvania Governor Raymond Schafer noted that twelve thousand state employees earned poverty-level incomes. About 10 percent of Pennsylvania state employees earned three thousand dollars or less a year. After taxes, insurance, and retirement deductions, a worker earning $3,560 took home an average of fifty-two dollars a week, or $2,700 a year. As Wurf said, "It is no less hellish to be employed and impoverished than it is to be out of a job and on welfare."

As his chief Pennsylvania organizer, Wurf chose Jerry McEntee, son of William McEntee, who had founded the Philadelphia AFSCME council. The younger McEntee, from his earliest boyhood, remembered that "my father would get home from work and then spend about half the evening on the phone talking to people. I would hear things like 'steward' and 'delegate,' and things like that that you didn't hear out on the streets or in schools." McEntee majored in economics and labor relations at La Salle College in Philadelphia, with the "feeling that if I was going to work in some way, I was going to work for the union. It came into my mind many years ago, without anybody really talking about it, or setting the direction."

After military service, McEntee was interviewed by Tom Morgan, the AFSCME organizing director, and went into the field at four thousand dollars a year, first in Washington, "trying to get a feel and understand the union," and then in New York, where he worked with Wurf in the 1958 hospital organizing campaign. "He was bold in his ideas and in his concepts," McEntee noted. Although Wurf tended to be "disorganized" once a campaign ended, "When it came to dealing with the campaign and a strike situation, I've always thought Jerry Wurf was the best field person I've ever met."

McEntee then returned to Philadelphia where he worked with his father's District Council 33. Although William McEntee supported Arnold Zander during the Wurf challenges, relations remained civil. McEntee continued working in Philadelphia for several years after Wurf's election, then received a summons to Washington.

Wurf told him, in effect, "Given the ethnic makeup of AFSCME in Philadelphia, the council there is eventually going to be run by blacks. There is no future there for a young Irishman, and I don't give a damn how bright you are." At Wurf's urging, McEntee became AFSCME director for Pennsylvania and New Jersey, with the emphasis on the former.

Times were ripe for labor legislation. With strong support from the AFL-CIO, McEntee managed to persuade the Pennsylvania legislature to pass a law giving unions the right to organize public sector workers, and requiring employers to negotiate contracts. The law was a boon for AFSCME, which had only a few scattered members outside Philadelphia. McEntee knew the state, however, and he sensed how an organizing campaign should be run. In geographical terms, Pennsylvania is vast, stretching from Philadelphia to the Great Lakes; residents in the Northern Tier counties have more interests in common with persons in, say, Montana, than with steel workers in Pittsburgh.

McEntee drove to Washington, stopped at a map store and bought two huge maps of Pennsylvania. He marked out the state by sectors, took the maps into Wurf's office, and spread them on the desk.

"Well, what do you want to do?" Wurf asked.

"Organize the state employees," McEntee replied.

"Which state employees?"

"All of them," McEntee said.

Wurf turned away. "Ah, that's bullshit," he said. "I just came off a losing campaign in the State of New York, and we just got rubbed out all over the place." Wurf wanted to go for specific targets, rather than state employees overall.

"Look," McEntee said, "I'm telling you, we can wipe them out. If you go with me, and roll some dice, I'm telling you we can blow them away, all of them." By "them" McEntee meant other unions that would be competing for state workers.

They talked longer, and McEntee pointed to odd crannies in the map. Wurf finally said, "All right, all right, I'll roll the dice with you. You put it together and let's go in as if we're going after all of it. I'm ready to make the investment."

To McEntee, AFSCME's chief advantage was that "we had an understanding of how to organize public sector workers and what the needs of the public sector workers were, and how as a union . . . we could relate to them." Because of his lobbying on behalf of the collective bargaining bill, McEntee knew the intricacies of the new rules. Win the first major election, he reasoned, and write a good contract, and "then use the contract to bounce into the other bargaining units and really roll with it."

McEntee's strategy, approved by Wurf, was to organize all employees in a state agency into a single bargaining unit. Competing unions, in contrast, tried to create separate locals for each group of workers. The first major contest came over the workers of the Penn-

sylvania Department of Transportation or Penn-DOT, and maintenance workers in state hospitals. AFSCME's major opponents were
the Teamsters and a combine of the Service Employees and
Operating Engineers known as "Penel."

Somewhat to McEntee's surprise, the first election ended with
AFSCME in a runoff with Penel. Wurf hurriedly called for reinforcements. Ernie Rewolinski and Vincent O'Brien, who had taken
other assignments in New York following the AFSCME defeat
there, were called to Washington for a strategy meeting with Wurf
and McEntee. Wurf was blunt. After what had happened in New
York, "It was a life and death struggle in Pennsylvania." Lose
there, Wurf said, and AFSCME would lose so much organizing
momentum that it would be "washed up as a major union." Wurf
promised that AFSCME's full resources would be thrown into
Pennsylvania. "There were no ifs, ands, or buts about it," Rewolinski said. As he listened to Wurf, Rewolinski also saw his own
career on the line. "Geez," he thought, "why am I getting caught
up in this one? I got killed in New York, I'll get killed in this one.
With my [lack of job] security and unblemished record of no-wins,
what is my future in the union?"

For the renewed campaign, McEntee divided the state into three
sectors. O'Brien was dispatched to Pittsburgh, to direct organizing
in the West; Rewolinski to Scranton, to cover the eastern part of
the state. McEntee worked as coordinator and chief organizer in
Harrisburg, the capital. Communication was frequent, to ensure
that, as McEntee put it, "everybody was going in the same direction." The Teamsters, in contrast, singled out individual transportation yards in the state, with no overall campaign.

Rewolinski, who concentrated on hospital workers, analyzed the
first-round voting and made some decisions. With only three to
four weeks to campaign, he did not have time to persuade people
who had voted for the Service Employees International to switch to
AFSCME. "But if you added up the people who didn't vote and
those who voted no-union, and put them with what we got the first
time, we won." So Rewolinski made contacts in individual hospitals, and AFSCME supporters helped him seek out votes.

AFSCME won both elections by comfortable margins, becoming the exclusive bargaining agent for about seventeen thousand highway and hospital workers. The first contracts negotiated by Wurf and McEntee contained landmark provisions. Previously, for instance, state employees had paid about thirty-five dollars monthly for health insurance. Under the AFSCME contract, the state paid the premiums.

The bargaining election was concurrent with the 1971 gubernatorial campaign. The Democratic candidate, Milton Shapp, bucked his party's organization to win the office, and thus was not beholden to machine politicians when he won the election. Nonetheless, the change of administration from Republican to Democratic worried Jerry McEntee because of a peculiar Pennsylvania patronage system known as "macing." Several thousand low-level jobs in the transportation department—laborers and truck drivers—could be filled by local political bosses; each time party control changed, the incumbents were fired and new political favorites hired.

Many of these people had just voted to accept AFSCME as their union. Concerned about their jobs, McEntee appealed to Shapp, who wrote him on February 11, 1971, that his administration had "no plans for blanket discharges" of the road workers. McEntee and Wurf took the letter as a promise that macing was dead—but a few months later, the state summarily dismissed three thousand blue collar transportation workers. McEntee said:

> The really lousy thing about it is that these guys are not really political kingpins. Rather, they are hard-working men with families to support. Many of them live in areas where jobs are scarce, and most make less than $5,000 a year. In the name of political payoffs, the state is literally going to starve these guys, unless we prevent it.

An angered Wurf flew to Harrisburg, and he and McEntee went to the Governor's Mansion to remonstrate with Shapp. They made their case, and Shapp said, "Hey, you know, these people are all Republican leaders."

"What, are you *crazy?*" Wurf shot back. "We're talking about a guy who drives a truck in Bedford County, Pennsylvania, or a flagman in Columbia County, Pennsylvania, and if you are going to tell us that they are the real leaders of the Republican Party, you are pulling our leg. Policy makers that work for the state, that's different. You do what you want with policy makers and top level administrators. But you are talking about the rank-and-file worker who has nothing to do with policy. It's our union's mission to protect them, and protect them we're going to."

"Well, let me think about it, and I'll meet with you tomorrow morning," Shapp replied.

But when they returned the next day Shapp was not there; instead, a second-echelon official appeared. Wurf angrily stormed out. "There's no sense in trying to reach an agreement with these guys," he told McEntee. "We've got to play tough."

AFSCME went to court to block the firings. When the state denied the dismissals were politically motivated, AFSCME had some six hundred workers appear in court, each ready to say they had been fired because of their politics. The state backed away after several of them testified and stipulated that the firings had been related to patronage. In another publicity ploy, fired workers appeared en masse at public assistance and food stamp offices. They told reporters the state had forced them onto welfare rolls. Newspapers normally unfriendly to labor applauded AFSCME, the *Philadelphia Inquirer*, for instance, praising the fight against the "ruthless purges."

The case dragged to the Pennsylvania Supreme Court. The ultimate decision: any worker fired after AFSCME's contract had taken effect was to be reinstated with back pay. About fifteen hundred men regained their jobs.

Thereafter AFSCME ensured that any contract negotiated with the state specified that a worker could not be discriminated against because of "race, creed, color, sex, age, national origin, union membership, *or political affiliation.*" That a union that traditionally supported Democratic candidates would go against a Democratic governor to protect Republican employees gave AFSCME inestimable credibility in Pennsylvania and elsewhere. Coupled with the contract gains, "we really started to roll," McEntee said. "We showed that we could deliver, and the people listened. In three and one-half years, we picked up the bargaining rights for seventy-five thousand people." Although state law did not force workers to join the union, about 80 percent chose to do so.

AFSCME bounded ahead in other states those heady months of early 1971. In Hawaii, Al Bilik negotiated a merger with the Hawaii Government Employees Association and its 19,200 members, and with the United Public Workers and its 8,400 members. In New Jersey, AFSCME won bargaining rights for about eight thousand health care and rehabilitation workers, beating three other unions. In Washington State, four thousand public assistance employees voted to join AFSCME by a margin of four to one in the largest representational election ever held in the state. In the first four months alone, AFSCME gained 56,600 new members.

A jubilant Wurf wrote in *The Public Employee,* "We are beating the pants off our opposition, particularly those two private sector unions [the Laborers and Service Employees] that have moved hungrily into our jurisdiction. We are finding at the state and local government levels . . . that public employees want full-time public employee unionism, not part-time private industry outfits dabbling in government unions." Further, Wurf detected a "clear change of direction by employers. I can sense it in my public appearances before employer associations and in my meetings with them. Public employee unionism is increasingly accepted and the knowledgeable employers and employees are reacting accordingly. They are assuredly not going out of their way to be nice to us, but they are starting to accept bargaining and bilateralism in the public work place."

However, AFSCME's explosive growth brought internal pains. With so many members coming into the union, AFSCME had trouble finding enough competent staff people to service them. Organizing campaigns such as that in Pennsylvania were costly; AFSCME would spend tens of thousands of dollars before receiving dues from a single member. "Jerry didn't hoard money," one staff member said. "If AFSCME managed to build up a surplus, we didn't go buy CD's [certificates of deposit]. Jerry would look around the country and say, 'Let's go organize there.' To Jerry, money had only one purpose: Use it to organize." In 1973 AFSCME actually operated in the red, at a loss of $470,000, and it had to go to the banks to finance purchase of a new office building (at 1625 L Street, Northwest, in downtown Washington).

Sophisticated—but essential—technical programs brought by Wurf into AFSCME also cost money. The research department, under Donald Wasserman, analyzed the many variants of collective bargaining laws passed by states and cities and advised AFSCME locals and councils on how to obtain model bills. Wage data for each AFSCME bargaining unit was computerized; thus a local in Minnesota representing highway workers could find out within minutes the salaries paid comparable workers in Rhode Island. Wasserman's department studied each of the hundreds of individual contracts negotiated by AFSCME units each year, pointing out possible pitfalls. "AFSCME has always stressed local autonomy," Wasserman said, "but at the same time, the international has the obligation to make sure a small local isn't suckered into signing a bad contract. City managers certainly have sophisticated guidance through their organizations."

An AFSCME economist, James Savarese, analyzed budgets of cities and states with which the union was negotiating, sorting myth from reality, seeing "what they had in the way of money." AFSCME learned early not to take published budget figures at face value. "Of course, when negotiations began, they would always cry poor. It might be to our seeming advantage that public budgets are just that—public. But they hide the stuff [the extra money] and finding it isn't easy. Historical data is meaningless; what we need to know, and accurately, is how much money the government actually will have in hand for the period in question. You can't let a government get away with phony projections. In a sense, our analysts get to know more about the figures than the state budget people, because we are interested in accuracy rather than in hiding the true financial situation."

Frequently, Savarese said, AFSCME would play a governor against the legislature, or vice versa. One truism of state finance is that the governor always tries to stash away a pocket of money which he can "find" at the time of a crisis to avoid an unbalanced budget. "Even if they come from the same party, the governor and the legislature are frequently at odds. If we find one of these caches of money, we can threaten to make it public, or quietly to give the other party the exact amount that is available. The legislature is always looking for ways to cut spending; knowing that the governor has forty million dollars stashed away would be valuable information for them. So we'll make a deal: We'll keep quiet about the existence of the forty million dollars—provided AFSCME receives half of it in the form of pay increases. The governor is permitted to continue hiding the other twenty million dollars for use when needed, and everyone is happy."

There are times, however, when AFSCME will not permit a governor to continue hiding money even when the union might find it advantageous to strike a deal. If the governor insists no money is available for Medicaid, for instance, AFSCME will blow the whistle on him to the legislature. "But we wouldn't do the same thing for the highway crowd," Savarese said.

Savarese devised a system whereby AFSCME routinely ran revenue projections for the twelve largest states, so that negotiators would know within tight bounds how much money would be available during contract talks. "We did this better than the states themselves," he commented. "Econometric studies gave the negotiators the sort of raw intelligence they needed when they got down to serious bargaining. Further, you only have to do this one time. The next time around, the other side won't make revenue an issue, because you've convinced them you've done your homework, that you rely on hard information and not just what the governor wants to tell you."

Wurf had no control over another AFSCME problem: A Nixon Administration economic program that in his view was harsh on cities, states, and the people who worked for them. In early 1971 as a means of curbing Vietnam-era inflation, the administration imposed a system of wage and price controls that Wurf, and every other labor leader, felt treated workers unfairly. Although profits continued at their highest levels in history, the administration's Pay Board—dominated by business figures—imposed a lid of 5.4 percent on wage increases. No similar mechanism dealt with prices. As Wurf noted, businesses quite happily cooperated with the government in restraining wages, but did as they wished with prices.

An anomaly of Wurf's relationship with other AFL-CIO barons was that while publicly clucking at his militancy, they often privately urged him to use his anger to their advantage. One instance vivid in Don Wasserman's mind came during Pay Board deliberations. Wurf was appointed as one of the labor representatives to a subcommittee on health care, an area considered responsible for a disproportionate share of the inflation rate. The chairman was Professor John Dunlop of Harvard, a man for whom Wurf had had a long-standing antipathy. ("George Meany's mouthpiece," Wurf called him.)

Wurf started the first meeting by getting into a tedious squabble with Dunlop. The unions would not stay on the panel unless they were listened to, Wurf said; he had no intention of wasting his time on a cosmetic committee. Dunlop argued that he could not pledge any decisions made by the subcommittee would be binding; but Wurf stood his ground, and after two to three hours of "haranguing," Dunlop yielded to the extent that he said it would be a "major catastrophe" if the administration went against the recommendations of the panel.

Wurf happened to miss the next meeting. Afterward, other union members complained to him that a management representative—a lawyer hired by the hospital association—was taking what seemed to be an unduly hard line on wages. Could Wurf teach him some civility? Yes, Wurf said, he thought he could.

Don Wasserman watched what happened:

> Jerry went into the next meeting. This guy says "Good morning," or something like that, and Jerry unloaded. He

proceeded to kick the stuffing out of the guy. The committee was going to break up, and it was all this lawyer's fault, because he was "creating disharmony."

The guy began pleading for "understanding," insisting he was not the villain. The other management people were afraid to say anything.

During a break, the other union members told Jerry to cool off, that he's ruining things, that he's going too far. He replied, "I'm doing what you asked me to do." When the management people returned, all was calm. Jerry had made his point. Later, he grabbed me, and he said, "The more I act like a baby, the more I get my way."

Wurf's explosion at the Pay Board would have been no surprise to AFSCME staff members and officers. Anyone in the union with even minimal exposure to Wurf could relate temper-tantrum stories, either as target or witness. "Jerry was a chronic meddler," said one staff person still with the union. "He would send you on a job, then drive you absolutely nuts with phone calls, telling you what to do." Life around Wurf, for his staff, was a cacophony of shouts, curses, threats, and general thunder and noise; at times his rage was so great he would appear to lose physical control of himself. "Jerry would humiliate a person in a meeting, then wonder why he was sore," said one former aide. "I think that he could turn his anger on and off at will. He could be perfectly calm, then call in someone with whom he had a problem. His face would turn red, the veins on his neck would expand, he would breathe harder, his eyes—well, they would be wild. He would explode, throw the guy out, then be as calm as anyone." Said another person, "Jerry got his way all his life because of his anger; he just never learned to turn it off, regardless of the circumstances."

Some persons could weather those storms and accept them as a quirk of Wurf's personality; others could not and left AFSCME. William Lucy, for one, considered that "by and large his hollering and yelling had no relationship to the issue that was up. . . . So long as you understood that, you could deal with it. His blustering, for lack of a better word, or his impatience, wasn't that big an issue. He'd rant and rave and yell and carry on like he was known to do. Well, we had sharp confrontations, but if you didn't defend yourself with Jerry, you weren't destined to be around very long." Further, Lucy stated, "you could argue with him, you could quarrel with him about ideas, differences in ideas, and have it taken as constructive criticism."

During AFSCME's busiest organizing years, Wurf spent much of his time running fire-brigade missions all over the country. Day-to-day direction of AFSCME fell to Joseph Ames, the secretary-treasurer, whom Lucy called "pretty much the anchor person in the office."

But in mid-1971 Ames became concerned about conduct of the Judicial Panel, the "mini-court" established in 1965 to mediate internal disputes. The chairman, John Zinos, had had recurring political problems in his home district council in Milwaukee, and although he excused himself from dealings when Milwaukee cases reached the panel, Ames and others felt he nonetheless exerted subtle influences. In July 1971 Ames wrote Wurf a lengthy letter listing other defects in the panel. "More and more," Ames wrote, "the panel membership has been made up of unsuccessful candidates for vice president, present or potential opponents of vice presidents who are being bought off, and political supporters who are being paid off. Without question, you and I must take a large share of the blame for this."

Ames proposed that the chairman be full-time, with salary and privileges equal to those of the secretary-treasurer, and that any panel member be ineligible to run for union office for the full length of his three-year term. The panel's jurisdiction would also be extended to include election contests, which at that time were decided by the president.

Ames sent Wurf the memorandum a few days before a scheduled leadership retreat at a resort in Piney Point, Maryland. Receiving no response, Ames finally walked to Wurf's office, told the secretary to hold any but emergency calls, and closed the door. "He went through the whole thing in my presence, and said, 'I agree with everything you've said. Only one problem. I don't believe there's anybody that I could trust to handle that kind of job.'

"I said, 'Yes, there is.'

" 'Who?' he asked.

"I said, 'Me,' and he nearly fell out of his chair. He couldn't believe that I'd give up the secretary-treasurer's job."

Wurf insisted that Ames talk to his wife before taking the new position. As Ames left the office, Wurf called, "What'll we do for secretary-treasurer?"

"You don't have any choice," Ames said. "You run Bill Lucy." Wurf did not commit himself.

A few days later they met again, and Ames said he was willing to take the Judicial Panel chairmanship. The talk then turned to Lucy and his elevation to secretary-treasurer.

"We ought to get Bill in here and tell him," Ames said. "You know, we're sitting here over a desk deciding his future, as well as some matters of considerable importance for the union, and I really think he ought to be called in."

So Lucy was summoned to hear the plan. Wurf spoke in circular fashion, gradually nearing the point at which his next sentence would be, "Bill, Joe and I think you ought to run for secretary-treasurer." Then the phone rang. The caller was Paul Hall, who rambled for half an hour while Ames fidgeted and Lucy sat in puzzlement. "I don't know how Lucy felt," Ames said, "but he must have been very uncomfortable, not knowing what the next sentence was going to be."

Wurf finally said the key sentence, and Lucy asked for "constant reassurance that we thought this was a good thing for the union." Then he accepted. Ames said, "He came to me later to have me assure him . . . that this wasn't some complicated plot at work to kick me aside."

Later, AFSCME mythology had it that Wurf promoted Lucy because, with the union's increasing black membership, and the

Memphis experience, a black was needed in a high and visible position. Several Wurf obituaries stated this version as fact. Ames says flatly it is not true.

Lucy had organized and held office on the local level; he had worked for the international staff in major trouble-shooting assignments, he was what Ames called "a number-one staff person. There just didn't seem to be anybody else that was a logical choice. Lucy was my suggestion, not Jerry's, and certainly not Lucy's. He didn't even know there was going to be an opening."

Thus Lucy moved into the post of AFSCME secretary-treasurer, making him one of the ranking labor officials in the country. Ames was named Judicial Panel chairman.

A photograph exists of Wurf, Lucy, and Ames standing at the convention podium, smiles wreathing their faces, their arms draped over shoulders in comradely fashion. The unity was real. But the changes voted that day were to lead five years later to a most serious political cleavage.

No one could have suspected such a storm cloud at the time, however. Wurf was concerned with a more immediate battle: with George Meany and the AFL-CIO, over both politics and labor policies.

CHAPTER SEVEN

At War with George Meany

In 1972 a reporter shared an elevator in a Miami Beach hotel with an AFL-CIO vice president just before a session of the executive council. "What do you intend to do today?" the reporter asked.

"I don't know what's on the formal agenda," the vice president replied without a flicker of a smile, "but my main concern is to make sure I don't have to sit between Meany and Jerry Wurf."

Meany and Wurf never actually came to blows during their many confrontations in the AFL-CIO executive council; but they often ended arguments at full-shout volume, filling the air with innovative profanity and shaking the table with pounding fists. "A lot of people say their differences were philosophical, not personal," one vice president recollected. "Well, that might be true, but those guys could put on a pretty lively show."

Wurf's admission to the executive council the fall of 1969 had no effect, visible or otherwise, on AFL-CIO policies. Although most press and public attention focused on his break with the AFL-CIO position on Vietnam, other strictly trade union issues were far more important to Wurf.

Even though AFSCME continued its thousand-member-a-week growth, Meany persisted in treating public employee unions as an interesting curiosity. Wurf had specific and legitimate requests. He felt the public employee unions were large enough to warrant having their own department within the AFL-CIO, as did other major groupings such as the building trades and maritime unions. These departments, with their own staffs, worked on such issues of common interest as lobbying, organization, and jurisdictions. Their unity gave them strength when they took a position before the Congress. Through cohabitation, they ironed out many family differences before they became serious.

When Wurf asked for a Public Employees Department, Meany would not say yes, Meany would not say no. "Let's talk about it," he told Wurf, time and again.

Creation of such a department was vital to AFSCME. After the initial surge of popular enthusiasm for public employee bargaining laws in the late 1960s, the climate had abruptly changed. Don Wasserman, a veteran AFSCME staff member, said, "States were not enacting legislation, and those that did were doing so in ways that provided lesser rights than those specified in the National Labor Relations Act [the act covering private sector employees]. We decided that the only way we'd get justice was through federal legislation, not through the states." What AFSCME wanted was legislation requiring that states and their political subdivisions bargain collectively with their employees. The rationale for federal jurisdiction in the matter was the interstate commerce clause of the Constitution.

Wurf knew that pushing such legislation through even a Democratic Congress would be difficult; therefore he needed as much collective lobbying power as he could muster. Hence his strong desire for a Public Employees Department, through which he could enlist the lobbying support of the federal employee unions. Wurf explained his case in great detail. Meany still said no.

Frustrated, Wurf tried to strike informal alliances on his own. For years he had kept an arm's distance from the American Federation of Teachers, an AFL-CIO affiliate that represented teachers in most large Eastern cities. AFSCME and the AFT had had frequent rows over raiding. There was also personal animosity between Wurf and AFT president Dave Selden and his top lieutenant, Albert Shanker. "Three volatile New York Jews, of roughly the same age and background, competing in the same profession," said one man who knew them all. "Jealousy, competitiveness, contempt—these are not qualities that make for a smooth relationship."

Nonetheless, Wurf tried. He went to the AFT convention in August 1970 and appealed for unity. Public employee unions should "stop pussyfooting around" and recognize that their sector was of near-equal strength to the building trades. They had to tell the Congress it had an obligation to make possible the development of a trade union movement for public workers. However, that would only be possible if the public employees achieved the same united front as the building trades.

> They [the building trades] have quarrels. They have disagreements. They scream at one another. . . . Nevertheless, they have a solid coalition of people who have a particular outlook on life—a solid coalition of people who have similar economic and social concerns.
>
> And what I am saying to you is that the time has come when we in the public employee sector need no longer depend upon other people to play the trade union tune that we will dance to. As a matter of fact, I think the time has come when we can put a musician or two of our own in the band.

Wurf's appeal was fruitless. The AFT leaders thanked him for the speech and said he made sense—but they would not help him pressure Meany for a public employee department.

So Wurf cast around for another ally. One tempting partner was the National Education Association, with its 1.1 million members. NEA was an anomaly. It was not in the AFL-CIO because its members sternly insisted that NEA was an *association*, not a *union*. Where AFT was predominantly a big-city union, NEA had its strength in the grass roots. As one observer said, "NEA is like the phone company; it is everywhere." NEA's membership was also *very* conservative.

In Wurf's view, about all NEA had in its favor was Terry Herndon, its executive director. Donovan McClure, who ran AFSCME's public affairs department in the 1970s, said "Although Terry was a staunch liberal, the NEA membership loved him, and regularly reelected him by healthy margins. NEA was basically a staff-run union." NEA's advantage in aligning with AFSCME was that it would secure a link to the labor movement, without becoming a formal member.

The deal was struck, and in March 1971 Wurf and Helen Bain, a Tennessee teacher serving as NEA president, announced formation of the Coalition of Public Employee Organizations (two years later to be regrouped as the Coalition of American Public Employees, or CAPE). The organizations pledged to lobby for common purposes, at all levels of government, and to try to arrive at consensus positions. The formal announcement invited other public employee groups to join the coalition.

That Wurf would make common cause with a group outside the AFL-CIO piqued Meany, although typically he said nothing publicly; Meany preferred to handle family squabbles at home. However, Meany recognized Wurf's action for what it was: a warning that AFSCME wanted a better deal for public employee unions. And he recognized that Wurf was not going to be bound by traditional AFL-CIO subservience to policies dictated by Meany. Wurf soon confirmed Meany's suspicion, and in dramatic fashion.

Neither Jerry Wurf nor AFSCME played any significant role in the 1964 and 1968 presidential elections. Wurf had been in office himself only a few months in 1964, and had had more important things to do than add AFSCME's weight to President Lyndon B. Johnson's landslide. AFSCME made no formal endorsement in 1968 because its conventions met before either the Democrats or Republicans had nominated a candidate; but Wurf and Joe Ames made their positions clear in an editorial in *The Public Employee:* "As the two full-time officers of this union, we are taking the liberty of making a recommendation," they wrote. They asked support of the Democratic candidate, Vice President Hubert H. Humphrey, on the basis of his record and his "amazing 100 percent pro-labor record." The editorial attacked the Republican candidate, Richard M. Nixon, for his opposition to social and labor legislation, and his silence on the right of collective bargaining for public employees.

Wurf did not intend for AFSCME to remain on the sidelines in 1972. He abhorred Richard Nixon and his economic and foreign politics. "The man is a hater," he said. "He just doesn't like people, unless they are rich and able to do something for him. I was obsessed with getting him out of office." Wurf also wanted a Democratic candidate who was both right on the issues and electable. He knew that he could not depend upon the AFL-CIO's political arm, the Committee on Political Education (COPE) to push for the nomination of a candidate favorable to public employees. At Meany's direction, the AFL-CIO took no acknowledged role in the nominating process, preferring to work in the shadows for its preferred candidate—though the sham fooled no one; any AFL-CIO political operation, by virtue of girth, is unconcealable.

By federal law, unions cannot spend dues money on elections; hence they create shadow organizations. In the summer of 1971, AFSCME formed its political arm—Public Employees Organized to Promote Legislative Equality, known by the acronym PEOPLE. The formation meeting came at a time when AFSCME was denouncing the Nixon wage-price freezes. Understandably, reporters asked Wurf, "Why are you doing this? Is it aimed at Richard Nixon?"

"We are not out to get Nixon," Wurf replied. "We are out to get the mentality which says workers in general and public employees in particular must take a back seat to corporate interests in this country. Unfortunately, Mr. Nixon embraces that view."

AFSCME did have complaints with Nixon beyond wage-price freezes. It charged the Labor Department with manipulating public service jobs programs in ways harmful to state and local governments, and contrary to Congressional intent on the rehirings of laid-off workers. Nixon also opposed bringing public employees under the Fair Labor Standards Act, which would have guaranteed them the same minimum wage and overtime pay as private sector workers. And Nixon was withholding ("probably illegally," said Wurf) twelve billion dollars in aid for cities and states, forcing them to lay off workers.

PEOPLE set a goal of one million to be raised by contributions and to be used "in such a manner as the [steering] committee considers appropriate for the achievement of the legislative goals of the federation." Wurf made plain, however, that PEOPLE's initial thrust was to be directed against the reelection of Nixon.

The problem then was: Which Democratic candidate had the desired qualities of suitability and electability? The AFSCME executive staff was sharply divided. William Hamilton, an articulate and slightly-built Texan—and a strongly-motivated man who was to become a force in the union—preferred Senator George McGovern. So did political operatives. Paul Minarchenko and Girard P. Clark. John Hein, Wurf's administrative assistant, preferred Humphrey, for whom he had once worked.

As Bill Hamilton related, "Because of his anti-war position, Wurf was inclined towards McGovern, but a number of people dissuaded him from saying anything at first." In early 1971, various Democratic hopefuls had already begun to campaign, the initial favorites being Humphrey and Senator Edmund Muskie of Maine.

The decision was made at an all-day meeting one Sunday in early 1972 at Wurf's home. Some staff members felt AFSCME should make no commitment so early, that the situation was too fluid. Hamilton said, "Jerry found the idea of identifying with Muskie early as a way to get recognition for the union. It was a good meeting, and after about five hours, Jerry made the decision. AFSCME would go with Muskie."

Both Humphrey and McGovern had reason to expect the endorsement, and so Wurf decided that they should be informed of the decision before any public announcement. Telling Humphrey would be particularly hard, in view of his pro-labor record and his friendship with Wurf. Bill Lucy quoted Wurf as saying, "Do we go and tell him?" Lucy replied, "No, *you* go and tell him." Wurf flew to the Midwest and talked with the campaigning Humphrey for three hours; at the end, Humphrey was unhappy but not bitter.

Breaking the news to McGovern was much more painful. By McGovern's account, Wurf said that although "he had a great regard for me personally . . . he was skeptical about whether I had any real chance. In a nice sort of way, he was saying, 'We're a big, powerful union, and we want to be effective, and there's no point in throwing our influence away on a loser.' "

At McGovern's invitation, Wurf came to his home. What Wurf said was a refrain McGovern had heard often during his campaign: "I was closer to his own personal views [than Muskie] . . . he was very much against the Vietnam deal . . . [which] led him to feel very uncomfortable about supporting anyone other than me because, intellectually, he was all for the positions I was outlining, especially with reference to the war . . ."

Wurf said, "You know, frankly, George, I just don't think you can make it. In fact, I don't think you've got a prayer of a chance of winning that nomination with Muskie in there and if Muskie doesn't make it, we'll probably go to Humphrey. . . . I hope you'll understand."

McGovern replied, "No, I don't understand it at all."

I was very tough on him. I said, "I just think it's outrageous for you people to be coming here and saying you agree with my positions, but there's no way of supporting me.

"What if the labor movement had started out that way, saying that it's a good thing to have collective bargaining, but it's not possible, so we're going to endorse the NAM [National Association of Manufacturers] position?"

It wasn't an angry thing. It was an indignant, tough reaction, because I wanted to make it just as painful and difficult for him as I could. I thought it might begin to wear on him, and that he would reverse his position.

Speaking of the episode a decade later, McGovern said that he "was a littly shaky" talking so tough to Wurf. "I really felt that these endorsements at that period from that wing of the party were going to hurt, that it was kind of making it difficult for us to get any momentum going nationally." But "I didn't let Jerry off the hook at all. When he got up to leave, I know he was very distressed, because I think . . . Jerry was an intellectually honest man and also something of a fighter and crusader. If I didn't have such a high regard for him, I wouldn't have given a damn about his position. I just would have figured, well, it's another guy who's playing the angles and so on. . . . I didn't think that if the tables were reversed, that he would have let me off."

As Wurf left, he said, "I hope there's no resentment on your part."

McGovern replied, "Well, Jerry, as a matter of fact, there is, because I think this is a wrong judgment and I just want to tell you something. When we win that nomination next July, you're going to look pretty foolish telling me [now] that I don't have a chance." Wurf left "in some distress."

AFSCME sought maximum publicity for its Muskie endorsement, presenting him at a press conference at which nineteen of the twenty-one AFSCME vice presidents concurred in the endorsement. Unfortunately, Muskie lasted only weeks longer. He lost in New Hampshire, and in Pennsylvania and Massachusetts. Soon his campaign, in Hamilton's words, was a "corpse looking around for a place to be buried." Accepting the obvious, Muskie "deactivated" his campaign, although pledging to remain available should the convention deadlock.

Muskie's demise left Wurf and AFSCME high and dry. Wurf talked about sitting out the remainder of the campaign, but George Meany and Al Barkan, the AFL-CIO political director, drove him back into it. At their urging, Humphrey and Senator Henry Jackson "were ganging up on McGovern, whose fierce opposition to the war had pissed off Meany," Hamilton said. "Jerry didn't especially like McGovern [as an electable candidate], but he was furious with Meany and Barkan."

An incident in May convinced Wurf that Meany would ultimately side with McGovern, despite his intense opposition to the Senator. Meany called a meeting on an obscure New York labor matter, and the talk turned to Vietnam. Another labor leader present "pressed on what would happen if McGovern got the nomination, and George made two points that were important.

"First, he said that, in the AFL-CIO, he didn't get involved in primaries, which was a measure in bullshit." Then Meany turned to the question of McGovern, saying, "I hate his guts on the Vietnam issue." He pointed to Wurf. "You, Jerry, will think it's because that's the only reason." Meany felt that McGovern was also unacceptable because of "grain sales and quotas and shipping and very complex business that affected maritime unions." Then Meany made what Wurf recalled as the most significant statement:

> But let me say, if he gets the nomination against the kind of son of a bitch the Republicans are putting up, a son of a bitch like Nixon, my feeling would be that our feelings on Vietnam and this other legislation shouldn't bring about any hesitation in supporting him.

Wurf had no reason to distrust Meany, who prided himself on keeping pledges. In this instance, Meany would disappoint Wurf.

Before the convention, held in July in Miami Beach, Wurf reestablished contact with McGovern. The senator was "pretty tight," in Bill Hamilton's words, but he accepted Wurf's offers of help in good grace. Abraham L. Zwerdling, the AFSCME counsel, helped McGovern over several legalistic hurdles, while Wurf, a delegate from the District of Columbia, roamed the floor, looking for signs of the AFL-CIO and other mischief. To his outrage, he saw an Israeli diplomat, a man he knew personally from the Washington embassy, on the floor, talking with delegates and "really working hard to stop McGovern." Wurf grabbed the man and hustled him to the side of the convention floor and told him, in blunt terms, that he considered his presence "outrageous." The diplomat left.

To Wurf—a master at propaganda himself—the AFL-CIO's most vicious move against McGovern at the convention was circulation of a "scurrilous white paper ... [which] charged that McGovern had been a tool of the big wheat exporters in his opposition to legislation requiring that half our grain exports be hauled in American ships; that he had double-crossed labor by once voting against the repeal of Section 14(b) of the Taft-Hartley Act* ... ; and that he had been undependable on issues requiring a hard line

---

* Section 14(b) permits state right-to-work laws weakening union security. Labor has tried to repeal 14(b) for more than three decades. Opposition to 14(b) is one of the litmus tests for a candidate desiring labor support.

against Communism." In fact, even the AFL-CIO's own COPE could fault McGovern for only five "wrong" votes during his Senate career, while crediting him with seventy-two "right" votes. And, Wurf noted, "Two of those 'wrong' votes were shared by most liberal senators who voted against [government funding for] the supersonic transport and Lockheed, bills favored by labor." By contrast, Wurf pointed out, Nixon as a congressman and vice president "had a miserably low score" on the COPE list—13 percent "right" during his Senate years, plus vetoes of fifteen bills of benefit to workers during the first forty-two months of his presidency, ranging from the creation of federally-funded day-care centers to support of public service jobs.

To Wurf, these issues were excuses dragged out by Meany and Al Barkan to conceal their own mistakes. When the Democratic Party decided to reform its delegate selection procedures following the riotous Chicago convention of 1968, the AFL-CIO leadership decided not to participate in drawing up new rules. "Perhaps they didn't take them seriously," Wurf said. "Some party regulars and no doubt some labor leaders were suspicious that it was all part of a plan by the 'new politics' crowd to take over." As Wurf wrote in *The New Republic* after the convention: "One might have expected labor to be in the forefront of reform—figuring, if nothing else, that the discipline and comparative orderliness inherent in union structures could give unions a leg up in dealing with the new rules. Reform presented an opportunity to say goodbye to the bosses and to mobilize the membership and encourage them to go to the polls and precinct meetings as advocates of change." Consequently, the AFL-CIO was left out of the reform movement, and could do nothing to alter its course. "We had a golden opportunity to bring working families access to power through the Democratic Party—and we blew it," Wurf wrote.

McGovern won the nomination on the first ballot. Several days later Meany called the executive council into session to urge that the AFL-CIO declare neutrality. Wurf argued that the question was too important to be settled by the executive council; he suggested that it be referred to the AFL-CIO General Board, composed of the presidents of each of the 117 unions in the federation. The motion lost, 25–5. Wurf's procedural objection brushed aside, Meany then called for a vote on the main neutrality motion. This time only three members voted no.

At a press conference after the meeting, Meany said that affiliated unions were "of course, free to endorse and support any candidate of their choice." But he, personally, "will not endorse, will not support, and will not vote" for either McGovern or Nixon. Asked by reporters why the labor movement was retreating from what Meany had earlier called "a major aim," the defeat of Nixon, he replied, "because a man named McGovern got the nomination" of the Democratic Party. "We don't think this man is good for labor."

In Wurf's view, the executive council went along with Meany, despite many misgivings, because of "profound loyalty" built up over years of progress in civil rights, social and economic legislation. Ironically, Wurf noted, had it not been for the Voting Rights Act and the Civil Rights Act, both of which had been pressed for by Meany and labor, "the gifted young blacks and chicanos and other new faces who dominated the Democratic convention might not have made it there."

Meany's repudiation of McGovern was treated by the media as a major political event, which it certainly was—the first nonendorsement by labor of the Democratic Party since 1952. But what happened in the weeks immediately after the executive council vote was perhaps equally significant: Following Wurf's example, half the members of the council tacitly repudiated the neutrality resolution, and in their capacity as leaders of individual unions, declared support for McGovern. Stephen C. Schlesinger, an aide to McGovern at the time, later wrote that "a genuine and widespread rebellion erupted in union ranks." By the end of August, thirty-three of the 117 unions in the AFL-CIO had come out in support of McGovern. So, too, had two large unions outside the AFL-CIO: the United Auto workers and the National Education Association. Paul **Wieck,** computing the extent of the defection in *The New Republic,* wrote that these unions "not only have a clear majority of all

AFL-CIO members (over seven million people), but with the single exception of the United Steelworkers, include all the major unions that traditionally have given a lot of money and manpower to campaigns."

Wurf knew McGovern's cause was doomed. "I can count votes, I knew the guy was going to get his ass kicked. But I didn't want that bum Nixon to get a free ride home, and I wanted to show Meany that he was not the total damned labor movement." So PEOPLE bought full-page ads in *Time* and elsewhere, featuring a Nixon caricature and a campaign quote of October 9, 1968: "Those who have had a chance for four years and could not produce peace should not be given another chance." Bill Lucy attended the post-convention COPE meeting and announced that AFSCME would not be making any further payments; other unions followed AFSCME's example. And Wurf took a hard shot at Meany in *The Public Employee:*

> It is clear that the AFL-CIO and President Meany will prevent state federations of labor and central labor bodies from supporting the McGovern campaign. We must fight to keep the American labor movement in this election. The stakes are too high for us to pretend the outcome makes no difference. It is important to remember, also, that the real issue is Richard Nixon, not George Meany or the AFL-CIO.
>
> George McGovern won the . . . nomination through sheer grit and hard work—starting at the grass roots level and working his way up when few people thought he could make it. That's not a bad way to go about things—whether it's building a union, selling an idea, or electing a president.

McGovern, of course, lost the election by an overwhelming margin, Nixon winning all electoral votes save those of Massachusetts and the District of Columbia. In the end, AFSCME's post-convention endorsement proved irrelevant, for not even a unified American labor movement could have saved McGovern.

But for Wurf, his spirited support of McGovern, and his direct criticisms of George Meany, meant that AFSCME could expect an increasingly sour reception from the labor establishment.

Wurf's 1971 alliance with the National Education Association proved largely symbolic. In 1973 he revived the idea, but this time with the addition of a large AFL-CIO union, the International Association of Fire Fighters (IAFF), which numbered more than one hundred and fifty thousand members; and the smaller National Treasury Employees Union. The new organization, the Coalition of American Public Employees, or CAPE, was intended as a direct rebuff to the AFL-CIO for its refusal to form a Public Employees Department. The firefighters union president, William H. "Howie" McClellan, was installed as CAPE president.

Creation of the alliance "drove Meany crazy," according to one AFL-CIO staff member. Meany demanded of Wurf, "How could you link up with a non-AFL-CIO member?" "You know what I wanted, you had your chance," Wurf responded.

In retaliation, Meany decided to bring Albert Shanker of the American Federation of Teachers onto the executive council. Shanker's union was the foremost rival of the NEA. Further, Shanker was not even the president of his union, so his election would constitute a double slap at Wurf.

Shanker's nomination went before the executive council at a meeting in Bal Harbour, Florida, in 1973. "Jerry jumped all over this one," said a labor source. "And for one of the few times in history, the council said 'no' to something George wanted.

"George came back with the statement that a press conference had already been set to announce Shanker's election, and that word had gotten around to labor reporters. George figuratively threw his body on the table. 'If you want to force me to go out and tell the press that Shanker has been rejected . . .'

"The executive council backed down. Some members even felt that George was so strong for Shanker because he considered him a possible successor."

For at least three years, Meany had promised Wurf he would

"study" the idea of a Public Employees Department for the AFL-CIO. Formation of CAPE jarred him into action. In 1974, at Meany's direction, the executive council formed just such a department. In a neat political maneuver, Meany also lured the fire fighters union out of CAPE by offering its president, Howie McClellan, the presidency of the new department. McClellan, to Wurf's disgust, accepted the bait. (Two of the milder descriptions of McClellan heard around AFSCME thereafter were that he was a "total turkey" and/or an "amiable ass.") Thomas Donahue, a key Meany lieutenant,* boasted around labor circles that "CAPE will survive another year at the most, no more."

Putting aside his better judgment, Wurf decided to bring AFSCME into the Public Employees Department, although he retained membership in CAPE as well, matching NEA's $10,000 monthly contribution. He considered the PED a farce. Meany opened its membership to any union with public employees on its rolls—which included the building trades, even though the bulk of their members worked in the private sector. Twenty-seven unions, more than one-fourth the AFL-CIO affiliates, ultimately joined the department. The Building and Construction Trades Department, however, did not extend reciprocal privileges to AFSCME, many of whose members worked as carpenters, steamfitters, and the like.

Wurf tolerated this situation for several years, and the evidence suggests he did so just to demonstrate to Meany that he could operate both within and without the AFL-CIO. There was much press speculation about Wurf taking AFSCME out of the AFL-CIO and forming a new labor center with the NEA, the United Auto Workers, and the United Mine Workers, which had recently shed itself of corrupt leadership. If one looked no further than basic arithmetic, such a mass wedding would have produced a federation of considerable size. But unions involve more than numbers. Were Wurf to leave the AFL-CIO, AFSCME would no longer be protected by the constitutional strictures against raiding. Don Wasserman, the veteran AFSCME economist, maintains secession from the AFL-

---

* Since 1980, the AFL-CIO secretary-treasurer.

CIO was never discussed, much less considered. "Those things that got to the press I wrote off as uninformed staff chatter," Wasserman said. "Wurf was not about to put AFSCME into a situation where it could be raided without protection by the Laborers and the Building Service unions. No chance at all."

After a year in the PED, Wurf realized he would never bring the AFL-CIO into support of a federal collective bargaining law in a form that would pass the Congress. The politics were intricate. By Wurf's estimate, the American Federation of Teachers, the Service Employees, and other AFSCME competitors feared passage of any such legislation because it would mean they would have to go one-on-one with AFSCME in representational elections. One Wurf aide of the era (no longer in AFSCME) said, "AFSCME made no real progress in cities such as Chicago and San Francisco because we wouldn't cut any deals with the local politicians. Had legislation existed forcing the other unions into city-wide elections, we'd have won everybody in sight."

For obvious reasons, the AFSCME competitors could not state their objections openly, so they devised a strategem by which they could kill chances for any such legislation by "being more pure than pure." The technique was simple: the AFL-CIO would not support any bill that did not guarantee that "the right to strike [was] a fundamental right of all workers."

Those last two words meant that the strike privilege had to be extended to policemen and firemen, and were included in an American Federation of Teachers resolution that went before the AFL-CIO convention in San Francisco in 1975 that ostensibly supported the federal collective bargaining law. Companion resolutions by the Communications Workers, the AFL-CIO Public Employees Department, the Service Employees, and other unions, contained variations of the same language.

Wurf knew Meany and other unions were gang-tackling him, and why, and he fought back in an emotional, but ultimately futile, floor speech. "The first time I had the courage to open my mouth on the executive council," he said, "it was to speak in favor of the unlimited right to strike for public employees.

"But I think the time has come to recognize some hard realities and to deal with some reasonableness, both as it affects our society and as it affects us as trade unionists."

Wurf saw a need to preserve public order and safety "without compromising the ability of those employees charged with maintaining order and safety, so that they may have a dignified and reasonable work situation." (Although Wurf did not raise the point, AFSCME long had required its police locals to put a no-strike provision in their constitutions. An Illinois local that violated this rule and struck in the late 1960s was ejected from AFSCME within hours. The ban on police strikes was dropped in the early 1970s.)

"But the basic fact of life is that . . . it is not possible to get a law through the Congress that makes it possible for public safety officers to strike. What we are in effect doing by insisting that there is an unlimited right to strike by public safety officers is in effect saying, 'We don't want a federal collective bargaining law.' "

Wurf suggested a trade-off: "Public employees should be given access to binding arbitration as an alternative to strikes." Already eight states had binding arbitration for police and "for the most part these laws work."

Delegate after delegate spoke against Wurf's position, a procession of speakers that signaled Meany wanted AFSCME buried. Taking no chances, Meany ended the debate by taking the floor himself to speak against Wurf. With appropriate, although false, indignation, Meany declared, "I hope I never see the day that the AFL-CIO sitting in convention will ask Congress to impose compulsory arbitration on anybody anywhere at any time." Meany returned to the podium amidst loud applause. The convention resolution passed with the right-to-strike proviso intact, ensuring certain death for any federal collective bargaining legislation.

As events developed, the U.S. Supreme Court mooted the entire issue before the Congress had a chance to act on the legislation. In 1974 Congress had extended federal wage and overtime standards to all state and local government workers, acting under the commerce powers of the Constitution. The National League of Cities challenged the constitutionality of the law in court, in a suit joined by numerous state and local governments and their trade organizations. The Supreme Court sided with the cities, ruling the act illegal.

The broader implication of the decision was that the Congress could not use those commerce powers as a grounds for legislation requiring states and cities to recognize and bargain with unions. As Don Wasserman of AFSCME stated, "This effectively finished, for a while, any chance for public employee collective bargaining legislation at the federal level." Thus AFSCME would be forced to return to the state level, and try to wheedle bargaining legislation from increasing hostile politicians.

By 1975, meanwhile, Wurf had tired of the charade of the Public Employee Department. New York City was struggling through a financial crisis, facing bankruptcy. When Wurf raised the problem at a department meeting in Bal Harbour, the building trades unions responded with a yawn: Most of their members worked in the private sector, they could care less about city employees. "Howie McClellan sat at the end of the table and smiled at Wurf, as if he was powerless to do anything."

When Wurf left the meeting he told Donovan McClure, his public affairs director, to announce AFSCME's withdrawal from the PED as soon as he returned to Washington. McClure learned, however, that McClellan planned a press conference that very day to "boast of the great things the Public Employees Department had achieved." With Wurf's approval he decided on some mischief. As McClellan began the press conference, McClure came into the room and handed reporters the AFSCME withdrawal statement. McClellan could see the flurry at the rear of the room but did not know what was happening until the first reporter's question: "What's this about AFSCME pulling out of your department?"

"Howie stood there flabbergasted, a look of utter astonishment on his face," McClure said. "He couldn't think of anything to say. Jerry and I later agreed that although this stunt was great fun, it was bad politics. That is something you do to the employer, not to your own folks."

Although CAPE never performed to Wurf's expectations, it did achieve some significant victories. In New Jersey, for example, Governor Brendan Byrne was in serious trouble when he sought re-election in 1977; the polls at one time showed him seventeen points behind Republican challenger V. Roy Bateman, the state senate president. Bateman pledged to do away with the state income tax if he was elected. "Jerry always argued that tax reform had to come from the left, otherwise it would come from the right," McClure said. "But Bateman was making points because these were Prop-13 days." (McClure referred to the California constitutional amendment, Proposition 13, which drastically cut property taxes, chiefly for businesses.) Political wisdom dictated that Byrne avoid drawing attention to the issue, so Wurf dispatched CAPE director James Farmer to Trenton to pose questions to Bateman: How in heaven's name, Farmer asked, did Bateman intend to fund New Jersey programs without the one billion dollars raised annually by state income tax? Farmer's speech caused other persons to ask the same question.

AFSCME did not want to be out front alone in the Byrne campaign, for it wished to show that essential services were at stake, not just salaries. New Jersey schools were already hurting, and the state supreme court had intervened several times to keep the income tax in force so they could operate. But the NEA state director, Fred Hipp, had never involved his group in state politics. "I'll take care of Hipp," promised Al Wurf, now director of New Jersey Administrative Council One. He asked Hipp what would be required to get NEA into the campaign. Hipp mentioned a technical matter concerning teachers. Byrne agreed: He would mention the point in a speech that very day.

"We all listened, and the governor passed by the point where he should have mentioned Hipp's issue," McClure said. "Al gets up, **and goes backstage,** and in a moment an arm is tugging at Byrne through the curtain. Al hands him a piece of paper. The governor reads it, then says this great thing about education. This wowed Hipp. He had never seen anything like it before."

Byrne overwhelmed Bateman, winning reelection by some twenty percentage points.

CHAPTER EIGHT

"The Best of Times . . . the Worst of Times"

Jerry Wurf turned to Charles Dickens's *A Tale of Two Cities* for language appropriate to describe AFSCME's situation in opening the 1976 convention:

> It was the best of times, it was the worst of times, it was the age of wisdom, it was the age of foolishness, it was the season of light, it was the season of darkness, it was the spring of hope, it was the winter of despair. . . .

AFSCME was forty years old that summer, and the minute band of Wisconsin civil servants had grown to an organization with more than 700,000 members, up 81,798 since the 1974 convention. Good financial management by William Lucy, the secretary-treasurer, and James O'Malley, the business manager, had enabled AFSCME to shake off its debts, and in fact accumulate a cash surplus of $1.1 million. Payments on the three million dollar headquarters building were on schedule.*

In the twenty months preceding the convention AFSCME faced other unions at the rate of more than one representational election daily; of 628 contests, AFSCME won 470, about 75 percent. Wurf

---

* AFSCME paid off the mortgage in five and one-half years, ending in 1980. The 1982 market value was more than ten million dollars.

insisted on being informed of each result, even if it meant a 3 A.M. phone call to his home.

Mildred Wurf learned to tuck her head under the pillow and go back to sleep when the phone rang. "For a while I would say, 'Jerry, what difference does it make if you wait until you get to the office to hear the results? You can't change anything.' He would say, 'If I didn't know, I wouldn't sleep anyway.' "

That heady year Wurf exulted in his reputation as the man who ran the union that was taking aboard members literally faster than they could be counted. As AFSCME economist James Savarese remembered, "We were the port of first call for young idealists who came to Washington. You wouldn't get rich at AFSCME, but you made a decent living, and you knew you were *involved*. We were the guys out pushing the programs on the Hill, and showing the AFL-CIO how a union could—and should—be run."

There were quality top-level hirings as well. Jack T. Conway, long a top aide to Walter P. Reuther of the United Auto Workers, and then director of Common Cause, joined AFSCME as executive director. William Welsh, executive director for governmental affairs—i.e., lobbying and politics—had long served as a key aide to Senator Hubert H. Humphrey. Donovan McClure, the public affairs director, had a background in journalism in his native West Virginia and in San Francisco, had held a Peace Corps position, then helped Governor Jay Rockefeller in West Virginia. William Hamilton remembered, "There was a vibrancy of ideas. This was a job where I liked to work in the morning."

But Wurf remained the demanding taskmaster, one who expected a devotion to AFSCME equalling his own, which meant total. His personal thunderstorms were frequent and dramatic. Once he stormed at Don McClure, "Get out of this office, get out of this union, go home, you're fired." McClure did as directed. The next day his phone rang at home. "Where the hell are you? This meeting is starting."

"You fired me, remember?" McClure said.

"Oh, don't take that sort of shit seriously," Wurf said. "Get on down here."

Other firings were more permanent. One high-risk job was editorship of *The Public Employee*. Wurf read each story, each headline, saw each photograph. He could not always tell the editor in advance what he *wanted*; after reviewing an edition, he was quick to tell an editor what he had not *liked*. The editorship turned into one of the more rapid swinging-door positions in Washington. At least one editor did not survive even one issue. "I sent the stories and the layout up to Jerry, and somebody called and said I should leave the building immediately; my check would be mailed to me."

Wurf made no pretense at gentility. During the mid-1970s he began to withdraw from the old friends who had surrounded him during his rise to power in AFSCME. Al Bilik had been in and out of AFSCME, formally, twice; informally, many more times. Wurf finally ran him away for good in 1976, and then made him squirm to qualify for a union pension. In Joe Ames's estimate, "Jerry seemed to be deliberately isolating himself from the old crowd, as if he had decided he wanted to be by himself all the time. He took a liking to these new guys, Bill Hamilton, for instance, as if the people from the old days had been sucked dry of ideas, and had nothing left to offer."

When Joe Ames spoke those words in December 1981, he was embittered at his own treatment a few years earlier by Wurf. However, Ames, who had had a leg blown off in combat, also recognized something else working on Wurf those years: pain. "He hurt," Ames said. "You have to have a bad leg to know how a bad leg can hurt. I got one. I know. He hurt."

Based upon my own observations of Wurf his last months, I agree with Joe Ames. Wurf once spoke to me of his pain. We were in an automobile, I did not take notes, hence I am quoting Wurf indirectly.

> There are times when I form this black circle in my mind, and I make it expand until it blots out everything else in my existence, even the pain in my foot. This is something you should know about.

I told Wurf I had a fouled-up knee that even after surgery gave more accurate weather reports than the Weather Bureau.

Yeah, but you feel that when you are walking. I feel this foot even when I am sitting down. I'm in a nice restaurant eating a good meal and maybe watching a pretty girl across the room—nothing serious, just watching—and I move the foot and it's as if I had put it into a bucket of fire. That, you big Texan, that is pain.

But some people who came to work for AFSCME learned to adapt to Wurf's moods, and work around him and with him. Kathi Howarth, hired originally as an executive floor secretary, demonstrated under Wurfian fire that she was a capable manager and arranger. "When he screamed, I trembled. I said to myself, 'I'm leery of this man, I'll give it a week.' Within three days there was a three-hundred-and-sixty-degree turn in the way he worked with me. I told him, 'All I want to do is my job. I can't do it unless you deal with me.' "

Thereafter Kathi Howarth was one of Wurf's closer confidantes within the union. A quiet-eyed, blond woman, in her mid-twenties when she went to work for AFSCME, Ms. Howarth was quickly involved in Wurf's personal life as well as his professional life. She went with Jerry and Mildred Wurf when they attended official functions. "He was always telling me, 'Get the name of that guy I was just talking with, I'm supposed to call him tomorrow.' "

An early riser, Howarth was often at her desk by eight in the morning. Frequently Wurf would call and ask "What's happening?"

"I would say, 'Jerry, this building is still empty, what *could* be happening?' " As Ms. Howarth interpreted these calls, Wurf fed on information, and he did not want anything happening of which he was unaware.

Ms. Howarth had another role as well. When Wurf entered the AFSCME building each morning, the switchboard operator, whom he had to pass, made an instant judgment on the question,

"What's his mood today?" and telephoned Howarth. If Wurf was dour, Howarth would discourage staff from asking him to approve projects; but if he came to the office in a happy mood, the gate would open. Interpreting Wurf's moods, and knowing when to discuss a project, were among the keys to success in AFSCME. Don McClure said, "My rule was *never* to throw an idea to him when he was flying somewhere to make a speech. Although Jerry was one of the best natural speakers I've ever known, a man who could ad lib an hour on almost any subject, he tended to get uptight. But once it was over, and if he had gone over well, he would listen to anything, and most likely agree."

Wurf began to spend more time outside the union. He joined the board of the Twentieth Century Fund, the New York foundation that commissions public policy studies. Wurf took the appointment seriously, and his confrontational style alarmed many other persons on the board. "Jerry would use . . . well, let us say *demagogic* tactics to get his way," said one Fund staff person. "Jerry was very protective of labor. If he felt a proposed study was unfair to the labor viewpoint, he would raise his objections, loudly and often profanely."

One such instance arose in May 1977 when the Fund was considering a study of the New York City budget. Previous studies by the proposed author had been sorely criticized by New York public employee unions, including AFSCME's District Council 37, for what Wurf called "seriously deficient and inaccurate presentation of data." Any objective study, he urged, must be conducted by someone not involved in the city's political-governmental-academic axis. Wurf's protests killed the project.

Wurf was active in other social and political areas as well. He served on policy planning committees for the Democratic Party. He joined the steering committee of the Democratic Socialist Organizing Committee (a throwback to his Yipsel origins, but dedicated to reforming the capitalistic system, not overthrowing it).

In talks with his inner circle, Wurf gave the impression that he was bored with the daily routine of running a seven-hundred-thousand member union. AFSCME now had a more or less self-

sustaining momentum. Future growth was a factor of internal organization, for if AFSCME could sign all the public workers for
which it had bargaining rights, its membership would double. (Few
states or cities had the so-called "agency shop," under which workers paid union dues regardless of membership, on the theory that
they benefited from union-negotiated contracts. Bringing these
"free-riders" into the union was—and is—a constant problem for
AFSCME.) So Wurf turned his anger to issues peripheral to unionism, but essential to humanity.

De-Institutionalization

In the mid-1970s big-city Americans began to notice a new social
phenomenon: "bag ladies," women who had stuffed the posses-
sions of a lifetime into paper or mesh bags, or a stolen shopping
cart, and set out to live on the streets. The bag ladies roamed aim-
lessly by day, often babbling incoherently, lost in private worlds of
despair and dementia. Passersby came to recognize the "regulars"
in a particular area—the woman who would drape clear plastic over
her pitiable pile of bags and sit on a park bench during a summer
rain, the man who would wash his face and feet daily in a park
fountain. At night the bag ladies merged with another subspecies of
their urban culture, the "grate people," homeless derelicts who
would huddle for warmth over the grates covering heating shafts of
buildings.

American liberalism is at its very worst when it conceives and ex-
ecutes programs without regard to the best interests of the persons
most directly affected. One such scheme came to be known as de-
institutionalization, and that the idea bears such a cumbersome
name is no accident. As George Orwell wrote in his essay, "Politics
and the English Language," men in power "try to make indefensi-
ble politics acceptable by describing them in incomprehensible
terms." As AFSCME consultant Henry Santiestevan wrote in his
study, *Out of Their Beds and into the Streets,*

'De-institutionalization' has emerged as the high-sounding name for a program that purports to transfer patients from dehumanizing institutions into community-based care centers. But, more often, this fad involves budget-cutting by state administrations and profiteering by unscrupulous private interests.

De-institutionalization was the bad result of good intentions. Notoriously understaffed and underfinanced, mental institutions for more than a century had been warehouses, with no treatment deserving of the name. In the early 1960s civil liberties lawyers won court decisions declaring that persons could not be confined for mental illness unless they received adequate care. Other decisions set strict standards for treatment in these hospitals.

These rulings more than trebled state mental health costs, from around six dollars per day in the 1950s to twenty dollars in 1975. As Santiestevan wrote, "The courts were handing down complex court orders that called for major improvements in institutional care. For financially pressed state governments, the easy way out of the cost squeeze was to cut hospital budgets and send the patients to private nursing homes eligible for federal Medicare, Medicaid and Social Security payments."

The Congress's intent was for discharged patients to continue to receive treatment through community health centers. Legislation passed in 1963 envisioned some two thousand centers, to be built with federal assistance. Twelve years later, only five hundred had been constructed. AFSCME supported those centers, even though they threatened the jobs of scores of thousands of members who worked in state hospitals. "I was sold, along with everybody else, that this was a good idea and a humane way to get people out of these horrible hospitals," Wurf said. He called de-institutionalization "a humane idea gone amok. Geez, I was wrong, but at least I was in good company." In 1975 the centers had only twenty thousand beds, compared with three hundred and sixty thousand in state and county hospitals.

Nonetheless, the mass exodus began. California alone cut its mental hospital population from 34,955 in 1963 to 7,264 in 1973. Many of these people became street roamers, the juveniles the targets of sexual exploitation, the elderly ignored as they shuffled along the streets. New York's hospital population the same years dropped from eighty-five thousand to thirty-eight thousand; instead of being on wards, the patients now slept in subway stations, doorways, and in cardboard boxes on the street. By 1979, according to a survey by the *Philadelphia Inquirer*, more than one million former mental patients were going without proper care or treatment.

"This is one of the anomalies of American society that infuriates me," Wurf said of de-institutionalization. "When I started pointing out the inequities, these damned politicians would say, 'Oh, listen to Jerry Wurf, all he wants to do is save jobs for his members, he doesn't care about the patients.' Well, that's rot, pure *rot*. The politicians weren't willing to spend the money for community centers. Throw these people out in the street, let some poor old lady stumble around until she gets lucky and freezes to death."

Wurf urged a moratorium on discharges of mental patients until the community had facilities to receive them. "You take a guy out of a hospital and dump him in some flophouse room, you're signing a death penalty for him," Wurf said.

Why, Wurf was once asked, do you spend so much time on this subject? Wurf seemed surprised that the question had been posed. "Who the hell else speaks for them?" he said. "If I couldn't go to bat for people in trouble, I'd find another line of work."

De-institutionalization was one of the many issues on which Wurf spoke but was not heeded. Four days after his death, the *New York Times* published some comments from a woman of about sixty-five, "neatly dressed, proud of her appearance," who spent her nights at a subway entrance in Grand Central Terminal. She looked at other people huddled around her and said, "It must be some kind of experiment to see how long people can survive without food or sleep."

Contracting-Out

The pro-business *U.S. News & World Report* exulted in August 1976: "A new weapon has emerged in the struggle to hold down the costs of state and local governments. It's called private enterprise." The publication referred to a new fad of government officials, the "contracting-out" of jobs formerly done by public employees, with claimed cost cutting.

When this supposed panacea for city budgets appeared, Wurf greeted it with indifference. "You see schemes where some local mayor doesn't have the guts to go for higher taxes, they try all sorts of gimmicks." But as contracting-out spread, Wurf spoke out, and strongly, that the cities were trying to cover up their own management shortcomings. As Wurf told the 1976 AFSCME convention:

> Contracting out public services and public service jobs has become a new source of political patronage subject to fantastic rip-offs and corruption. Most workers, public and private, want to do a day's work for a day's pay. As responsible men and women it's important to us. . . . It's a source of satisfaction. But productivity in the public sector depends upon good management. And as long as public officials hand out jobs to their political pals, cries for great productivity are a red herring.

AFSCME did a systematic study of contracting-out situations in selected cities. What seemed on the surface an easy way to cut costs turned out to be something else entirely, once the programs had a few years' experience.

Wurf gave some examples to the 1976 convention.* Warren,

---

* Many of the histories cited by Wurf were compiled by John D. Hanrahan, a *Washington Post* editor who refused to cross picket lines during a pressmen's strike in 1975. The *Post* broke the strike with scabs and remote printing facilities ("a great fucking liberal newspaper that put its pocketbook before its principles," Wurf said of the *Post*). With Wurf's approval, Donovan McClure had Hanrahan research and write a major study of contracting-out entitled *Government for $ale*.

Michigan, had private contractors pick up garbage for two years, then canceled the experiment because no money was being saved. Memphis, Tennessee, ever alert to get rid of its militant sanitationmen, was on the brink of contracting-out its trash collections until a study showed a private firm would cost far more than what was already being spent. The University of Denver tried a private collector for a year, then took back the functions.

Wurf objected to contracting-out on other grounds as well. Private firms that do contract work for cities have a record splotched with notorious instances of corruption. And Wurf repeatedly challenged the mayors' trade lodges to offer studies proving that public employees were any less effective than those of private firms doing contract work for government. None appeared that convinced him.

Tax Reform

Tax reform is one more of those perennial issues to which the public and politicians devote much anguished-brow attention, but about which nothing of true substance is ever done. In his speeches throughout the 1970s, Wurf preached several things. To Wurf, tax reform was important "because the existing regressive tax system is one of the principal deterrents to popular support to the needs of public service." Almost seventy-five cents of every dollar raised by state and city governments "are generated by regressive property and sales taxes." Wurf related this fact directly to public opinion of public workers:

> That's why people get mad at us. Those taxes are unfair because they are not based on the ability to pay. That's why we . . . favor . . . a program that places limits on the amounts of property taxes that low-income homeowners and renters pay.

Wurf offered a variety of ideas. The key one was the so-called circuit-breaker. The circuit-breaker—one form or another of which was already adopted in many states—provided a uniform system of tax credits or rebates on property tax liability for those with low incomes, especially elderly citizens. Homeowners below a certain income level—say $10,000—would be exempted from a portion of their property tax liability. Property tax liability would be gradually removed at lower rates of income. Thus, income level is what "breaks" the property tax "circuit."

Wurf recognized early in the 1970s that public concern over unfair property taxes would eventually lead to a voter backlash unless equitable changes were made. "This is an issue on which the right-wing and the left-wing are in agreement," he told an AFSCME conference in 1974. "Well, if 'reform' is to be done, I'd rather have it done from our side."

Just as Wurf predicted, California voters imposed a strict limitation on property taxes in the famed Proposition 13 referendum engineered by a rightist named Howard Jarvis. "I would agree with Jarvis on one point," Wurf said. "The tax situation in that state is ridiculous." Because of a runaway real estate market that increased home values by upward of 20 percent annually in California, many homeowners found themselves paying almost as much a month in property taxes as they did for mortgages. "Jerry Wurf has often been in the situation where I can say, 'I told you so,' " he said tartly after Proposition 13 was passed. "I say it again. I told you so."

Nervous that the "Prop 13 fever" would sweep other states, cutting funds available for public services, Wurf spoke out often in the late 1970s, both in opposition to further such initiatives, and in positive promotion of AFSCME's own reform programs. He went head-to-head with Jarvis once, on a Washington television talk show. The debate was a curious one. Each time Wurf tried to argue the facts about tax reform, the burly Jarvis would exclaim, "horse manure," or "fertilizer," and criticize Wurf and unions personally. At one point he even said that Wurf, as a union president, had a "racket." Wurf pinned him down: Are you really calling me a "racketeer"? he asked. Jarvis stuck with the word.

Then the program credits began rolling at the end of the show. With the audio still on, the interviewer insisted—even begged—

that Jarvis retract the "racketeer" charge. "I withdraw it," Jarvis finally said. Wurf, in the background, muttered angrily, "Outrage, this is an absolute outrage, what you are letting him do."

When Wurf came home an hour or so later, he told Mildred, "Well, I almost paid off our mortgage in Wellfleet tonight. [The Wurfs had just purchased a summer home on Cape Cod.] Old Jarvis libeled me, and then the station let him squirm off the hook." Wurf would not permit his public affairs staff to book any further debates with Jarvis. "It's a waste of time talking with that sort," he said.

When Wurf used the Charles Dickens quotation that opened the 1976 convention and this chapter, he was thinking, among other things, of the agonies suffered by New York City during its recurring fiscal crisis of the mid-1970s. For months the city skittered along the edge of bankruptcy. In the end, it was saved financially by a restructuring of its long-term debt, loans from pension funds of the major public employee unions—including AFSCME's District Council 37—and a host of other measures. The New York situation was so muddled, so controversial, that it defies capsulization. To the general press, the public employees, with their "bloated salaries, fat pensions, and cushy working conditions" were the villains. Long-range factors, such as the flight of the middle class and their replacement with the poor, also played a part. Regardless of the facts, however, the New York mess, and the grim possibility that the nation's largest city would go broke, shook public confidence; and the public (and the press) was quick to assign public employee unions the lion's share of the blame.

Wurf refused to accept any such responsibility. Rather, he pointed to three interlocking reasons: the soaring inflation of the Nixon-Ford years, which drove interest rates on government bonds to record levels; the willingness of New York banks to continue pumping money into those profitable bonds, despite evidence of fiscal irresponsibility on the part of city officials; and overall poor management of the city government.

Although President Gerald R. Ford was to claim in 1975, "The record shows that New York City's wages and salaries are the highest in the United States," the "record" actually showed something else. Ford cited one particular group of workers, the sanitationmen, members of the Teamsters union, who after three years earned nearly $15,000 a year, a four-week vacation, and attractive retirement benefits.

But as Wurf pointed out in rebuttal to Ford, using figures from the Bureau of Labor Statistics, New York City municipal workers' salaries ranked behind those in major cities elsewhere. Average monthly salaries in 1975, according to BLS, were Los Angeles, $1,180; Detroit, $1,144; San Francisco, $1,094, and New York City, $1,062.

Nor did New York City receive its fair share of federal tax revenues. In 1974 New York City residents paid twenty-six billion dollars in federal taxes. In return, the federal government returned about three billion dollars. Of the federal revenue-sharing program of six billion dollars, New York City received $263 million—about 4 percent of the total.

Before the National Press Club on July 10, 1975, Wurf spoke at length of New York's problems and gave both his interpretation of the causes and some solutions for cure.

> The administration, the media, and even some of our friends in Congress have made New York City a sacrificial lamb—a scapegoat for the failures of national policy. They've held out New York as an example of unparalleled municipal profligacy. . . .
>
> I organized and represented workers in New York for eighteen years. I watched while the city government responded to various pressures to increase expenditures without increasing tax revenues at a comparable rate. Often, this was covered up by disguising current operating costs as capital expenditures, rather than placing them in the expense budget where they belong. New York City's financial crisis didn't catch me . . . by surprise.
>
> But much of the pressure has come from the federal gov-

ernment's failure to assume responsibility for financing health
and education—and by the city's own commitments to operate city colleges, municipal hospitals, and an extensive welfare system. More than half of New York City's budget is devoted to the children, the aged, impoverished, and those in
need of medical care. . . .

The banks that dominate municipal finance throughout
the nation have their homes—but, most certainly, not their
hearts—in New York City. And, like any enterprise, the city
requires access to credit.

This year, by their own admission, the banks decided to
teach their own city a lesson. They formed a 'consortium'—
or, in plain English, a cartel—to jack up interest rates [for the
city] to a usurious and tax-exempt 9.5 percent.

That was last winter—when New York needed short-term
loans.

This spring, when New York needed short-term loans, the
banks simply refused to lend the money—although neither
Moody's Investors Service nor Standard and Poor doubted
[the city's] ability to repay. The bankers then demanded, and
received, a controlling voice in how [the city] manages its
own affairs.

The solution, the Municipal Assistance Corporation, helped
New York convert three billion dollars of short-term debt into
long-term debt. For ten years it was to monitor the city's budget
and receive all the city's sales tax and stock transfer tax revenues.

What Wurf wanted was increased federal aid, a tax on the banks'
bond interest income, and an equitable statewide real estate tax,
rather than leaving it in the hands of timorous local officials.

Municipal unions in New York, including AFSCME, voluntarily deferred contractual wage increases totalling one hundred and
fifty million dollars to help the city out of the 1975 crisis; they gave
up benefits worth an additional thirty-five million dollars. They also
used pension funds to buy $3.5 billion in Municipal Assistance
Corporation bonds. "In terms of going deep into the pocketbook,"

Wurf said, "we did a hell of a lot more than any of the banks. Yet we still ended up the villains."

Indeed, AFSCME and other public employee unions were depicted as the black hats of the financial problems that wracked America's cities in the 1970s. Wurf's major fight in the 1960s, his first years as AFSCME president, was to achieve public acceptance of the right of his workers to form unions and bargain collectively. By 1971 Wurf would speak of these rights as "established facts." Now he found himself and AFSCME facing an even graver crisis: attempts by politicians to strip away the rights for which public employees had worked so hard.

Mayors and governors made no secret of what they intended; they discussed strategy openly at their conventions, with each seemingly trying to outstrip the other in anti-union oratory. Their reasons were politically cynical. In the summer of 1975, pollster Louis Harris told the U.S. Conference of Mayors that the way for them to get reelected was to get tough with public employees. "How you got elected the last time could well be the last time you might ever get elected that way," Harris told the mayors. "The key to tomorrow . . . [is to] ask the public and city employees to make the sacrifices necessary to achieve quality performance of these services." The mayors itched for a fight with public employee unions, and complained when none occurred. As Mayor Edward Hanna of Utica, New York, told *Business Week* in late 1975, "I can't get anyone to go on strike against me. I think city government needs a showdown with the unions." (In a memorandum forwarding this article to Wurf, Donovan McClure wrote, "In my book there is a mayor who is itching for a strike.")

In late 1975, Mayor Charles B. Wheeler, Jr., of Kansas City, Missouri, asked the National League of Cities to adopt a mutual assistance pact under which a "flying squad" of non-union fire fighters would be trained and paid to serve as strikebreakers whenever and wherever fire fighters went out on strike. (Wurf called the flying squads "a task force of goons." Nothing ever came of the idea.)

What galled Wurf was that the governors and mayors became so carried away with their own scare talk that they would not listen to his proposal for compulsory arbitration in fire and police strikes—a procedure that would alleviate the officials' most basic fear. The most intransigent opposition (save perhaps that of George Meany) came from management organizations—the National League of Cities, the U.S. Conference of Mayors, the National Governors Conference, and the National Association of County Officials. As McClure commented in a letter to the editor of the *Kansas City Times,* "These organizations always have had a morbid fear of sharing responsibility with public employees. They have had an irrational dread of letting an impartial third party enter into labor relations and examine employer policies. They fear reasonableness more than they fear strikes. Also, many public officials have decided it's good politics to provoke strikes. They would rather take a strike, and use the strike for political aggrandizement."

The American press, by and large, is indifferent or hostile to organized labor—a reflection of the fact that newspapers are businesses, and the people who control their editorial policies are guided by the same societal values as, say, people who manufacture cardboard boxes or automobile transmissions. Although Wurf got along famously with most labor reporters on a personal basis, he and AFSCME were regularly savaged by editorial writers and columnists, who disregarded facts and either misunderstood or misstated the union's positions. The theme was consistent: Government workers "have notoriously had a soft life" and "have become sacred cows," and are grossly overpaid as well. The words are from the *Hartford Times* in December 1975; uncountable other newspapers said much the same. To the *Tallahassee Democrat,* Wurf was "demagogic" for suggesting that arbitrators settle public employee disputes with governments when all other means failed. The *Honolulu Star-Bulletin* charged that "high salaries and unbelievably high pensions for municipal employees" led to New York City's recurrent financial crises.

One canard that haunted Wurf and AFSCME for years was a remark falsely attributed to him during a Baltimore strike in the summer of 1974. AFSCME's relations with government in Balti-

more were historically stormy, usually climaxed by what William
Lucy called "the annual Baltimore strike." Sanitationmen were out
in August, and one Saturday Wurf and Lucy drove to Baltimore to
walk a picket line. As Lucy related what happened:

> The police differ. Guys who understand their job will react
> in one way, guys who are ambitious and want to be a sergeant
> . . . will react in another way. It just depends on who you got
> out there that particular day.
>
> As fate would have it, we had a shift change, and some guy
> came out who was bucking for something, and he was going
> to impose a set of rules different than the guy who just
> left. . . . We could not accept these kinds of restrictions with-
> out echoing our opposition . . . and the more we confronted,
> the more they had to enforce their authority.
>
> Some cop got pushed or we refused to move when he said
> "move" and they pulled out a paddy wagon.

Wurf, Lucy, Peter Morolis, the AFL-CIO political director in
Baltimore, and Frank Hutchins, a staff representative, were hauled
off to jail. Lucy continued:

> Jerry's notion of going to jail and mine differed. He was
> still struck with the liberal notion that you go down, they look
> at you, and you tell them who you are and you leave. It didn't
> quite work like that. We kept talking about our constitutional
> rights and the guy kept saying, "Yeah, we'll get around to
> them."

Wurf and Lucy were stuck in a holding cell; by then the police
realized they had arrested the ranking officers of one of America's
largest unions, and the governor's office was demanding that they
be freed immediately. Governor Marvin Mandel did so not because
of any liking for Wurf—the two men detested one another—but
because he knew he would be negotiating with Wurf the next week
and did not want him unduly angry. However, in classic bureaucratic fashion, the "machinery wouldn't work, they couldn't get the

papers right." So Wurf sat in the cell and fumed, with Lucy alternately calming him and laughing at the situation.

Then in walked an earnest young social worker, intent on doing an "intake interview" of the new prisoners.

> By this time I had really sort of quieted Jerry down, at least from the last incident, and this guy started out with, "Where was he born? What was his background?"
> But the fella didn't know who was in jail either. Jerry was just one more case with him. He asked him about his profession. Jerry said he was a professional trade unionist, and the guy asked him about his income. Jerry said, "$80,000 a year."
> The guy says, "Yeah, sure, yeah, I understand, right."

Lucy managed to keep Wurf from throwing the social worker bodily from the cell, and late in the afternoon they were released. The next week, police joined the strike, and Wurf and Mandel met in a hotel to try to reach a settlement. Later, Mandel told the press, "Mister Wurf, at the height of the strike, warned me that Baltimore City would burn to the ground unless the city gave in to his demands."

"An absolute lie," Wurf countered. "Nothing of the sort ever passed my lips. Mandel is loathsome." Challenged to substantiate the statement, Mandel could offer no evidence ("chiefly because none existed," Wurf said). Three weeks after the statement, AFSCME sued Mandel for libel in the U.S. District Court in Baltimore. Wurf later lost interest and did not press it.

Wurf's denial, however, and the law suit, did not stop repetition of the charge. The right-wing journalist Ralph de Toledano used the statement in slightly altered form as the title for *Let Our Cities Burn*, an anti-union book published in 1975. Senator Clifford Hansen (Republican, Wyoming) repeated it, in a privileged forum, in a floor speech on March 6; reprints of his speech were widely distributed by anti-union groups. One such organization, the so-called Americans Against Union Control of Governments, used the reprints in a fund-raising appeal that netted eight hundred and fifty thousand dollars. (AAUCG's main reason for existence is to oppose federal collective bargaining laws for public employees.) AFSCME sent editors a three-page background memorandum on the spurious origins of the charge; nonetheless it constantly resurfaced during the next several years. Peter A. Jay of the *Baltimore Sun* used the quotation in a column as the justification for terming AFSCME "bloody-minded." Jay acknowledged that Wurf denied ever making such a threat, but then he added that the alleged remark "was personally and philosophically in character."

Wurf, in frustration, finally tried to counter anti-AFSCME propaganda with a million dollar advertising campaign designed to bolster the union's image, and to increase public perceptions of what its members actually contributed to society. So Americans soon were seeing a TV commercial that preached the message:

After the parades,
After the promises,
Someone has to work
to keep our states
and cities runnin'
A – F – S – C – M – E
AFSCME! AFSCME!

This ditty, written by the J. Walter Thompson advertising agency in New York, was not intended to replace "Solidarity Forever" as a labor anthem. As Wurf told one interviewer, "Just as corporations have done for decades, we're reminding people that our members perform necessary services." Other series of ads depicted AFSCME members performing their myriad jobs—cafeteria attendant, parks worker, highway maintenance—and asked how cities would function without them. And a "public affairs" series attacked bloated defense spending and restrictive immigration quotas.

The cumulative effects of the anti-union agitation, and of AFSCME's attempts at rebuttal, cannot be measured on any objective scale, but as a visible and controversial figure, one of less

than universal popularity even within the labor movement, Wurf
was a natural lightning rod. When an official of the Republican
National Committee charged that Wurf "has this country by the
throat," he replied with a laugh to an interviewer, Henry B. Burnett, Jr., of *Skeptic.* "As a matter of fact," he said, "I am unable
even to get hold of a toenail. I couldn't even call a strike of twelve
computer operators in our union. I don't have the authority to call
anybody out on a strike—or to settle a strike, either." Wurf continued:

> If we're so powerful, why does every mayor and governor
> try to make his political reputation by fighting our union? If
> you sat in this office all day, you'd get the impression that
> every public official in the United States thinks he can win his
> epaulets by declaring war on our members.

Attacks by his enemies Wurf could accept as legitimate political
debate. What cut him deepest during those years, however, was the
realization that even his supposed friends could become anti-union
when elected to office. In one such instance, he found himself on
opposite sides from the key figures of the civil rights coalition that
had helped the AFSCME sanitationmen in Memphis in 1968.
Now, however, the onetime aides of the late Dr. Martin Luther
King, Jr., sat on what Wurf called "the bosses' side of the table, and
they sure the hell behaved like bosses, too."

It happened like this: AFSCME's chief figure in Atlanta was
Leamon Hood, who had joined the union in 1962 while working as
a school custodian, then moved to the position of water pollution
control operator, at an entry level. When he put in for a promotion,
"The city wouldn't give me the job, even though I placed number
two on the written examination." In the oral interview supervisors
quizzed Hood closely on "whether or not I was a Muslim . . .
whether I had any civil rights activity or background. Quite frankly,
I didn't but I was appalled, and I expressed it, and I think that was
part of why I never got the position."

When Wurf was elected AFSCME president in 1964, Atlanta
locals were white-dominated, even though men such as Hood had

helped organize them. Wurf immediately ordered the locals integrated; when one protested, he installed a trusteeship, and the local eventually disappeared.

Wurf's attitude impressed Hood, so he readily accepted when offered a slot in the Staff Intern Training Program. The next four years he worked in Ohio, organizing college maintenance people; in New York state on the hospital campaign; in Michigan, as area director; and in Memphis, in the aftermath of the 1968 strike. Then in 1971, when Wurf decided to increase AFSCME organizing in the Deep South, Hood became area director for a six-state district: Tennessee, Alabama, the Carolinas, Georgia, and Florida.

In AFSCME Hood gained the reputation of a man who, although outwardly easygoing, had an inner layer of iron. One of his locals represented guards at the Brushy Mountain Prison in Tennessee. "To watch a black man go in there and deal with these white guards, who had all the racial hangups of the South at the time, was wondrous to behold," noted one AFSCME person.

Because of his background, Hood gave especial attention to Atlanta, the so-called Capital of the New South, a city that had sloughed off the racial baggage that plagued other cities in Dixie. Beginning in 1974 Atlanta's mayor was Maynard Jackson, long active in the civil rights movement, both locally and nationally. Jackson had been a friend of the union in the past. In 1970 Local 1644 had reached an impasse with then Mayor Sam Massell over wages, hours, and working conditions and had gone on strike. Jackson, the vice mayor, had marched on AFSCME picket lines, and proclaimed the workers' low pay "a disgrace before God." In one address he said, "It is the obligation of the city to anticipate the needs of its workers and be creative and resourceful in meeting these needs. That means everybody—garbagemen, sewer workers, policemen, firemen, and everyone else."

Thus when Jackson ran for mayor in 1973, AFSCME gave him full support. According to Hood, "A lot of resources—money, manpower, political training—went into helping get Maynard Jackson elected." And he turned out to be a disappointment to

AFSCME from his first days. "After he was elected, it became impossible to get an audience with him or to get him to return a phone call. He would have somebody in another department return a phone call. Most of the time you couldn't even get the mayor's secretary. It would be the secretary to the secretary."

When Jackson was sworn into office in early 1974, AFSCME had been participating in city budgetary talks for some months. Jackson threw them out on a technicality, saying the Civil Service Board with which they were meeting was improperly constituted. AFSCME members had to picket City Hall to get a satisfactory pay increase. The next year, 1975, Hood complained that "a lack of creativity was again shown by this mayor, who said that for him to balance the budget, workers would be furloughed for a week without pay." Once again, AFSCME members marched and demonstrated outside City Council chambers, and Jackson canceled the furloughs.

All the while, Jackson was boasting each January of operating surpluses in the Atlanta budget—$6.5 million in 1974, $7.6 million in 1975. But by the middle of 1976, according to Hood, "Our people had gone for about thirty months without receiving any real pay increases. They'd received about ten cents an hour in '74, and that was it."

In 1976 Hood decided the time had come to push Jackson. The Congress had just passed the so-called counter-cyclical funding program, under which the federal government would give direct grants to cities with a certain percentage of unemployment. Atlanta qualified. Again, Jackson refused to talk with any AFSCME local leaders; so Hood telephoned Wurf, who in turn contacted Representative Andrew Young, formerly Martin Luther King's chief deputy, now a Democratic congressman from Atlanta.

Wurf, Jackson, Hood, Young, and others met in the mayor's office in City Hall on a sweltering Sunday night in July, with the air conditioning off for the weekend. By Wurf's computations, Atlanta's share of the counter-cyclical funding would give five hundred dollar annual raises to the five thousand lowest-paid workers. Jackson argued that "it would be illegal and improper." Wurf, who had played a major role in having the counter-cyclical legislation passed, disagreed. He finally told Jackson, according to Leamon Hood: "I'm prepared to make a commitment, if the local [AFSCME] people approve it, that if the counter-cyclical monies cannot be used for pay increases for city workers, then we will accept the position the city has given: that there is no money for pay increases."

Jackson replied, "Well, I'll make this commitment. If there are no legal restrictions or prohibition for using that money for pay increases, I will commit to giving it all to the low-pay employees." Andrew Young asked a few questions to ensure that everyone understood the agreement. A few days later Senator Edmund Muskie, chairman of the Senate committee that had written the legislation, telegraphed Jackson that the money could be used as agreed.

"But the mayor changed the whole position," Hood said. "Instead of giving it to those people who were supposedly . . . the low-paid workers, everybody got it except the commissioners of departments and the mayor himself. So that's how it was." With so many persons dipping into the pool of money, the share that went to low-paid workers dropped considerably.

Hood was now deeply suspicious of Maynard Jackson. Although Wurf had warned him repeatedly, "Don't believe anything a damned politician tells you, even if he swears it on his mother's grave," Hood felt fundamental decency was involved: If a man made a promise, he should keep it.

Relations went downhill in a hurry. Jackson opened 1977 by announcing yet another budget surplus, $9.3 million, which could be carried over to the new year. An AFSCME financial analyst from the International staff told the City Council finance committee in February 1977 exactly where funds could be found in the budget for pay increases. Average starting salary for Atlanta city laborers was $535 a month; the average for all workers was $7,400 a year, $2,200 less than what the U.S. Department of Labor said was required to support a family of four persons in Atlanta, even on a "low-income budget." When AFSCME submitted a list of demands, Jackson refused even to consider them. Although

AFSCME had lowered its requests several times, Jackson would not talk. "He said zero when we started talking with his representatives, and they were still saying zero when the budget was finally about to be adopted," Hood said. Angered, Local 1644 flooded City Hall with about eight hundred members demanding an audience with Jackson. Hood related: "The mayor came out of his office and said he had nothing to say to us, that his representatives had conveyed that the city had no money and there was no money for pay increases and there was nothing else to discuss. That was it. And all of those people who were there heard it and they were very—well, they were angered by it."

The members reassembled downstairs and someone called for a strike vote on the spot. Hood, sensing a runaway situation, suggested they wait a day or two. No, the crowd insisted, some eight hundred of the union's fourteen hundred members were there, including the top officers. The issue was debated as members stood on stairwells and in corridors. AFSCME prides itself on grass roots democracy, and in Atlanta that day, the overwhelming decision was to strike.

When Hood finally reached Wurf the next day to report what had happened, "He was not happy with the strike having to take place in that fashion." But he would give what support he could.

Wurf realized, in fact, that the Atlanta strike had the markings of a major defeat. Georgia had no law requiring public employee collective bargaining. Nor was there any effective mechanism for bringing public pressure to bear on Jackson to settle. The two Atlanta newspapers, both owned by the Cox chain, opposed the strike from the start. This precluded objective coverage from the press, much less sympathy, when it struck. Don McClure, who spent most of the strike days in Atlanta directing AFSCME public relations, said the newspapers were "really puff pieces for the city—like Chamber of Commerce publications."

The most grievous blow to AFSCME was that the "black middle class set it out," in McClure's words. William Lucy, who spent many days in Atlanta—just as he had done in Memphis during the 1968 strike—cited several reasons for lack of community support.

Atlanta, I think, reflects more of a cultural separation between the working poor and the middle to upper class, both on the black and white side. There's sort of a paralysis in Atlanta. It's more motivated by education than it is about understanding. . . . Educated Atlanta only identified with uneducated Atlanta in speeches, as opposed to action. This may sound harsh on the city, but it's sort of a fact.

One disadvantage AFSCME carried into Atlanta was a deliberate decision not to mention Dr. King's past support of the union in Memphis. That was done, according to Lucy, "so that we weren't perceived as riding on King's image—the idea that we could do no wrong. . . . We've gone overboard the other way, in trying to protect the image of the union in that regard." The night in 1968 when Dr. King was killed, Lucy and other AFSCME staff members had met in the Lorraine Motel with the top officers of the Southern Christian Leadership Conference (SCLC), King's main organization. "Our commitment was that the union would not exploit the death of Dr. King."

But AFSCME did use James Farmer in an attempt to shame Atlanta's black leadership into supporting the strike. Speaking outside City Hall, Farmer recollected his participation in civil rights fights for decades, and declared, "Now public employees are the niggers of the '70s." Waving his arm at City Hall, Farmer called, "Maynard, where are you? Why aren't you out here?" The rally ended with the crowd singing, "We Shall Overcome." Shaken, Jackson turned to an aide in his office and said, "If anyone had told me four years ago that today I'd be on the wrong side of that song, I'd have called them a liar."

Leamon Hood, the day after the strike began, called on leaders of the Ministers' Union, the alliance of black churchmen in Atlanta, to ask support. After he made his case, one of them replied that he thought "it would be bad for . . . the city of Atlanta if black ministers came out against the first black mayor and [gave] their support to a union directed by outsiders, white folks." "They were taking a position," Hood said, "that the white folks in Washington were directing black folks in Atlanta to strike against the first black mayor." In fact, Wurf probably knew less about the actual strike situation than did the ministers.

Lacking mass community support, AFSCME had to embarrass Jackson with guerrilla tactics. AFSCME printed hundreds of green T-shirts emblazoned, "Maynard's Word is Garbage," and clusters of pickets dogged his steps at each public appearance, including some outside Atlanta. AFSCME bought a block of centerfield seats for the opening game of the Atlanta Braves baseball team. Each time the cameras panned the outfield, hundreds of strikers arose and brandished their slogan.

The city's position was hard-line from the start. The strikers were immediately fired; when they came to City Hall to attempt to meet with city officials, they were denied admittance. There were scuffles in the hallway, and several AFSCME members were taken away in handcuffs. When two private citizens tried to start mediation, Jackson refused to talk until the strikers acknowledged defeat and returned to work.

It was about that time that AFSCME suffered two body blows—one an accident of timing and the other a gesture of contempt by the black community that signaled that the strike would never be won.

Several weeks before the strike began, Atlanta had launched a self-promotion campaign in newspapers and magazines across the country, calling itself the "World's Next Great City." The intent was to lure new, clean, labor-intensive businesses out of the Northeast, as well as to attract regional headquarters of national and multinational corporations. The Chamber of Commerce spoke of the New South and called Atlanta "the city too busy to hate," and promoted the slogans with three hundred thousand dollars annually. Although the ads avoided any covert anti-union statements, corporate bosses knew how to read the subtleties: What Atlanta offered was a "good business climate," i.e., a town with no strong labor tradition, whose work force would tolerate wages less than those paid in the North. Preservation of such a climate depended, of course, on keeping unions weak.

Before the confrontation with Jackson came to a head, Wurf had decided to answer those ads with an AFSCME advertising campaign showing that Atlanta was not all that great a city. The intent was to demonstrate that lower-paid city workers in Atlanta were not treated well, and that the city should do better by its own people. As Wurf told Ken Bode of *The New Republic,* "The Chamber of Commerce is buying up a progressive image on the cheap. They expect to build their hotels and banks and businesses on $3.50 an hour wages, no medical care and no pensions. Maynard Jackson wants to work both sides of the street, come off as a liberal mayor who cares about the working man and at the same time keep Atlanta an open shop."

The AFSCME ads, published in major newspapers and magazines, derided Atlanta's boosterism. "The Falcons aren't the only losing team in Atlanta," one of them stated. "Try City Hall." Charging four years of "bickering, squabblings, phonyism, and cronyism" under Jackson, AFSCME asked, "Will Atlanta join New York and the other troubled cities of the Northeast? It could. Unless Atlanta can put together a winning team at the top. The Falcons have hired a new coach. It's time for one at City Hall." What the ad did not point out—but everyone in Atlanta knew—was that Jackson was up for reelection that year.

Everyone involved at AFSCME later conceded that the timing of the ads was a disaster. Bill Lucy, for one, had opposed running them outside Atlanta. "If we ran an ad in New York and condemned Atlanta, basic instinct would cause people to come together. Their reaction was, 'You're not really doing this to enlighten us, you're really doing this to embarrass us.'" But as Lucy said, "Jerry disagreed. I think others probably agreed with me, but weren't going to jump off the bridge about it."

The ads did just as Lucy predicted: They caused Atlanta to form tight ranks around Mayor Jackson. An even more telling blow came when a group of strikers went to King's Ebenezer Baptist Church on April 4, the anniversary of his assassination, to hold a memorial service. As Leamon Hood states:

They sent out somebody to tell us that we didn't have permission to have a prayer session. So I asked who did we need to get permission from, and they said from Daddy King. [The Rev. Martin Luther King, Sr.] I went in and talked with him and he said that we hadn't gotten his permission or anybody else's permission, and that the King family had voted on it. . . .

Hood argued that the city had the money to pay the requested increases, whereupon the Rev. King had his daughter phone an official he knew at City Hall. "He told him, 'Charlie, I got this union guy in my office and they're claiming that you got money down there for a pay increase.' He made me get on the phone to hear. I heard [the man] say, 'No, Daddy King, we don't have no money now.'

" 'That's all I want to know,' " King said, and hung up. He told Hood he did not like "all this controversy and you guys creating a disturbance.' "

"Well, Daddy King," Hood replied, "it's ironic you would say that because nobody was more controversial than your son, a person who we came to respect at his grave." The Rev. King gave the demonstrators permission for a fifteen-minute service—no longer—and forbade them to return.

Later that day, at a press conference at the Atlanta Chamber of Commerce, the Rev. King joined prominent white businessmen in expressing support for Jackson "in his dealings with Local 1644." When a reporter suggested his position seemed to conflict with that of his late son, Daddy King replied, "I didn't want to get into the Memphis business. We are never out to destroy, we are out to build. . . . Now, if you do everything you can to accommodate them [the strikers], then I say, 'Fire them.' "

In early May leaders of Local 1644 sadly sent a telegram to Jackson: "This is to inform you that our membership has acknowledged that you have succeeded in breaking our strike, and we have recommended that all striking workers return to work immediately." The decision and the circumstances that forced it stung Wurf. As he told AFSCME people later, "I'm going to keep the union in Atlanta if it takes every damned dollar we have." Local 1644 survives. Maynard Jackson won reelection. Jerry Wurf had learned, again the hard way, that alliances in any form are ephemeral. But even as the Atlanta strike ended in quasi-disaster, Wurf was looking elsewhere: to the election of a president of the United States who owed his nomination in large part to AFSCME support.

CHAPTER NINE

Another Georgia Disaster

Early the morning of April 3, 1975, a slightly built man with a toothy smile came into the lobby of the AFSCME building, and told the guard he had an appointment with Jerry Wurf. The guard did not catch the man's name, but he did understand his title. He telephoned the seventh floor executive offices and said, in effect, there's a man down here who says he's a former governor of Georgia, and that he has an appointment with President Wurf.

Jimmy Carter indeed struggled with anonymity in those early days of his campaign. The political satirist Dick Tuck was to write of him in *Playboy* the following March, "Jimmy Carter will get a little run for his money, but I can't help it that to most people he looks more like a kid in a bus station with his name pinned on his sweater on his way to a summer camp than a President on his way to the White House."

Wurf, however, was willing to listen to Carter over Danish and coffee in the anteroom off his office. Receiving Carter was more a matter of courtesy toward a former governor than anything else. "I wouldn't have gone six steps to see him," Wurf said. But Carter in the flesh was initially impressive. "The thing that struck me the most about him was that he was low key, he was comfortable, and while he was comfortable, and while he sometimes gave you simplistic answers to questions, he also showed a capacity for dealing with the complex."

At home that evening, Wurf said to Mildred, "I met a nice little guy today."

Mildred replied, "And to a New Yorker I know what that means."

Wurf continued. "You know, after that son of a bitch Nixon, and Vietnam and the race problems we've had through the years, maybe he's the kind of guy—even though ideologically he's far away from Brighton Beach—that might be able to pull this country together."

Thus the first stirrings of a most unusual political marriage: the Brighton Beach Jewish socialist and the born-again Georgia Baptist. This initial empathy was to do much to help Jimmy Carter acquire first the nomination, then the presidency. However, Wurf's feelings about Carter's actual performance in office—his program as compared with his promises—ultimately resulted in one of the final of many disillusionments of his career. Jimmy Carter, for all his Southern glibness and earnestness, in the end proved not much different from any local alderman: He would say what was necessary to get into office; thereafter he would do what he wished.

Jerry Wurf needed a political winner in 1976. His break with George Meany and the AFL-CIO executive council over George McGovern did attract him favorable publicity, but in the end his candidate was a spectacular loser. In the 1974 gubernatorial primaries, he and AFSCME supported numerous losing Democratic candidates, including Howard Samuels in New York, Robert Quinn in Massachusetts, and Bob Moretti in California. A month before the first Carter meeting, Christopher Lydon had written in the *New York Times,* "Long an abrasive irregular in the AFL-CIO, Mr. Wurf . . . is still discounted in some labor circles as an impulsive plunger on political losers. . . . Adversaries at AFL-CIO headquarters expect Mr. Wurf to 'guess wrong' again about Presidential politics in 1976, but Mr. Wurf says he sees no candidate strong or attractive enough to warrant any pre-convention endorsement."

Wurf by no means intended to stay out of the nomination process, however, even if it involved another confrontation with George Meany. Wurf felt it hypocritical for Meany to have the

AFL-CIO remain officially neutral, while spending labor money and influence in behind-the-scenes boosts to his perennial candidate, Senator Henry Jackson of Washington. Al Barkan, head of the AFL-CIO's political wing, the Committee on Political Education, briefed state and city federation leaders in late April 1975. Jerry Clark, who attended the meeting for AFSCME, told Wurf the key points in a memorandum. Although the AFL-CIO would "stay out of the delegate selection process," international unions could be expected to seek delegates on their own. But Barkan wanted state federations and central body officials to "keep it cool" and "play it low key." COPE would not be "looking over the shoulder" of these local efforts on behalf of candidates, and "would rather not know about it." Barkan also said, according to Clark:

> Does this mean that we are going to sit out the 1976 campaign as we did in 1972? Absolutely not! Mr. Meany feels that the Democratic leaders have learned their lesson—that they cannot nominate someone from the right, a Wallace, or someone from the left, a McGovern.
>
> Mr. Meany feels that the Republican Party will come up with a conservative candidate—Ford or Reagan—and that the Democratic Party will come up with a candidate we can endorse, as they did in 1956, 1960, 1964 and 1968.
>
> He has told me personally and has told others in my presence that there are six or seven candidates who would certainly be endorsed—Kennedy, Jackson, Humphrey, Muskie.

According to Barkan, Meany consistently listed the "acceptables" in this order, with the occasional addition of Senator Birch Bayh of Indiana. Jimmy Carter was never on the list.

Through 1975, Wurf "was somewhat interested in Birch Bayh, but concerned that no one took him seriously." In a conversation with Leonard Woodcock, the United Auto Workers president, in mid-1975, Wurf ventured that "I thought George [Meany] was playing his cards close to his vest . . . that labor takes no position until conventions, when he chooses the best of two." Quietly, however, Meany "would do everything he could to push his own fellow forward. His ideal would be Jackson, and I didn't think that was in the cards." Wurf opposed Jackson as archetypal of the pro-Pentagon, pro-military spending senator with insufficient concern for cities and states.

In the meanwhile, Carter assiduously courted Wurf, as he did other potential strong supporters. When Carter learned that Wurf was addressing a gathering of public officials in Atlanta, he politely asked, by an intermediary, if Wurf would mind "if he came into the room and shook hands with the fellows." Wurf replied, in a note, that "I was a guest like he was, and I had no objections." Carter came, and spoke of Wurf in "warm, tender terms." The kind words flattered Wurf, for they were not what he usually heard from governors, and especially Southerners.

Yet Wurf was not ready to make a commitment; he wished to see which candidates emerged from the pack. A grouping of unions not satisfied with the AFL-CIO's strategy put together an informal coalition to work in the delegate selection process: AFSCME, the United Auto Workers, the National Education Association, the International Association of Machinists, the Communications Workers of America, and several small unions. According to William Hamilton, Wurf's executive assistant at the time, "We had two broad goals: to maximize the number of delegates unions would have at the [Democratic] convention, and to stop George Wallace, who was taken most seriously at that time." The coalition did not attempt to agree on a candidate (other than that Wallace was unacceptable). In Iowa, for instance, the UAW worked for Representative Morris Udall (Democrat, Arizona) while AFSCME divided between Carter, Bayh, and Udall.

Carter's early strength impressed Wurf, however, and so they arranged another talk. This time Wurf made some specific demands. Wallace was marshaling strength in Florida, a state with a peculiar political mixture of rednecks and liberal retirees. Wurf and other liberals felt the Wallace menace had to be stopped there. Wurf was blunt: If AFSCME helped Carter in Florida, it would do so in a way that might cost Carter other Southern support, because AFSCME would go after Wallace as a racist. "It's early enough for

us to kiss you goodbye on the cheek, and for you to kiss us goodbye," Wurf told Carter. "Do what you wish," Carter said. "I would
like your support." "Come back and see me after you win Florida,"
Wurf replied.

Wurf was still unwilling to make a total commitment to Carter
at this point, according to William Hamilton; his appeal was as a
Southerner who could beat Wallace, and run well in the South-
west. Privately, according to Hamilton, Wurf called Carter a
"cracker." Nonetheless, "That wasn't unusual. To Jerry, anyone
south of New Jersey was a cracker."

By his own admission, however, Wurf temporarily laid aside
AFSCME's best interests to work for Carter in Florida. AFSCME
was in an organizing campaign, and many state workers in the
northern counties "felt very strong about Wallace."

Carter did win in Florida; as invited he came again to Wurf's office—but this time not as the solitary figure with a briefcase, but as
the center of an entourage of aides. At that meeting Wurf pinned
Carter down on specific programs. As Hamilton related, "Wurf got
Carter to make some fairly significant commitments: revenue sharing, counter-cyclical spending, collective bargaining for public employees [via a federal law]." But Wurf wanted something more
binding than conversation:

> I'm a hard-nosed son of a bitch when it comes to the bread
> of our people. That's a proud boast. I got a letter out of him
> about the right of public employees to organize and bargain
> collectively.

There were reservations. William Lucy, for instance, felt that although "he sounded good, he looked good, he looked determined, I
didn't think he was really that deep as a candidate." But Carter had
collected genuine support in the reform primaries and caucuses,
and "I think it was fair to say that he was talking about the kinds of
issues in the way that we thought made sense." Carter was also
ideologically acceptable to AFSCME rank and file, Lucy felt.

The 1976 AFSCME convention in Miami Beach preceded the
Democratic nominating convention by several days, and Wurf en-

countered some opposition in obtaining an endorsement of Carter's candidacy. When he had first met Carter, Wurf said, "we thought he was a nice fellow with a lot of guts and a lot of *chutzpah*. We began pressing him on issues that were of importance to us," and Carter's answers, in the whole, were satisfactory. One delegate, however, Joel Black, of Local 1583 in Michigan, read a letter to the convention that Carter had written in 1971 to Reid Larson of the National Right to Work Committee. Carter, then the governor-elect, had written, "I stated during my campaign that I was not in favor of doing away with the Right to Work Law and that is a position I still maintain." Black noted the letter was being widely circulated by the Service Employees International Union, one of AFSCME's chief organizing rivals.

Wurf exploded. The letter, he charged, was a ploy of George Hardy, the Service Employees president, a supporter of California Governor Jerry Brown. "Who the hell are you quoting here!" Wurf exclaimed. "I would rather have Reid Larson quoted than a man named Hardy who talks to a labor caucus at the Democratic Convention in Kansas City and says, 'After all, you are free, white, and 21 and you can make the decisions on this convention.'

"That's who you are quoting in that goddamned letter. It is true that Carter signed that letter to Larson. He has now said that he supports collective bargaining for public employees by federal legislation. It is true that Governor Brown did his best to blow a collective bargaining law that was before the California legislature less than six months ago. . . ." Delegate John Folcarelli agreed. "For God's sake don't kill him because of one mistake."

The endorsement carried by overwhelming voice vote. Speaking to the convention over a long-distance telephone hookup the next day, Carter made no specific promises other than to work for tax reform and to "give to those who work in government the recognition that you so richly deserve." Much of the rest of the talk— which lasted about three minutes—was platitudes. He was silent on the right of public employees to organize. He said nothing about extending the Wagner Act to public workers. He did say, "You'll have a friend in the White House if I'm elected there."

Some six hundred delegates to the Democratic National Convention were labor representatives. The largest contingent came from the National Education Association, AFSCME's partner in the Coalition of American Public Employees, but AFSCME itself had quite a few. As Wurf stressed, however, AFSCME exerted no control over its members who were delegates. "We have a rule in our union. If you're elected a delegate, you go to your convention, Republican [or] Democratic. You never get told what to do. You get your expenses paid—what we call hard money—to get there and while you're there.

"You're asked to come to a meeting once a day where the leadership ventilates its ideas and everybody else has an idea to ventilate. After that, let your own conscience be your guide. It's a brilliant rule. It's much better than totalitarianism."*

Carter won the nomination on the first ballot. Days before, Wurf had involved himself in the selection of a vice-presidential candidate. Carter recognized he needed labor's support to unseat an incumbent president. As the first major union president to endorse Carter, Wurf—with more than seven hundred thousand members behind him—knew he would have a voice. Wurf encountered George Meany at a luncheon at the Israeli Embassy soon after the convention.

"What the hell are you doing about a vice president now that you've picked a president?" Meany asked. "Fritz Mondale," Wurf replied.

"You know, that ain't a bad idea," Meany said. "Why don't we talk about it?"

Wurf assured Meany that Leonard Woodcock would support

---

* Wurf had strong opinions on many elections, but when AFSCME's interests meant supporting a repugnant candidate, he could hold his nose. In 1974 Earl Stout, head of the AFSCME district council in Philadelphia, called Wurf to announce he was supporting Mayor Frank Rizzo for reelection. Wurf exploded. "You're a fucking crazy man. This is the bastard who paraded blacks through the streets naked. You're a black. Have you lost your mind?" "Come talk to me," Stout said. Wurf hustled to Philadelphia, where Stout told him he had signed a contract with Rizzo giving AFSCME a 12.8 percent pay increase. "Go ahead," Wurf said. Stout's endorsement meant many black votes for Rizzo; within two years, however, Stout broke with Rizzo.

Mondale. Meany interjected that "ideologically" he would prefer Senator John Glenn (Democrat, Ohio) but that Mondale would make a "good ticket."

Carter considered numerous possibilities for his vice president. Most of the interviewees, however, were brought to him for ego reasons. According to Wurf, once he suggested Mondale, and Meany agreed, the nomination was never in doubt. Some of the elaborate political histories of the Carter vice-presidential selection devote great detail to other candidates who were tested and then rejected. Given the combined influence (and votes) of Meany and Wurf, Mondale was the assured candidate once he was presented.

Some early performances of the people supporting Carter offended Wurf, however. To muster Jewish support, a reception was put together in early July in Washington at which, in Wurf's words, "the Carter people would explain their relationship to the Jewish community." The evening was an unrelieved disaster. A Georgia hostess greeted Wurf at the door, "Isn't it marvelous that a man with your kind of handicap, coming from where you did, achieved what you did." Wurf, not favorably moved by condescension, controlled his tongue. There was more. Morris Abrams, the New York civil liberties lawyer and a Georgia native, went through what Wurf called "that cracker shit." Abrams defended some past Southern politicians who had had to be "backward in regard to race" to be reelected, but who nonetheless had been competent legislators. "I couldn't help but overhear whispers around me noting that some of these men also represented prosperity and privilege in addition to racism," Wurf said. Abrams talked at length about the Southern Protestantism from which Carter came, saying it was neither racist nor anti-Semitic. As Wurf wrote in a memorandum the next day:

> As an old smeller of audiences, I don't think he was making it with progressives, conservatives or moderates. During the question-and-answer period, he was asked where Carter stood on issues, and Morris, in essence, made the point that Frank-

lin Roosevelt and John Kennedy had run on issues like the missile gap and balanced budgets, but were altogether different once in office. I am not sure the audience agreed that two wrongs make a right.

Nor did the Carter campaign organization show any signs of expertise or understanding. Nationally, AFSCME's political arm, PEOPLE, concentrated on states where the polls showed Carter and President Ford in close races. The intensity of AFSCME's work on behalf of Carter is shown by some figures from District Council 37 in New York. Working weekends, fourteen hundred AFSCME volunteers made tens of thousands of telephone calls on behalf of Carter-Mondale. All one hundred and thirty thousand members and retirees received postcards reminding them to protect their jobs and pensions by voting Democratic. The union's printing presses churned out more than 4.5 million posters, leaflets and palm cards for the Democratic candidates. (The candidates paid the cost of this printing, as required by federal law.) Included were posters reproducing the famed *New York Daily News* headline, "FORD TO CITY: DROP DEAD."

But much of this campaigning was done without any meaningful input from the Carter campaign staff. Although Victor Gotbaum, the District Council 37 director, offered to work with Carter campaign people, according to Wurf "they did terrible things to Vic. They sent him knuckleheads. They sent him people who were so beneath him intellectually that he couldn't hold a coherent conversation with them. . . . We got troops in New York, real troops. We got blacks, Chicanos, we got them trained. Well, he [Gotbaum] couldn't get with anybody to put the thing together, and they kept changing leaders on him." Gotbaum finally proceeded on his own and told the Carter people to get out of his way. Carter carried New York. Crediting AFSCME for his election would be a claim difficult to document, but Carter did acknowledge his labor support, and especially that of Wurf and the National Education Association.

On the surface, relations between and Wurf and Carter remained civil for months. Wurf appreciated small gestures Carter made toward him. During the transition period Carter telephoned the Wurf home one evening. Wurf was out, but the President-elect talked to his daughter Abigail for about fifteen minutes, a thrill for any school girl. "Wurf found that part of Carter very moving," remarked William Hamilton.

Carter satisfied Wurf on a larger issue as well. In Democratic administrations, organized labor is generally heeded on the appointment of the secretary of labor. George Meany wanted the position to go to his old friend John Dunlop, a Harvard professor who often did trouble-shooting missions for the AFL-CIO, especially in jurisdictional disputes. Wurf said no, loudly and effectively. During Wurf's fight to unseat Arnold Zander, Dunlop had played a role in the printing of Leo Kramer's book, *Labor's Paradox*. Wurf also considered Dunlop was a captive of Meany and the building trades. "I didn't get much out of Carter," Wurf said, "but one thing I did get is that Dunlop did not become secretary of labor." Wurf's choice was Representative Frank Thompson, Jr., (Democrat, New Jersey), chairman of the House Education and Labor Committee. "For various reasons Jerry decided Thompson was more useful to labor in the House," Mildred Wurf said. When the name of Raymond Marshall, a labor professor at the University of Texas, was proposed by Carter as a compromise, Wurf accepted him.

The significant part of this maneuvering was that Jerry Wurf had asserted a veto power over a candidate backed by George Meany.

But Wurf's good feelings toward Carter were not to last a year. Carter used AFSCME to get into the White House; he would now not even solicit AFSCME's opinions on issues, much less heed them. In his eagerness to disassociate himself from the Washington establishment, Carter chose subordinates with no knowledge of the areas for which they were to be responsible. "Fresh ideas from fresh people makes sense," Wurf said, "but you don't deliberately seek out dumb jerks to run the country just so you can say you aren't depending on Clark Clifford and a bunch of other lawyers." In William Hamilton's opinion, "Landon Butler, the guy Carter picked for labor liaison, was about as logical a choice for that job as

I would be for pope. He did not know the unions, he did not know the people involved in the labor movement; he by no means appreciated the issues. Hell, he didn't even know what the initials stood for—you mentioned the IAM [International Association of Machinists], you had to explain you were talking about the machinists."

In a July 1976 speech to the U.S. Conference of Mayors, Carter had promised a massive initiative to provide public and private jobs. He promised public works, welfare reform, operating subsidies for mass transit, new programs for housing and urban development, an urban development bank, and revitalization of the railroads. "America's number one economic problem is our cities," he affirmed.

"Welfare reform"—Carter's people called it that, at any rate— was the first of these programs to go to the Congress, in the fall of 1977. The plan was concrete evidence, in Wurf's opinion, that President Carter was a vastly different man from Candidate Carter. The keystone of the plan was creation of 1.4 million public jobs for welfare recipients and other low-income persons.

The program was riddled with obvious holes. The workers would receive only the minimum wage, not the higher prevailing wage rate. They would be denied fringe benefits given other workers. They would be laid off for five weeks each year. The jobs would be financed by eliminating $5.5 billion from the Comprehensive Employment and Training Act (CETA). In 1977 about seven hundred and fifty thousand CETA workers, all previously unemployed, held jobs alongside regular public employees. They were integrated into existing work forces, earned entry-level wages, were trained properly for their jobs, and offered opportunities for permanence of advancement. In some cities, such as Buffalo, Cleveland, St. Louis, and Hartford, CETA workers comprised at least 20 percent of the city work force.

Wurf felt the Carter plan displayed a contempt for public employees. "The placement of 1.4 million minimum wage workers in the public sector will undermine employment standards, fragment government services, create a dual structure of second-class work-

ers, and play havoc with public sector labor relations," Wurf told a
House committee.

In Wurf's view, Carter's conceptual approach to unemployment
was wrong. Here Wurf took a position that in a sense ran contrary
to the narrow interests of AFSCME. Were 1.4 million workers to
be added to public payrolls, the law of averages meant that thousands of them would join the union. This sort of membership Wurf
did not want, although he was intensely proud of AFSCME's position as the fastest growing union in America. In a major address to
the National Press Club in March 1978, Wurf detailed his opposition to the Carter plan, and offered his own solution to city problems.

> As president of the nation's largest union of public employ-
> ees, I reject the concept of government as the employer of last
> resort. This theory, this slogan, is a sure and proven loser.
>
> Public jobs are vital, but public employment cannot work
> as a system of welfare.
>
> This is a capitalist society. It is unreasonable to expect such
> a society to work without capital. The availability of private
> sector jobs is a prerequisite for the health of American cities
> as well as the foundation of a prosperous American society.

Wurf felt that private sector employment "must be the linchpin
of true urban recovery." Incentives for private recovery "are the key
to a workable program or of urban progress." He continued:

> The present need for assistance to the indigent should not
> disguise the need for a long-range solution. In the long run,
> the present recipients of inadequate largess must be inte-
> grated into the mainstream of our society.
>
> By and large, we have taken a ward-of-the-state approach to
> solving the urban crisis. If we choose, we can continue to fol-
> low that course.
>
> The city can be tethered to a federal life support machine.
> Food stamps and welfare payments can be funneled in
> through tubes. Artificially created public sector jobs can

project the illusion of useful employment. Inadequate food, shelter, and clothing can be pumped in through the umbilical cord.

The key to urban revival, Wurf argued, was an equitable tax program. Regressive taxes on real estate and wages cause moderate income families to flee to the suburbs, to be replaced by the poor. "The cost of delivering public services actually increases. Taxes are hiked again. More taxpayers leave. More jobs disappear. The tragedy deepens. . . ." If Federal welfare and assistance programs were to continue, they should be more carefully targeted. "Federal grant programs should reward progressive taxes and investment incentives which can help stem the hemorrhage of jobs from the hardship cities." Carter was to propose no such tax reform program.

By 1978 Carter's telephone pledge to the 1976 AFSCME convention—"You'll have a friend in the White House if I'm elected"—was quoted in mocking terms by Wurf and his staff. When the administration announced an "anti-inflation" program that spring, labor leaders were not consulted or informed. One surprise in the program was a 5.5 percent "cap" on annual pay increases of federal employees, a decision surely to be considered a guideline by states and cities. But Carter, to AFSCME's surprise, went a step further. Without warning, "we woke up one morning to find out that they [Carter et al.] had sent out letters to the governors and mayors" asking them to adhere to the 5.5 percent pay cap, complained William Welsh, Wurf's executive assistant. However, the cost-of-living increase was running at 9 to 10 percent annually, meaning inflation would outstrip any pay increases. Wurf felt this limitation absurd. "We find it hard to take three-year contracts that leave us helpless while prices continue to rise," Wurf said. "We must insist on automatic cost-of-living increases. . . . [W]age increases for us have fallen below the inflation rate. That gap is intolerable, it must be closed. Public employees pay an equal share of taxes, we bear an equal cost of living. We deserve equal compensation with all other American workers."

After months of private fretting, Wurf went public with criticisms of Carter at an AFSCME leadership conference on January 10, 1979. "Unions must start facing the truth," Wurf said. "One of these truths is . . . what the President is doing to that budget will destroy our jobs and destroy our ability to get raises and will have no effect upon inflation. The President knows it as well as we do." Wurf continued that Carter knew "this terrible infliction of unreasonableness" on the "have-nots and the public employee" would not slow inflation. Carter, Wurf said, "is playing a public relations game, a political game, and you are the patsies." Wurf said Carter had agreed to meet him and the AFSCME international executive board two days later: He continued:

> We can get so enthusiastic about electing a public official . . . that deep in our gut we're really not disappointed when he screws us after the election is over. This means that we need an arm's-length relationship with the boss that has sometimes been missing.
>
> I intend to tell the President on Friday that what we think has been happening is an outrage. I have no desire for a confrontation with Mr. Carter. I also intend to let him know in the clearest possible tones that if confrontation is necessary, we are quite prepared for it.

Two days later Carter listened to Wurf's criticisms of his programs; he said nothing of substance in reply. Later that spring, the White House staged an elaborate reception to mark the merger of the Amalgamated Meatcutters and the Retail Clerks unions into the United Food and Commercial Workers. Wurf was invited, he had business elsewhere and could not attend. Nonetheless, the White House, in naming the invited guests, included Wurf on the list of "Carter supporters." This disinformation infuriated Wurf.

A month later, in July 1979, Carter apparently realized his presidency was crumbling. Over a period of several days he had various national leaders flown into Camp David for talks about what could be done to reverse the "malaise" he claimed was throttling America. Wurf was told the meetings were off-the-record and that Carter would appreciate frank talk. Each day some twenty-five people would assemble around a conference table with the President. One person who preceded Wurf was a Southern governor. "I listened to this governor try to tell him how strong he was, that he should just get up there and be the old Jimmy Carter. He [Carter] nodded his little pointy head in agreement and I just thought he was getting a lot of shit from these people." When Wurf's turn came he chose his words with care; he tried to avoid any hint of hostility. Wurf made no notes of his remarks, but he reconstructed what he said this way:

> I told him that fundamentally the economy was failing, that Americans were all mixed up . . . this moving from position to position without any stability was chaotic. I simply did not understand [Carter's] domestic policy, that I was fearful that he, like other presidents, was getting so involved in international affairs that while he gave a lot of lip service to domestic affairs, things were screwed up, and that in the long run we were in for inflation and unemployment.
>
> I said that one of the reasons I supported him so vigorously as a candidate [was] . . . because I was firmly convinced that he really wanted to make this a better America and that he was not playing clubhouse politics with the well-being of the American people.

Vernon Jordan, president of the Urban League, sat next to Wurf. When Wurf finished, Jordan slipped him a note. "Don't ever lose that fire."

An informal lunch followed the discussions. Carter seemingly went out of his way not to speak to Wurf. As Wurf reflected later, "The Camp David meeting was a real revelation of what I consider one of Carter's great weaknesses. He was incapable of accepting criticism, however well-intended."

The day after Camp David, Wurf spoke to the National Press Club. What he said put Wurf on many front pages. Jimmy Carter had defaulted on his promises of 1976; the Democratic Congress had not carried out the promises of the 1976 party platform. Labor had some new choices in 1980:

We can take a new look at the Republican Party. No longer can we allow the Democrats to take us for granted— and the Republicans to write us off. Next year, we will evaluate candidates on the basis of their records and their programs, not their party labels.

If a responsible Republican, with a sound platform, emerges as a serious contender next year, then our union and other unions will not support a less adequate Democrat.

Wurf's personal preference at that time, although he did not say so outside his inner circle, was Senator Edward Kennedy. In the speech he did note that if Kennedy announced his candidacy "he would begin his campaign with the support of a majority of the members of our union." But Kennedy must run actively and not wait for a draft. "America needs a leader as president—not a man who is led to the presidency."

Carter never restored himself, in Wurf's estimate. Wurf and progressive unionists spent much of 1979 and 1980 trying to coax, pressure, or beg Kennedy into opposing Carter. When Kennedy did move, he sounded for weeks like an ersatz Carter. Through an emissary, the political journalist and activist Tom Mechling, Kennedy at one point informally agreed to withdraw as a candidate, but continue campaigning on the issues, with the promise to release his convention delegates to Representative Morris Udall. Douglas Fraser, president of the United Auto Workers, and William Winpisinger, head of the International Association of Machinists, both with a million-plus members, endorsed the idea. Joseph Rauh, the Washington lawyer, contacted Kennedy. The agreement was that Kennedy would withdraw immediately after the March 25 New York primary, where polls showed him trailing Carter by thirty points.

The electorate intervened. Angry at Carter over an anti-Israel vote in the United Nations, Jewish voters rebuked the President by voting overwhelmingly for Kennedy, and he won. The New York victory, plus another unexpected win the same day in Connecticut, breathed hope but not life into Kennedy's campaign. The Udall switch aborted, Kennedy continued campaigning, and Carter won.

Given the choice of Ronald Reagan and Carter, Jerry Wurf had no choice. His heart was not in the campaign, and people around him knew it. AFSCME went through the motions of working for Carter, but as James Savarese of the AFSCME staff said, "When the time came to resurrect Carter, the people wouldn't buy it. You could scare people with Ronald Reagan, but not enough."

However, Jerry Wurf had problems other than Jimmy Carter during the late 1970s. Internal dissension was threatening his control of AFSCME. Although Wurf eventually put down the revolt, through both his political skills and his grip on the loyalties of AFSCME members, the cost was the loss of two of his oldest and closest friends.

CHAPTER TEN

A Civil War Within AFSCME

In my first talks with Jerry Wurf, he raised what was to him a painful yet essential subject. To do the book right, he said, you must talk to a couple of guys who are important. They'll call me a [obscenity], but they know what went on. These men were Joseph L. Ames and Victor Gotbaum, each an ally in COUR when Wurf unseated Arnold Zander in 1964; each a major power in AFSCME thereafter. That Wurf would direct my attention to blood enemies was something I found refreshing—although these feuds were of such magnitude they would have come to my attention anyway.

This chapter must be preceded with a caveat. At my age I have witnessed the dissolution of many relationships, particularly marriages. My working assumption is that any outsider who purports to know the definitive reason for any break between spouses—or friends—is deluding himself. What an outsider can do is to present the stories of each side, plus the observations of persons who saw portions of the story. Candidly, I do not think even the principals of the disputes described below could give a reasoned account of what happened—or why.

A complicating factor—one that contributed to the ferocity with which Wurf fought his friends—was Wurf's health during the years. Partially because of his lame foot, Wurf paid minimal attention to physical exercise; his health suffered as a result. Through the middle 1960s, he smoked several packages of cigarettes daily; many photographs taken during his early years show him with the omnipresent cigarette—while negotiating, walking a picket line, even when posing for a group picture after he attended a summer labor school at the University of Wisconsin. Wurf developed a cough, he had trouble breathing, he consulted a doctor. The diagnosis was emphysema, an ailment in which the surface of the lungs become corky and do not absorb sufficient oxygen.

"What happens?" Wurf asked the doctor.

"Continue smoking, and I'll give you maybe another year," the doctor stated. Wurf thought of his two young children (as he told friends later) and he never smoked another cigarette. But the emphysema was to plague him the rest of his life. When he traveled, he carried a portable respirator, and he had to find a few private minutes several times a day to breathe pure oxygen and regenerate himself.

Other physical problems bothered Wurf as well. He underwent operations for cataracts and a prostate ailment. In the winter he had recurring bronchial infections. "Most people would get over a cold in several days," Kathi Howarth stated. "For Jerry, it was weeks of real misery." Coupled with his ever-aching foot, these illnesses, in the opinion of many persons around him, ultimately affected Wurf's temperament and his judgment. As Victor Gotbaum stated, "For years there was a method to go with Jerry's madness. In the last years, there was no method."

Wurf's first dispute was with Ames, who in 1977 was chairman of the AFSCME Judicial Panel. This struggle touched off a chain of bitter disputes that were to linger in the union literally until the day Jerry Wurf died.

Joe Ames had the reputation in AFSCME as being both the house intellect and the house character. Ames's knowledge of the AFSCME constitution and rules was legendary. Ames screened constitutions of newly chartered locals and district councils with a stern eye. He routinely presided over founding conventions of councils and larger locals, and he ensured that the rules were followed to the letter. "A brilliant, able guy," Wurf said of him, even after their break. Ames had served as secretary-treasurer from 1966 to 1972, when he had stepped aside in favor of William Lucy, and then became chairman of the Judicial Panel. Seldom, if ever, had the second-ranking officer of a major union willingly accepted a lesser office.

Ames was also known for his eccentricities. That the buttons of his shirt did not always find the proper holes seemed of no concern to him. If a shirt served him well one day, it would also suffice a second day. Some persons found it odd, and talked about it, that in 1972 Joe Ames suddenly grew a great and gray frizzly beard of the type sported by Gabby Hayes, the B-movie cowboy actor. (Ames had good reason: It covered the deep scars in his face. Once the beard began, during a vacation, he let it run its course and then kept it.)

Wurf's ties with Ames extended beyond AFSCME. Wurf's daughter Abigail and Ames's daughter Victoria were only eight days apart in age, and fast friends, as were the families. They regularly shared holidays such as Thanksgiving, and during summer vacations on Cape Cod the children of both families considered the houses interchangeable.

Under the AFSCME constitution, the Judicial Panel chairman was authorized to perform "such other duties" as the president might direct. Ames wrote this language himself when he resigned from the secretary-treasurer post to go on the Judicial Panel, for he had too much of his life invested in AFSCME to divorce himself totally from union policy. Under the catchall language, Ames wrote a column for *The Public Employee.* He helped AFSCME affiliates write their constitutions and rules, he frequently advised Wurf on policy issues. For instance, in a long memorandum to Wurf in December 1976, Ames suggested giving more power to district councils, in effect to permit their elective officers to control AFSCME operations in their areas. Ames discussed several alternatives, at length, and he concluded:

> Whatever final determination is made, the biggest danger to be avoided is creation of a situation where the staff be-

comes a political tool of either the international president or
of a vice president in the political rivalries that will surely develop from time to time.

Such a proposal meant a drastic diminution of the AFSCME's
president's authority. Ames told me, but did not convince me, that
the memorandum was an intellectual exercise, that its contents
were never considered by Wurf. But what happened in the next few
months suggests that Wurf considered the ideas contained in the
memorandum a threat to his office.

During the first five years of Ames's chairmanship, he and Wurf
had no disputes on Judicial Panel cases. Of the twenty-odd trusteeship cases that arose—instances where Wurf took control of a
council or a local—Ames upheld Wurf each time. Often Ames
talked with Wurf in advance of imposition of trusteeships. The
prescreening, he felt, gave Wurf the chance to back away from
weak cases without embarrassment. Ames emphatically stated he
did not wish to go counter to Wurf. Although the Judicial Panel
was set up "parallel" to the U.S. Supreme Court (that is, independent of the president), Ames did not use his independent position
to pick unnecessary fights with Wurf. Through mid-1977, so far as
Ames knew, Wurf did not take issue with any Judicial Panel decision.

The case on which Wurf and Ames split stemmed from a complex internal dispute in District Council 94 in Rhode Island,
formed in November 1976 by a merger of two other councils. Because the council had no money, Wurf appointed as acting executive director Frank Bucholtz, a member of the International staff.
The understanding was that Bucholtz was to serve forty-five to
ninety days, at which point DC 94 would elect its own officers. The
details of what happened thereafter would be of interest only to a
devoted student of labor technicalities. In sum, the leaders of DC
94 tired of Bucholtz and tried to elect a director of their choosing.
Wurf imposed a trusteeship on the council, effectively removing
control of its funds and activities to Washington. Disgruntled leaders responded with talk of withdrawing from AFSCME and form-

ing an independent union. They also appealed to the Judicial Panel to have the trusteeship lifted.

A three-person panel, including Ames, Al Church of Minnesota, and Wanda Walker of Pennsylvania, heard evidence in a one-day hearing. "There was no basis for what Jerry did," Ames said. "They [the international] simply did not have the evidence to support the trusteeship."

AFSCME's case had been presented by Michael T. Leibig, an associate in the firm of AFSCME general counsel Abraham L. Zwerdling. "Abe Zwerdling came into my office on an unrelated matter," Ames said. "As the conversation ended, he asked, 'How is young Mike doing?' I replied, 'He's doing a good job for a lawyer who has no case. His problem is that he doesn't have a single piece of hard evidence.' "

When the hearing resumed two weeks later, according to Ames, Wanda Walker wanted to dismiss the charges outright, but he and Church insisted they wait until they studied the transcript. Late that night he and Church split a bottle of wine and talked over the case. "We had no interest in embarrassing the international president and the union as an organization," Ames said. "We decided we would do nothing until the briefs were in from the opposing sides."

Back in Washington, Ames said he told Wurf, "We've got a problem." He had pored over the transcript. "There's nothing there, Jerry, we can't write a decision that would uphold you." Ames suggested that Wurf issue a statement saying that although the trusteeship might have been justified, circumstances had changed, and he was withdrawing it. To Ames, this was a graceful way for Wurf to retreat from an untenable situation.

"Jerry heard this very calmly," Ames said. "He repeated that he thought there were grounds for the trusteeship, and he would not end it. His utter calm scared me. I knew he was about to blow."

A few hours later Wurf called Ames's office. He had spoken with Church and Walker, who had agreed to meet him privately to hear the "real reason" for the trusteeship. Would Ames care to attend:

"I told him that if he really had two votes to my one, I would be wasting my time saying anything. He hung up."

Events of the next few days were muddled, and hurried. Wurf withdrew his suggestion to talk privately with the panel members, but he did insist on testifying. Through Zwerdling, he asked that it be scheduled in September, as he wished to spend August in Wellfleet. The request was made on either July 22 or July 24, by Ames's recollection. "I walked across the room and pointed to the date July 29 on a wall calendar. 'This is the last day, this is the day the decision is being announced,' I told Abe. 'See if Jerry will testify before that time.' "

Wurf's testimony did nothing to change the panel's opinion. When he requested an immediate decision, he received one: Ames, Walker, and Church voted to end the trusteeship. For the first time in Wurf's presidency he had lost on a major test of his control of AFSCME.

"This was on a Monday," Ames said. "By Friday, I had received phone calls from three different places in the United States. The international representatives [staff people in the field] had the word from Washington. 'Jerry Wurf is going to chop Ames's head off.' This isn't Jerry speaking, those aren't his words. But this is the message he gave the staff. They got the word that way."

Soon after Labor day, Wurf met with Ames and Zwerdling over sandwiches in the anteroom off his office. There was heated debate over Ames's decision, and whether it was unduly harsh in its comments about Wurf. The decision ended with a statement implying strongly that Wurf imposed the trusteeship because he did not want John Folcarelli, a former Rhode Island lieutenant governor, to become executive director of the council.

Wurf also spoke at length about the powers of the Judicial Panel and whether it had the constitutional standing to overrule an executive decision of the president. There are times, Wurf argued, when political wisdom dictated that not all relevant facts be put into a formal record. AFSCME had problems in Rhode Island, he did not want Folcarelli to use the union as a springboard for an intended bid for the governorship. AFSCME historically had kept its distance from politicians; why harbor a man whose ambition was to run for high elective office?

Ames replied that the Judicial Panel was an independent body, and that it had constitutional standing; he would not countenance any interference in its work.

"Wurf went into a rage, yelling and cursing," Ames related. "He stood with his hands on his hips, his face contorted. He yelled, 'All right, Joe, the meeting is over.'

"I got up and went to the door and opened it. Jerry screamed, 'Sit down, sit down.' I said, 'No, I'm not sitting down. You are standing. If you want to talk to me, calm down, and sit down, and we will continue.' I did not move away from the door.

" 'You go through that door and I'll refuse to sign your paycheck,' he screamed.

" 'Fuck you,' I said, and I walked out the door. That ended our relationship."

Within the next months Ames learned concretely of his loss of status. The paper flow now bypassed him. His clerical staff was cut. He was shunted away from the seventh floor to a drab office on the fourth floor. At one point he did not even have a typist. When a Judicial Panel member retired from office in his Detroit local, Wurf sent word that if Ames were seated at the head table at the farewell dinner, he would not attend. Ames sat in the audience between two secretaries; Wurf sat at the head table. No longer was Ames asked to review constitutions of new affiliates; nor did Wurf ask him to help plan conventions. Wurf was to reserve the final humiliation for the 1980 convention.

Such, anyway, is Ames's version of the break. Wurf died before I could obtain his side of the complex story. Abe Zwerdling, who as AFSCME's lawyer was at Wurf's side during the dispute (though he, too, later broke with Wurf), has another explanation.

"I first started dealing with union constitutions in the 1940s, when I worked with Walter Reuther," Zwerdling said. "I think I know a bit about them. The AFSCME constitution says that the constitution is to be interpreted between conventions by the board and between board meetings by the president." The meaning of the constitution is not "an exercise in interpreting sacred writ," Zwerdling maintains, "but that of following a living document adopted by living people. And both the board and the president are living, elected people, who must go before the convention." In other words, if Wurf overstepped himself, the convention could correct him.

Zwerdling felt—although he agreed he could not prove—that Ames nurtured a long-standing animosity toward Wurf dating to the COUR period, even if he did not recognize it. Wurf got the presidency, Ames eventually got the position of secretary-treasurer, only to yield it within six years to William Lucy. Ames's jealousy fermented for five years, in Zwerdling's view.

"I saw Ames as a frustrated lawyer, and he took the job of interpreting the constitution more seriously than I would have done," Zwerdling stated. To Zwerdling, Ames's decision in the Rhode Island case was contradictory. In carefully selected words, Zwerdling said, "It is my observation that over the course of the years, of the various cases that went to the Judicial Panel involving the reviewability of trusteeship cases, Ames never overruled Wurf. When Rhode Island came along, it is my belief that the factual situation no more warranted the Judicial Panel to overrule the president than it had in other cases."

Zwerdling also disputed Ames's statement that Rhode Island was the first evidence of a break with Ames. "The relationship with Ames and Jerry had frayed."

Zwerdling did not agree with Ames's depiction of himself as a cloistered judge, remote from daily union affairs. "You can't have it both ways. Ames was there originally and continually as a politician. He considered himself much more than simply a Judicial Panel chairman." Zwerdling also pointed to a coincidence: At the 1976 convention, Ames had been elected to a new five-year term as Judicial Panel chairman. Given his pension rights, Ames could look forward to a comfortable period, then retire. "He seized upon

Rhode Island as his first chance to slap at Jerry. Jerry knocked him down. Ames never forgave him."

The final chapter of the Wurf-Ames dispute was not to be written for several more years, but their clash did cause many persons in AFSCME to take a hard look at Wurf's performance.

Wurf had many legitimate reasons for frustrations in 1977. He had built one of the larger unions in the AFL-CIO, yet he consistently found himself a minority of one when he tried to shake the executive council off dead center. He began to despair of persuading the AFL-CIO to fulfill its potential as a political and social force in America. Wurf had helped lift an "obscure cracker politician" into the presidency, yet nothing had been given in return. Internal polls showed his own membership turning toward the right. (The shift was as much a function of geography as ideology. AFSCME was a big-city union when Wurf won the presidency. Because of organizing drives among state employees, a decade later the fulcrum shifted to the more conservative people to be found in such state capitals as Harrisburg, Pennsylvania, and Springfield, Illinois.) Because of his insistence upon total control of AFSCME executive functions, no clearly-anointed successor had been chosen.

In 1977 Jerry Wurf recognized the precarious condition of his health. He wheezed through many days, his troubled lungs now as much a burden as his withered foot. His prostate condition meant his staff had to consider the proximity of restrooms when scheduling his appearances. The cataracts threatened to curtail his luxury of reading.

So what would happen to AFSCME when he was gone? The question preoccupied Jerry Wurf during his last years. His honest anger had created an organization of which he was proud; indeed, an organization which had taken precedence over any other part of his life. "Jerry gave himself to AFSCME," Victor Gotbaum was to muse, a month after Wurf's death. "Jerry took it home with him, Jerry slept with it, Jerry woke up with it in the morning."

In rambling talks with his friends and his staff, Wurf talked about his successor, and possible changes in AFSCME's structure.

Grass roots democracy, with each local free to decide whether to strike, or whether to endorse a certain candidate, was a unique strength of AFSCME. Wurf felt local unions should retain their autonomy, yet he also tossed around a number of ideas about how the union could be made more cohesive. Here I must make clear a salient point: Wurf floated many trial balloons in many forms to many persons his last years. The persons hearing them were not always clear whether he was *testing* an idea, or *prompting* an idea. Wurf, similarly, was both guarded and contradictory in his discussions of the question of whom he would prefer to succeed him in the presidency. At various times, to various people, he said both nice and savage things about Gerald McEntee, the head of the Pennsylvania District Council 13; William Lucy, the AFSCME secretary-treasurer; and Joseph M. Bonavita of Boston. At one point, after two bottles of wine at Wellfleet, he even suggested that William Hamilton go to Florida for a period as a district council director, gain some field experience, and then run for president, with Wurf's support. AFSCME would be divided into "strong regions," with Hamilton serving as a chairman of the board. Several persons pointed out the obvious absurdities in this scheme. Hamilton, while a capable staff man, had come to AFSCME as a public relations man. He had no union background other than his experience as an assistant to Wurf.

One person who was not included in Wurf's discussions of a successor after 1977 was Victor Gotbaum, the person within AFSCME with whom he had long felt the closest personal and philosophical empathy. Strong-willed, emotional, skillful political manipulators, Wurf and Gotbaum could communicate in the verbal shorthand that marks a true friendship. They did so three, four, even five times a week, by phone or in person. "Vic was the guy who would hear Jerry's new ideas," said one of Wurf's former assistants. "They laced their talk with a lot of profanity. You'd think these were two brothers talking. They were that close."

From Wurf's viewpoint, the Gotbaum relationship began to lose its luster in 1975, during the New York City financial crisis. At one critical point, Gotbaum flew to Israel to fulfill engagements made months earlier. Wurf thought he should have canceled them. He said nothing publicly, but daughter Susan remembers many angry phone talks between Wurf, who was at Wellfleet, and Gotbaum while the latter was abroad.

During this same period Gotbaum was leaving an unhappy marriage, and striking up a relationship with a most vivacious younger woman, later to become the second Mrs. Gotbaum. Gotbaum is a lithe, physical man who exudes energy. To Wurf's distress, Gotbaum once bounded into an international executive board meeting in Florida clad in tennis whites, and tossed his racket into the corner, as if to signal, "OK, let's get this nonsense out of the way." Perceptions of this event differ. Abe Zwerdling felt that Wurf was offended: Not only was Gotbaum enjoying the company of a much younger woman, he was also displaying athletic skills denied to a man who had no choice but to be physically sedentary. As Zwerdling summarized Wurf's reaction, "It was difficult for him even to stand. The sight of Victor in his tennis suit must have been a horrible reminder of the physical differences between the two." Nonsense, replied Gotbaum, he had been locked out of his hotel room and he had not had time to chase down a bellman for an extra key, and then change. Although he had little respect for the AFSCME board, he would express his discontent in other ways.

Privately, Wurf would also gripe about Gotbaum "becoming a goddamn socialite." During the 1975 New York fiscal crisis, Gotbaum became friendly with financier Felix Rohatyn, the chairman of the Municipal Assistance Corporation and a partner of the prestigious house of Lazard Frères. Gotbaum was Rohatyn's best man at his wedding, and enjoyed weekends at his Southampton home. To Wurf such a tie was "outrageous—you don't pal around with the guys you bargain with."

Gotbaum, concurrently, compiled his own litany of complaints, most of them having to do with what he called "the marked deterioration of AFSCME as a labor union." AFSCME was a "hollow shell," Gotbaum maintained. His District Council 37, although only about one-tenth the size of the international union, had a larger staff in certain key areas. Wurf's "volatile and unsympathetic personality" drove away valuable people. (Jack T. Conway, and William Welsh, both hired with a flourish by Wurf, were among those who decided after several years they could no longer work with him and left AFSCME.) During one fifteen-year-period, by Gotbaum's count, *The Public Employee* had eighteen editors. Gotbaum would rage at Wurf in private—their conversations becoming more profane by the month—and he would challenge him in executive board meetings. But until the fall of 1977 he maintained public silence.

Two events that autumn turned him totally against Wurf. One was "his attempt to slaughter Joe Ames" in the Judicial Panel dispute. The other, and more important, was Wurf's plan for the restructuring of AFSCME, which he outlined to Gotbaum and Jerry McEntee one Sunday afternoon at his home. AFSCME would be realigned into eight districts, each headed by a regional director appointed by the president. Those regional directors and various national union staff officers would constitute the AFSCME board.

To Gotbaum, such a plan ran counter to AFSCME grass roots traditions; to replace elective council directors and executive board members with presidential appointees was a blow at union democracy never attempted by Arnold Zander. But when Wurf told him the idea, all Gotbaum said was "fine."

> He looked at me, he was nervous, and he says, "You don't disagree?"
>
> I says, "No, if they elect me, I'll be glad to take it."
>
> "No," he says, "they're not electing. I'm appointing you."
>
> I said, "Oh." I was playing with him, really. I says, "What if you unappoint me?"
>
> "Well, what are you talking about? Someone like you, Vic, I wouldn't . . ."
>
> I says, "Jerry"—and this was really the break, it was really that time—I says, "This international is strewn with too many of the bodies that you killed. I'm not going to be one of them."

And that was it. When I walked out of the house, I felt he had to be taken on. I knew he'd stop the plan, because McEntee wouldn't allow the plan either. So I knew he could never go through with it without us.

Gotbaum tried to persuade McEntee to run against Wurf. McEntee said, "I thought about it for I guess a minute and said no. I didn't want to run. I thought Jerry was unbeatable at this point." Then would you support me? Gotbaum asked. "I told him I thought he would make an excellent president, but I'd have to give some thought to that, because it could be a kamikaze mission." But he did not say flatly no for a while.

For unexplained reasons, Gotbaum never announced that he would oppose Wurf; he simply began campaigning. For two years he and Wurf fought viciously with one another at two levels. One was public name-calling. Gotbaum termed Wurf a "mad dog" who was "getting sicker every day" and was "incapable of running the union." Wurf responded that Gotbaum had been "co-opted by the Southampton syndrome . . . getting himself in deeper and deeper obligation to forces that oppose the interests of our members." In the shadows the fighting was more intricate but no less savage.

Wurf devised a multilevel strategy for beating down Gotbaum. Nat Lindenthal, head of District Council 37's health program until he broke with Gotbaum, was sent to New York to open an office. Ostensibly the reason was to service AFSCME members who were not affiliated with DC 37. In actuality, he was there to create so much mischief in Gotbaum's own territory that he would have trouble finding time to wage a national campaign. As a focus, Lindenthal used James Butler, head of Local 420, which represented fifteen thousand hospital workers. Gotbaum and Butler did not care for one another, and eventually Gotbaum tried to have him suspended on grounds of financial mismanagement. Wurf cheerily came to Butler's rescue and took his local out of DC 37, thereby depriving it of $150,000 a month in dues. There were rows and suits in state courts, and tedious debates before the AFSCME executive board. Wurf did not care about the eventual outcome: he only wanted to keep Gotbaum preoccupied with DC 37. The Butler situation so depleted DC 37 revenues that the council had to borrow $500,000 for operating expenses and cut its staff.

Wurf next worked on the vice presidents, knowing their support would be translatable to convention votes. When one of vice president David Trasks's children married in Hawaii, Wurf grudgingly left a summer vacation in Wellfleet for the long and uncomfortable trip west. Trask, who had been wavering, was moved, and supported Wurf. "Ten Little Indians," Gotbaum said of the board, "and he got them one at a time."

But Wurf's greatest coup was a surprise affiliation with the New York Civil Service Employees Association (CSEA), with two hundred twenty thousand members. The merger, consummated in April 1978, laid the groundwork for decisions that effectively doomed Gotbaum's candidacy.

Relations between AFSCME and the CSEA were always complex and often hostile during Wurf's early presidency. As related earlier, CSEA had roundly defeated AFSCME in the first representational election for New York state employees in the late 1960s. CSEA had begun as an organization whose chief purpose was to sell low-cost group insurance to state employees, most of whom wanted no affiliation with a labor union. Lacking the protective umbrella of the AFL-CIO's no-raiding provision, however, CSEA was a constant target for such unions as the Service Employees, the Laborers, the Teamsters, and various building trades groups. Furthermore, CSEA had problems negotiating contracts with state agencies that were comparable to those gained by other unions. One settlement in the mid-1970s called for no pay raises at all, only a one-time $250 bonus.

Wurf spoke frequently to the then president of CSEA, Theodore Wenzle, and found him strongly opposed to affiliation. Then two events occurred which changed the CSEA's collective mind:

—Wenzle was voted out of office and replaced by William McGowan, who had earlier been a member of the Railway Brotherhood and the Electrical Workers. Because of these associations with organized labor, "that made things easier," Wurf said.

—In April 1978, CSEA lost representational rights to forty-five thousand state professional, technical, and scientific employees to a coalition of the Service Employees and the New York State United Teachers, the state affiliate of the America Federation of Teachers. The coalition, the Public Employees Federation (PEF), made plain its intentions to go after other CSEA units in representational elections.

During the course of the PEF raid, CSEA lawyer James Romer spoke frequently with Abe Zwerdling, the AFSCME house counsel, on strategy. Zwerdling planted an idea with Romer: CSEA's safest move would be to take refuge within AFSCME. "Through these conversations," Zwerdling said, "we introduced them to a willingness to believe in the advantages of affiliation."

After the PEF raid "the door seemed to be open" to merger, Zwerdling said, though several barriers remained. One was a reluctance of the CSEA officers to submerge themselves—and their members—in a much larger union that would obviously be the dominant partner. "In a merger situation," Zwerdling noted, "you must recognize that the incumbents wish to preserve as much power and authority as they can. The incumbents . . . worry about their job security, about their pensions, about any number of things. . . . The other organization, the one prompting the merger, is thus well advised to accommodate you as much as it can."

Wurf got around what Zwerdling called "this ego thing" by promising that CSEA would have two seats on the international executive board, and that it would be an autonomous organization (AFSCME Local 1,000) rather than being put under a district council.

Another CSEA worry was money, and the services it could expect once it began sending hundreds of thousands of dollars annually to AFSCME. Wurf got around that problem by agreeing to rebate to CSEA all per capita tax payments the first two years of the merger—about four million dollars annually. Zwerdling said, "To Jerry, it was evident that they were concerned most about the continued control of this money. Now Jerry was basically an honest trade unionist, but he did not hesitate to use money for Machiavellian purposes; to him, money was an end to whatever means he had in mind, if he thought it in the best interests of AFSCME."

When the merger was on the brink of consummation, Zwerdling felt it prudent to sound a cautionary note to Wurf. The addition of CSEA would increase AFSCME's membership by 30 percent, but these new members "had their own attitudes, their frames of reference, their ways of doing things." He asked Wurf directly: "Do you want this big and potentially indigestible mass in AFSCME? It is a powerful organization in its own right, and this merger could change the entire character of AFSCME."

"Hell, yes, I want them," Wurf replied without hesitation. As Zwerdling commented, "A person with the self-confidence and imagination and the verve of a Jerry Wurf feels that regardless of the details of a deal, once they're in the union, he could meld them into our way of thinking."

Boards of both AFSCME and CSEA accepted an agreement on April 21, 1978. To Wurf, the merger was one of the more satisfying moments of his life. His union now had one million members, making it the largest international in the AFL-CIO. The United Steel Workers were next with 969,000; outside the AFL-CIO, other million-member unions were the National Education Association, 1.9 million; the Teamsters, 1.8 million, and the United Auto Workers, 1.3 million.

For the first time in months, Jerry Wurf smiled as he bustled around the AFSCME executive suite that day and took congratulatory telephone calls from friends. The kid from Brooklyn who had set out to organize cafeteria workers thirty-six years earlier now ran the largest labor union within the AFL-CIO.

As anticipated, CSEA decided to vote for Wurf in the presidential race at the 1980 convention. Jerry McEntee added his own endorsement shortly thereafter, meaning Victor Gotbaum had no mathematical chance to win; so he told friends in the New York labor press that he was abandoning the campaign—one that still lacked any official announcement of his candidacy—but would continue to contest Wurf on issues of importance to AFSCME.

Wurf would not let up. "Jerry was so turned on that he really wanted to destroy Gotbaum," William Hamilton observed. At the 1980 convention he even arranged for a strong third candidate, Charles G. Hughes, to challenge Gotbaum and the other New York City vice president, Al Diop. Despite his years in AFSCME, Gotbaum retained his vice presidency by only a 60–40 vote.

Wurf also used the convention to bring to a climax his feud with Joseph Ames. At his direction, the constitution was amended to reduce the term of the Judicial Panel chairman from five years to three. No longer would the chairman's pay equal that of the secretary-treasurer; it would be fixed by the president. Other more technical changes lessened the Judicial Panel's authority.

Supporters of the changes complained of Ames's domination of the panel. From June 1972 to January 1980 the panel had issued 309 decisions, including 31 appeal cases heard by the full panel. Of the 278 remaining cases, Ames had heard 262. Between 1974 and 1979 only three of 229 cases heard were conducted by panel members other than Ames. The amendments passed.

Joe Ames flew back to Washington and went to the AFSCME building to clean out his desk. A guard met him in the lobby and said he had orders to deny him admittance to the building. Ames turned over his leased-car keys and walked out of the building for the last time.

Charging breach of contract, Ames later forced AFSCME to pay him two more full years salary at $84,000 a year, $51,000 severance pay, and $10,000 a year for fifteen years in deferred compensation, plus his regular pension. The total package came to about half a million dollars.

Of the original COUR group that had seized command of AFSCME in the reform movement of the 1960s, only Jerry Wurf now remained. And his last months were not to be happy ones.

CHAPTER ELEVEN

The Last Days of Agony

By the summer of 1981 Jerry Wurf resembled the frail child in a wheelchair his mother had pushed to the boardwalk at Brighton Beach in the 1920s. To his many medical problems he now added an elusive stomach ailment that made it impossible for him to absorb proper nourishment. To walk even a few feet was a test of his inner strength. His face was haggard, and his eyes seemed to have receded deeply into their sockets. His appearances at the AFSCME office were infrequent and brief.

Then there were the pills. As one of his closest staff members said, "Jerry knew more about medicine than any doctor, just as he knew more law than any attorney." Frantic at the inability of physicians to find the cause of his painful stomach problem, Wurf doctor-shopped. If the prescribed dosage of medicine did him no good, he would unilaterally double, even quadruple the number of pills he took. I happened to see Wurf's pill case by accident at Wellfleet; I thought to myself, "That looks like a pharmaceutical salesman's case." Shingles further aggravated his pain.

Much of what Wurf did his final days must be put into context. His energy, his anger, his organizing ability, and his drive, put his union at the forefront of American labor. Given normal health, Wurf could have enjoyed his ranking for another decade and become a stronger voice in the AFL-CIO now that it had passed from the authoritarian hands of George Meany, who had retired in November 1980 and died the next spring, to the more flexible Lane Kirkland. But now circumstances were to deny him the enjoyment of his final days in power.

Sick and tired though he was, Wurf could still summon echoes of his old anger. He was an early and outspoken foe of "Reaganomics." From the early days of the Reagan administration he denounced the President's programs as starve-the-poor, feed-the-rich dogma. Listening to Wurf denounce Reagan was a reminder of the soapbox debates of his youth.

There was also the "dark Jerry," the man quick to snap at his personal staff, and to summarily fire those who crossed him—real or imagined, wittingly or unwittingly. No purpose would be served in compiling a complete roster of those who left him that final year; some of those exiled or fired outright during Wurf's last days are now back in the union, in one fashion or another. Others, notably Abe Zwerdling, who finally tired of Wurf's rages, are not, and do not speak kindly of him.

Wurf spent much of the summer of 1981 at his home in Wellfleet, the omnipresent telephone cradled on his shoulder as he talked with "my troops" around the country. There was a steady shuffle of staff between Washington and Cape Cod, and often during the luncheon break Wurf would gather a car of visitors for a drive to a favored restaurant, where he liked to linger for several hours over a sea food salad. He even invited Victor Gotbaum down several times to discuss some housekeeping remnants of their feud. But as close as they had been, neither man was willing—nor desirous—of making the first overture toward ending their split. (Discussing Gotbaum from his hospital bed that fall, Wurf jabbed a finger at the telephone alongside his bed. "From right here I can rattle his fucking cage any time I want to," he said. For a moment or so it appeared he would demonstrate. He did not.)

In September Wurf returned to Washington for the Solidarity Day rally; he was in and out of George Washington University Medical Center for tests. He was saddened when his old friend P. J.

Ciampa died in October, and he seemed to have a premonition that he would soon follow. At the wake, Wurf stood alongside Champ's casket, and Mrs. Ciampa heard him whisper, "I'll be with you before too much longer, old friend." Susan Wurf spoke to him by phone the day after the Solidarity demonstration, to congratulate him on the turnout and his speech. His voice was weary, and, after hanging up, she burst into uncontrolled weeping. "I knew he was dying."

But Wurf found the energy for a trip to an AFSCME convention in Detroit and to another in Pennsylvania. Still unable to hold nourishment, his body becoming seemingly weaker by the day, he entered the hospital in late October to build his strength for exploratory abdominal surgery. One afternoon after reading over some old COUR flyers he laughed and said, "Wow, those were the *days.* We were a bunch of kids with fire in our ass—to think that we could knock off the incumbent president of a union. Impossible. Impossible." He laughed.

That was November 1. That night Wurf began hemorrhaging from a perforated ulcer. In a nightmarish early morning scene he was wheeled into surgery. He never regained his strength; several times the fever and other side effects of an infection brought him to the brink of death. He was in intensive care, with tubes in his arms and throat, unable to speak, yet he clung to life with Wurfian ferocity.

The night of December 9, physicians decided upon further surgery to determine the cause of the infection. Wurf suffered cardiac arrest while on the operating table. He died the next evening, December 10.

Susan Wurf spent December 10 in Philadelphia, running a representational election in which employees of the Office of Housing and Community Development were to choose between AFSCME and a Teamsters local. She hurried to Washington when she learned her daddy was dying.

"This was the last election held by AFSCME before he died,

and I'm damned glad we won it. Daddy would have been happy, too."

In our first talk at Wellfleet, I asked Wurf one of those at-random questions writers use to provoke self-introspection by a subject. How, I asked, would you like to be described in history.

He did not hesitate. "I'm a labor organizer."

Sources and Acknowledgments

When Jerry Wurf suggested to me in the summer of 1981 that I write this book, the idea did not excite me. A decade earlier, I told him, I had spent two years doing a massive biography of George Meany, then the AFL-CIO president; my earnings barely covered my expenses. Further, I told him, "You have a reputation for being a pretty mercurial guy. You say that you'll cooperate, and you'll tell all. What happens if you get mad at me a year from now and tell me to go to hell?"

But we negotiated, and in the end we struck a deal. *Jerry Wurf: Labor's Last Angry Man* would be his story but my book. Wurf wanted the book "warts and all" (his words). He had some stories to tell, some records to straighten for history, and he felt the time had come. Looking at him that morning in Wellfleet—this was in July—I recognized that he was a seriously ill man, and I deduced, although I did not ask him, that he had decided to make a record before he died. Our agreement had these salient points: I would talk to his friends and his enemies, and I would write the book as I pleased. If someone "took a shot at Wurf"—i.e., criticized him, he would have the chance to respond. Otherwise, I was on my own. AFSCME, in return, would underwrite my expenses and promise to purchase enough copies from the publisher to make the book commercially feasible.

Wurf stuck to his side of the bargain, even suggesting the names and current whereabouts of persons with whom he had fought. He told persons in the union and in his family that he trusted me and that he wished they would cooperate with me. With one minor exception, this book goes to the publisher without having been read by anyone within AFSCME. One person had given an oral history to researchers elsewhere about an event in which he played a major role. Rather than have him rewalk the same ground again, I permitted him to read the draft of the section concerned. He caught an error in one man's name, in another person's exact title, and some transposed digits in the number of an AFSCME local. I am making this disclosure because of the suspicion with which "authorized" books are generally viewed. Given my sometime reputation for being an ornery bastard when I write about people and institutions, AFSCME's attitude was unique. I was not surprised. Jerry Wurf was also unique.

Because of Wurf's illnesses in 1981, we did not talk nearly so much as both of us had planned. Fortunately, Wurf spoke on the record, in so many places to so many interviewers, that a wealth of his story exists in his own words. I have drawn heavily from this material. I am especially grateful to Richard Billings and John Greenya for permission to use material about Wurf's early New York years that they obtained in lengthy interviews while writing their own book, *Power to the Public Worker* (Robert B. Luce, Inc., Washington, D.C., 1974). Harry Fleischman gave me permission to quote from an interview he did with Wurf on his Socialist wellsprings. Nat Hentoff permitted me to use quotations from two obituary articles he wrote for the *Village Voice.*

Other useful printed sources included Wurf interviews with Alan Westin in the *Civil Liberties Review* (Volume Two, Number 3, 1975); and Henry B. Burnett, Jr., *Skeptic* (May-June 1976); *Labor's Paradox,* by Leo Kramer (John Wiley & Sons, New York, 1962); *Governing New York City,* by Wallace S. Sayre and Herbert Kaufman (W.W. Norton, New York, 1965); *The Streets Were Paved With Gold,* by Ken Auletta (Random House, New York, 1979); *The Roots of American Communism,* by Theodore Draper (Viking, New York, 1963); and *At Home in America: Second-Generation New York Jews,* by Deborah Dash Moore (Columbia University Press, New York, 1981).

In the immediate Wurf family, I benefited from interviews from his wife, Mildred, his daughter, Susan, and his brother, Al. Wurf's former wife, Sylvia, also spoke with me. Other interviews included Gerald W. McEntee, William Lucy, Ernest Rewolinski, Don Wasserman, James Savarese, Donovan McClure, Kathi Howarth,

Father Albert Blatz, Earl Stout, Jack Merkel, Abraham L. Zwerdling, Eric J. Schmertz, Joseph L. Ames, Victor Gotbaum, Al Bilik, George McGovern, William Hamilton, Leamon Hood, Jack Howard, Phil Sparks, William Evans, Chuck Schultz, Bernard Harvey, John Herling, and M. J. Rossant. Several persons who spoke with me prefer not to be named. Sally Dickerson and Germaine Moran of the AFSCME executive staff helped me over some logistical bumps.

AFSCME archives for much of Wurf's presidency are maintained in the Archives of Labor and Urban Affairs, the Walter P. Reuther Library, Wayne State University, Detroit. Dr. Philip P. Mason, the director, and his deputy, Warner Pflug, were gracious hosts during my stay there, and they also answered numerous mail queries later. (Transcripts of many of the interviews in this book will be deposited at Wayne State in the future, as well as a source-annotated copy of the manuscript.) The Wayne State collection, in addition to documents, also contains tapes of many Wurf appearances on television and radio interview shows and at public speeches. More current AFSCME documents are in the Information Center at the AFSCME headquarters building in Washington; the director, Jodie Beck, was helpful.

An extraordinary mass of materials on the Memphis strike and its aftermath has been compiled in the Mississippi Valley Collection at the J. W. Brister Library, Memphis State University, Memphis. A group of civic activists headed by David Yellin and Carol Lynn Yellin, both with communications backgrounds, sensed the historical significance of this strike, and began collecting materials while it was in progress. Aided by scores of volunteers, the Yellins compiled some three hundred hours of taped interviews of persons involved in the strike, either directly or as observers (transcribed into 2.4 million words), and about thirty hours of TV and other film, plus crates of other materials. The existence of this trove was invaluable in my writing the Memphis chapter, and I am most grateful to David and Carol Lynn for their contribution to history. I am also appreciative of the hospitality of the collection curator, Eleanor McKay, and her assistant, John Terreo.

For research assistance on Wurf's tenure at District Council 37, I am indebted to Richard Steier. Tom Mechling of New York shared his own assessments of Wurf and permitted me to quote from an unpublished article he wrote about the 1980 campaign. Martin Berke and Rose Berke helped the book find a home. For typing a rather rough manuscript, I am grateful to Christine Herdell, Lucille Cohen, and Joan Boswell. And, for the second time, my wife Leslie Cantrell Smith learned what it's like to live with a writer who is living with a book. My appreciation. Sons Trey and Jim Craig also gave up some time for which they will be repaid.